I WOULDN'T GO BACK IF THEY BUILT A BRIDGE

Ardith Maney

Culicidae Press, LLC
PO Box 5069
Madison, WI 53705-5069
USA
culicidaepress.com
editor@culicidaepress.com

Ames | Berlin | Lemgo

ISBN-13: 978-1-68315-088-6

Library of Congress Control Number: 2024933848

Cover design and interior layout © 2024 by polytekton
Photos of the author by Lori A. McGinnis

twitter.com/culicidaepress – facebook.com/culicidaepress
threads.net/culicidaepress – instagram.com/culicidaepress

Our books may be purchased in bulk for promotional, educational, and/or business use. Please contact your local bookseller or the Culicidae Press Sales Department at +1-515-462-0278 or by email at sales@culicidaepress.com

Contents

Glossary 6

Acknowledgments 8

Preface 14

01 Introduction to Our Family Tapestry 18

02 Bradstreets Leave England for British
America and British Ireland 54

03 Lovett Families Living on Essex
County's Maritime Frontier 96

04 Scottish Families Emigrate to British America 140

05 I Wouldn't Go Back If They Built A Bridge 178

06 The Mothers of Us All 216

Bibliography 256

Glossary

Ancestral Line – This term can include all of the people whose DNA you share with your ancestors, your children, and their children whether you already know them or not.

British Empire – Countries and parts of countries where England was dominant during the period after 1707 when the king of Scotland assumed responsibility for governing England, Scotland, and Ireland plus Australia, New Zealand, most of North America, the East and West Indies, and parts of Africa and Asia.

British North America – Most of the British colonies located in North America, plus parts of Canada but not the West Indies. A very similar term to British America.

Clearance of Ireland – Unlike the Scottish clearance described below, the Irish Clearance was more focused on one set of events, the appearance of famine and disease that caused millions of Irish people to leave their homes, towns, and villages starting at the end of the first half of the nineteenth century and continuing throughout that century. People also left because of practices of the local landowners. The population leaving Ireland was a much higher percentage of the total population that was poor and the Irish went to many more countries than the Scots did.

Direct Ancestors – These people include someone's parents, grandparents, great-grandparents, and others further back in your ancestry, that is in the direct line of people from whom you get your genetic makeup.

DNA Matches – People who have some of the same genes that you have and show up in DNA tests done by companies such as Family Search and Ancestry.com. They are considered to be your distant relatives because some of your DNA is shared with some of them.

Genealogy Tree – This is the term for the descent of a person or family depicted by drawing a chart which includes your name plus that of your father, mother, any or all four of your grandparents, any other siblings you know you have, and other people with whom you share some of the same genes, such as a person who is or was a great-grandparent or distant cousin.

Genealogy Mini-tree – This term refers to one of the forms that a genealogy tree chart, as defined above, can take. See genealogy tree above.

Great Migration – The name that is often applied to the large number of people, mostly from England and lands among its many dependencies, who settled in what is now the state of Massachusetts starting in 1629 and continued into the 1650s. See also the terms migration, immigration, and emigration.

Indenture – A formal, signed contract between a worker and someone that person has to work for according to terms that both have formally agreed to, concerning how long the indenture will be, what work shall be done to end the indenture, and what money or other payment is formally required to show completion of the job. Signing an indenture was often used by poor people to pay for their travel to British America in general and to the Massachusetts Bay Colony in particular.

Laird – These are owners of Scottish estates. Lairds became the targets of the ire of local people during the nineteenth century especially when some of these landowners took active steps to close off their lands to people seeking to continue using small farm plots while the landowner, the laird, wanted to turn away local residents in favor of setting up big sheep farms which left very little space for small-scale traditional farms. In an unusual arrangement the Isle of Coll had two lairds, one from the MacLean clans and the other from a branch of the Campbell Duke of Argyll until the laird heading Coll's MacLean line moved from Scotland to Africa in the mid1800s.

Massachusetts Bay Colony – Also known as the MBC, this governmental entity was set up by the English government during the 1630s as the official economic engine. See also the entry for the Great Migration.

Maternal line – Like the paternal line, which runs through your father and his fathers to you, the maternal or female line is important for genealogical studies because it includes DNA from a person's maternal line of ancestors. Chapter 6 of this book focuses on the connections within the author's maternal line, i.e., the mothers of my mother.

Migration - In this book the term refers to one of the most common ways for leaving one's country of origin or location and seeking permanent residence in a different place or locality outside your country of birth. However, if you move from one place to another and do not have permission to live there, that is usually called emigration or immigration. Emigration emphasizes that you are leaving your own country to enter another country under that country's own terms for immigration.

Puritans – The first settlements in Boston and Salem in the 1630s grew quickly because of the large numbers of Puritans coming from England who wanted to set up towns that would be governed only by other Puritans holding religious beliefs similar to their own. Puritans were also widely spread within the population of England. In the MBC, families required religious tests before in-comers could purchase land and set up their own farms. The MBC also offered financial support to economic entrepreneurs during the period from 1630-1660.

Scottish Highland Clearance – People from highland and island areas of Scotland left their homes to move to British North America (BNA) starting in the late 1700s and continued doing so until the 1900s. Additional residents of these areas, including whole families, continued to leave for British North America after the end of the British war with France which was settled in the second decade of the nineteenth century. At that point in time, there were additional allies and voices supporting the movement out of Scotland especially to Canada and later to Australia and New Zealand.

Slavery - People from Africa and Europe were both taken against their will in order to work in slave colonies in the West Indies, and to other colonies against their will to serve prison terms or work under the condition of slavery. The British Empire abolished slavery in 1807 but the U.S. government and its states kept it until much later. Some historians also include Native peoples in North America under the category of slaves, especially people who were taken as slaves by the victors after losing on the battlefields in British colonies.

Acknowledgments

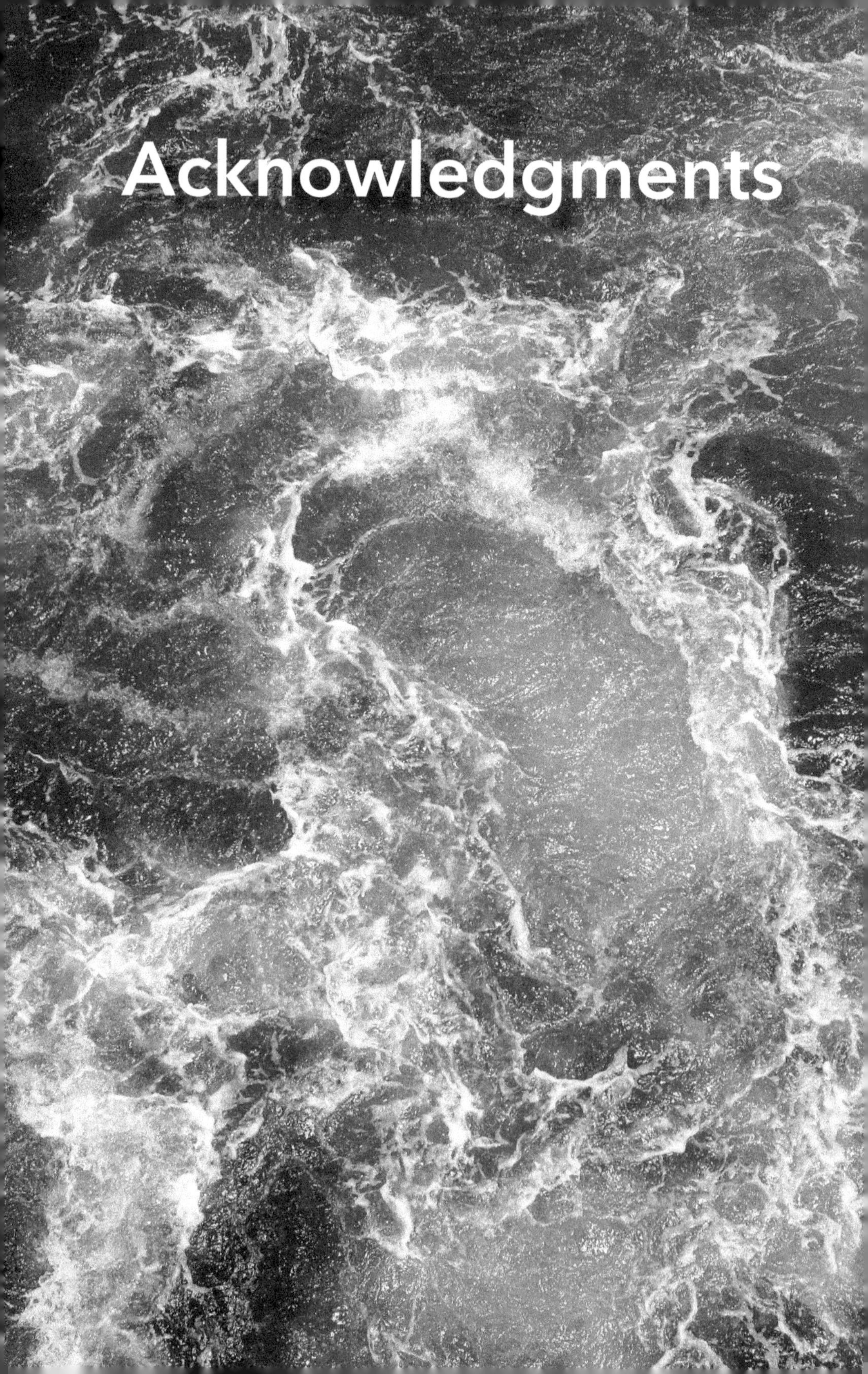

It is a worthy custom that authors acknowledge a few special kinds of sources in the front matter of genealogical and other books. So, I will happily do the same but with some modifications appropriate to the special contents of this genealogical memoir. The first group of people to be honored are my ancestors even though I have probably not been able to name and include all of them. My main ancestors are those who played important roles in my life and the lives of my relatives during their lifetimes and to their families when they lived somewhere in England, Ireland, Scotland, and/or Canada or on their way from a particular part of Europe to new homes and final resting places in various parts of North America.

The main evidence that I show in this book is the identities and lives of the people in my four main ancestral lines during each generation since the end of the 1500s. Also this tree has allowed me to look at evidence about proven DNA matches starting with those of my own siblings and myself in present time as well as cousins living in Massachusetts or elsewhere or in their other 'home' countries of England, Ireland, Scotland, and Canada whom I knew about before I started this project. Just as important to me, there were others whom I have found living in New Zealand,

Australia, and other places where I hadn't known that I had cousins. By looking for – and relying on – DNA matches, this book gives a strong foundation on which to generate ideas for future projects after work on this book is finished.

All of my direct ancestors left one or more of the home countries mentioned above, either willingly, or unwillingly. Some moved with family members to places in England from Scotland or Ireland or to places that were colonies of England in British America, such as Newfoundland, British colonies like Barbados in the West Indies for the rest of their lives, and other places that used to be British colonies or dependencies. As I researched and wrote about them, I discovered two additional subsets of people who needed to be acknowledged as well. The people who came to New England in the early 1600s were not all Puritans. Many others did not have sufficient funds to pay for their voyage to North America or to buy land there. Instead some people had to borrow money to come and some became established landowners only after the expiration of a loan in the form of an indenture.

Some other important groups and/or individuals show up in the introductory chapter of this book when I write about the methods that are used in genealogical research and in studies of local government and local history, which were the main subjects of my work life before I retired from university research, teaching, and outreach in the U.S. and in other countries. One group of these hard-working people are the historians and librarians who specialize in local history of the various countries and localities that are the subjects of this book. Another group is made up of the authors of books about various industries such as shoemaking, textile manufacturing, and other topics important to the local manufacturing industries like those in Essex County. All of that information may also include re-telling stories about what ancestors like mine said and did – or didn't say or do – to keep the information flowing.

In addition to the overlapping first two groups just described, there was also a third source of information that I needed to tap into. A good example of people in this category includes my cousin, Robert Lovett, a senior researcher and administrator for many years at the Baker Library at Harvard University's Business School. The affiliations of other such experts are identified and included in chapters devoted not just to people in my family tree but also included officials in libraries and historical societies in Lawrence, Beverly, Salem, and Boston, at the Public Library and the New England Historical Genealogical Society (NEHGS), and colleagues with similar responsibilities in Nova Scotia, Prince Edward Island, and various cities in Ireland, Scotland, and England who are mentioned later in this book. Another excellent researcher from whom I learned a lot was Dr. Annmarie H. Walsh, who held a senior position in New York City's Institute of Public Administration. I knew her professionally at the beginning of my career when I was studying for a PhD in local government and public administration at Columbia University. I also was privileged to work as her assistant for several years where I learned more about the process of using archival information in the research I did for my dissertation about the New York City Departments of Marketing, Licensing, and Consumer Protection for the PhD granted to me in 1975 when I stopped working at IPA and began searching for academic jobs.

The influence of colleagues is also explored in places in the book where I connect local government and administration. In all of the chapters of this book, I include images showing people, places, buildings, maps, etc. In sum, the reader will find a range of images in each chapter covering topics discussed in the text which range to include the triangular trade between Massachusetts and New England with England and Africa. The images also include people who attended my parents' wedding and even some of the buildings in England and New England that played a crucial role in the industrialization of mill work and shoemaking, in New England and in Stockport, EN.

I also want to show the reader that some of the people telling their stories or showing up in the records that I consulted were as important to the stories that I wanted to tell in this book as the people who came from middle class or well-to-do families ready and able to pay their own way to cross the wild ocean and continue their lives in the U.S., Canada, or wherever they and their families finally settled. Hopefully, seeing those images – as well as using photos to show the wild Atlantic Ocean – will allow readers to apply new information to their families' local and community history.

Finally, I want to thank some particular people who were very important to the final format of the book. The first person is the publisher of The Culicidae Press, Mikesch Muecke, for the hard work and insight he brought to the formidable tasks which doing this kind of book presented. Second is the important editing expertise and formatting work of my friend and former colleague at Iowa State University and hardy fellow traveler with me on trips to Scotland and Canada, Barbara Matthies. In addition, I need to thank my friend and genealogy guru, Rhoda Briggs, as well as my sister and brother for their great memories. And all members of this genealogy team appreciate the various cousins who helped me compare the experiences of the John Maney families of Lawrence, MA, with the William Maney families from Providence, RI, and elsewhere, not to mention Lovetts, MacLeans, and Bradstreets.

The author with some memories of Alvah and Bertha Bradstreet from the Maney Family Archive

Preface

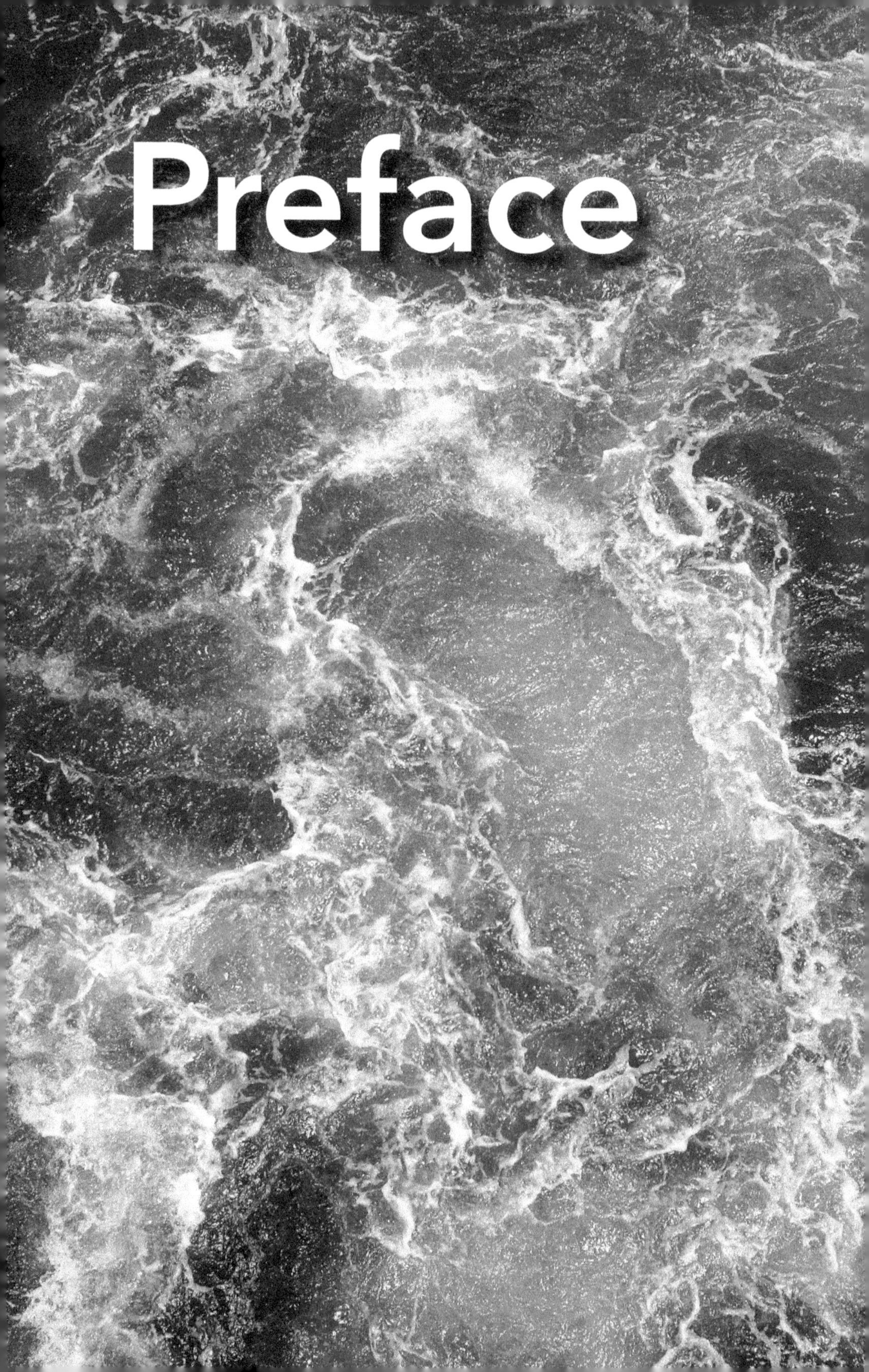

Uncovering my relatives' stories about their families' relationships with England's growing empire after 1600 is what drew me to the topics cited above and got me interested in writing this book from the perspective of the sea journeys from Europe to British America, Britain's various colonies, and other places where these relatives ended up living. From the beginning of the seventeenth century until the middle of the eighteenth century, Great Britain seemed to have developed a colonial model that was successfully working on the basis of the economic, political, and military hegemony that England still held over most of its former European partners and rivals such as France, Portugal, Holland, and Spain.

At the beginning of the seventeenth century, one of the biggest concerns that empire builders on the eastern side of the Atlantic world had about building new colonies in British North America was the relative likelihood of attracting people to do the work which needed to be done in order to build ships, supervise the work of slaves and others working on tobacco, sugar, and other plantations in various parts of North America, and manage the extraction, manufacture, and spread of these products back to the populations of the mother lands. By the time of the successful push for independence in the 1780s, more and more small steps were being taken, especially in Essex County, MA, which showed that industrialization was going to be one of the main economic development challenges during the nineteenth century.

At that time, seaborne transportation was still important for time-sensitive activities such as getting fish cured in Newfoundland, so that fish products could be transported by ship back to Roman Catholic countries dependent on it in Europe, as well as the growing market for fish in British America. However, more and more evidence is piling up to show current scholars and readers that there would be opportunities not just for men but also for women in various manufacturing fields in the nineteenth and twentieth centuries. Also high on the list would be jobs for women in various manufacturing sectors from shoemaking to textile mill work. In Massachusetts and other states the need for a widening labor supply was clear not only in big cities like Lawrence and Lowell, MA, but also in small towns like Danvers and growing cities like Beverly and Lynn.

01
Introduction to Our Family Tapestry

The concept of a tapestry appealed to me as a theme for this book for several reasons. First, dictionary definitions about tapestries emphasize the richness and complexity of the materials used. Certainly, the same thing can be said about the lives of real people who lived hundreds of years ago yet have connections with people living today. Secondly, the materials used in a tapestry may be quite different across one part of the design and another. The threads of a tapestry are like the lines connecting people with their own families and with their parents, spouses, children, and siblings over time and through the generations. How a tapestry is woven is also important because each person's activities and experiences may change the look and feel of it. Furthermore, in the case of a family tapestry made of peoples' lives, individuals and whole generations of families reflect the fact that each person is made up of DNA that a person inherits from some of the people who came before in their families. So, using a tapestry metaphor can convey that my parents, relatives, family, siblings, and I are all constructed out of slightly different materials that contribute to the complexity of the stories that will be told here.

However, while I was thinking about tapestries when I started this book, I didn't realize that I would soon be surprised and pleased that so many women and girls in these families would clamor to be recognized in the stories I wanted to tell. "What about women's work and working women like me?" were among their questions, and I have tried to provide some answers. Looking at the famous Bayeux tapestries,[1] which may have included the arrival of people from my Lovett and Eustace families, reminded me about the impact of government and history on the lives of the people whom I am researching. This aroused my interest in finding out family stories and reminiscences of individual family members, including mothers, daughters, and sisters, to use in this book. When backed up by available civil and vital records, such stories add to the richness of these human tapestries by helping the reader see the context of how our female and male ancestors lived their lives. If we can document where they lived and some of the obligations and opportunities they faced, this kind of information can be woven into their family trees which allows readers to better understand the lives that these people led.

Also important to understand is what obligations and penalties a given person might have faced at a particular time because of where she or he lived and what trouble might have been lurking around a nearby corner. Family history, in this view, includes both positive and negative effects of laws, police actions, and other important events, such as wars, insurrections, and epidemics on our ancestors and on us as well. One of the common experiences depicted in this five-family tapestry is that all of the

---

[1] You can see images of these famous tapestries at https://en.wikipedia.org/wiki/Bayeux_Tapestry which I accessed on 28 Jan 2021 at www.wikipedia.org. The Bayeux tapestries spool out a story of the invasion of Britain by Normans from France in the eleventh century; these tapestries also showed ships on which the soldiers sailed from France to Britain and Ireland, where the depicted battles took place after the invaders arrived.

people traveling to North America used sea voyages from Europe at some point to reach a new homeland in North America. I show the importance or impact of at least one emigration[2] in every family chapter. Whether it was a voluntary or forced decision is for the reader to judge as the tapestry starts to fill in. Another commonality in these five big families is that where the emigrants ended up was at least partially ensured by the protection that government, and especially an invading country's navy, provided for the most important sea lanes during the period from 1600 to 1950 which is the span covered in this book. Thus, it is important to know from the beginning of this book that, during the time ships were bringing these individuals and families across the high seas to British ports in or near North America, Canada, or Australia, all of my family members were British subjects, and the Atlantic Ocean was nearly as important in their stories as the people who made the journey.

The Structure of This Book

This book is written for generalist readers, as well as for family history researchers and enthusiasts, because members of both groups want to know how and where a certain set of their own ancestors came together in each generation; where they lived at the beginning, middle, and end of their lives; and what they passed down the generations about their lives before and after they left their home countries. I present information on these topics for people in five sets of families during the same time frame, which starts in the first quarter of the 1600s and ends in the middle of the 1900s. This introductory chapter previews the other chapters about specific family groups by focusing on the lives of my parents, John MacLean Maney (1914-1985) and Ethel Bradstreet (1917-2004), and pays special attention to their marriage in 1940. In this chapter, I show the last three generations in the families of these

---

[2] Please see the book's Glossary to read about concepts that apply throughout.

two people in order to help the reader better understand the later chapters, which focus more on Ethel's English families or John's Scottish and Irish ones.

The contents of each subsequent chapter are accompanied by one or more family mini-trees, including the names of people — and the locations where they were living — for each family line in a generation, that is, the mother and father and all of their known children, not just the main male line. In general, the mini-trees go back as far as my genealogical research has covered during the past twelve years and builds on the construction of one big family tree. This research is based on records available online at Ancesry.com and at various libraries and historical societies located in Canada, Ireland, England, Scotland, and the United States.[3] Information is also given in each chapter that provides context about where members of each family lived in a particular generation as well as what was going on in the worlds in which they lived. There are some "outliers," that is, people with whom Maneys now living have DNA connections even though I don't understand yet how their ancestors are related to the people I do know about.

For example, a person born in County Wexford, Ireland, might be distantly related — according to DNA records — to someone from Tipperary County, Ireland, even though I don't know exactly which person that was or how he or she is connected to me. Similarly, someone whose name corresponds with a fifth-great-

---

[3] The complete Maney family tree is located on Ancestry.com, and that is also where I have kept a check on DNA matches among the people in this tree. However, except for me, in keeping with rules endorsed by genealogical organizations, neither the names of other living persons in the Maney tree, nor the DNA information applying to members of the five main families belonging in the trees is given in this book. Some of that DNA information has, however, informed this book and may be further discussed in papers or articles which I may write in the future. So, for example, if I know that a cousin of mine and I have a common ancestor, I show it by citing public records, not by divulging that we may have a DNA match with a certain living person.

grandfather in one Scottish Campbell family was found in North Carolina records from the mid-eighteenth century. Whether he came on his own or with some other inhabitants from the same Hebridean island is not known at this time, nor is it certain yet whether it really is the same person, that is, someone from the Isle of Coll in Scotland who went to live in Britain's Carolina colony in the eighteenth century. I use maps in each chapter to show where particular families lived over time, as well as where they migrated to after crossing the Atlantic Ocean to North America — when that information is known — from a point of origin in Ireland, England, or Scotland.

Family stories and other anecdotes are included to put a human face on the findings from official documents and allow the reader to understand better what is in those official records. If personal stories have been handed down, or when someone in a family has written more specifically about their own ancestors' and/or descendants' lives, that will also be presented and evaluated in an appropriate chapter. Each chapter also includes footnotes and a gallery containing photos and other information about the people and places involved in that family's life. After reading a given chapter, you may have questions, as I still do, about why someone did some things or didn't do something else for which we do not have all the answers. The best face to put on such an outcome is to consider this and other attempts at family history to be like solving a giant jigsaw puzzle that was purchased at a flea market and turns out to have been sold with some key pieces missing. Hopefully, additional information will become available later that will allow you or me or someone else to make any needed changes.

I decided to write the book in this particular way because I wanted to go back in time looking for as many ancestors, female and male, as I could without respect for whether they were ordinary or famous, sweethearts, or scoundrels. Also important was to compare the families in each chapter within a common time period, starting in the seventeenth century and going forward in time to my parents, Ethel Bradstreet and John MacLean Maney. In retrospect, the decision to include mini-trees also gave me some advantages in my quest because many people connected with my grandparents lived less than twenty miles from each other in Essex County in the Commonwealth of Massachusetts (MA) at the end of this book, and that helped me compare similar events during the twentieth century from several different vantage points. Another advantage of the methodology is that it is possible to compare what is happening in the various geographical settings in which the main families were living at the same point in time — for example, in the Western Isles of Scotland, eastern and southern Ireland, and several areas of England — before and after these families moved to North America.

Throughout the past decade, I have been actively working to fill information gaps about these families, and this book is one of the results of that work. I started ancestor-hunting after hearing stories told by my mother's father about his family. In 1949, this grandfather finished writing a book about himself and his family titled *The Life and Times of Alvah J. Bradstreet*, after talking to local historical society experts and corresponding with similar people located further afield, all the while soliciting stories about his ancestors from family members and friends scattered around the United States. Another spur to writing this book came from my interest in what happens at the local or community level of society. That interest started when I tried to understand as much as I could about current events by reading newspapers while in high school, which led me to study history and political science at the local or community level for my bachelor's degree in college. There I learned that comparing communities can be done within one's own country or by comparing communities and regions inside England, Scotland, Canada, and the United States with one another over a particular period of time. It is up to the reader to decide whether how I applied information about local events and conditions to the actions of the people in the various family chapters is helpful.

In sum, this social history approach fits my interests, and I hope that others find it useful in order to ask and answer questions that are important for their families' histories. I am interested in showing readers *why* people in the four main families within this big family tree decided to leave their home countries, and what difference it made that by the end of the nineteenth century many of their descendants had settled in Essex County, a part of coastal Massachusetts, after one or more stops along the way. Maybe specific ancestors decided to "leave" or "escape" for their own reasons and that was successful, but members of subsequent generations moved again for the same or different reasons that were important to them. The *how* question is also important but more complicated. Whichever forms of transportation were in use at the times in question must also have played a role because they might make further movement more or less easy to reach some destinations and discourage movement to other particular places. Also, there may have been an economic reward for using transatlantic travel to leave one continent and travel to another. I hope to show the reader some of the answers to questions about motives of and benefits for people in these families.

Asking how people leave or escape a place also may mean that researchers have to expand the kinds of records to be consulted. Of course, birth, baptism, marriage, and death records are important, but land, tax, and probate records also give useful information. Where the usual records or tools of family history research are unavailable or do not provide answers, it may be necessary to include offerings from historians and other commentators and consider personal family stories and experiences, for example, how people planned and paid for the costs of moving in different periods of time or from different locations. Knowing some answers to such questions can lead to further answers to the *why* and *how* questions. Some of the most interesting kinds of family stories can be what may get written down or told orally to children and grandchildren. Also, what is included in a written obituary may be useful, whether it is mostly true — or a mostly cleaned-up version of what the person was like — but it may also provide information that will help the reader see that person in a different light.

This book's premise is that telling what we know happened to individual people and their families — and, where possible, citing what they said and wrote about these events — can enrich the findings of historians, who examine the context and sweep of economic, political, and social history topics; as well as of genealogists, who examine official records forward and backward over time in order to learn as many facts as possible about how people are related to one another. In addition, activities gleaned from records and stories can give new sources of written and oral information that other readers can use when they are doing histories of their own families. Accordingly, where possible, this book incorporates the stories of several English, Scottish, and Irish families who left Britain and arrived in either New England or Atlantic Canada.

Some people you will meet in this book crossed the Atlantic Ocean alone and others moved in family groups. Each set of travelers had their members' reasons for coming. The first family to arrive, that of Anne Dudley and Simon Bradstreet, came with a lot of people over a decade or more whom they didn't know, as did the Scots from the Western Isles. On the other hand, mystery still enshrouds the voyages made by John Lovett and his future wife, Mary Grant, but it is likely that each came with his or her own family members. Several children of one particular Irish Meany family either came separately or with their husbands and children while their mother came on her own after her husband died. And the first mother in the maternal chapter came with her husband and daughter and may have been accompanied by friends, family connections, and others from the same particular location in the west of England.

Seeing These Families Through a Social History Lens

The fact that the families whose stories are told in this book lived, worked, and raised their children in Essex County, Massachusetts, profoundly influenced the topics considered in the category of social history. All of the main people in the Lovett, Bradstreet, MacLean, and Maney families, as well as those who came from the west coast of England to northern Essex County, crossed the Atlantic Ocean from England, Scotland, or Ireland at different points in time, from the decade of the 1620s through the last quarter of the 1800s. The bulk of the English families began settling in what became Essex County in the Massachusetts Bay Colony during the 1630s and this book introduces readers to some of the Bradstreet cousins and descendants of John Lovett and Mary Grant who were still living in the same town, Beverly, in 1950, which was where these Lovetts had been living for more than three hundred years. When they did start moving, it was usually a short distance from where they had lived before and also close to where one of our Bradstreet families had lived in rural Topsfield.

Later these Bradstreets had moved to the urbanizing town of Danvers in 1860, which was located about nine miles away from where they had lived since 1660. Meanwhile, two MacLean sisters followed relatives from Nova Scotia to Ipswich, MA, after their parents had left Scotland's Western Isles for Nova Scotia. Furthermore, the parents of an Irish family included the newest arrivals, started married life together in 1874 in Lawrence, MA, one of the biggest mill cities in North America, after arriving in the United States from famine-stricken Ireland. One of the main aims of the research that produced this book was to find out what each set of newcomers expected from their decision to settle in Essex County, MA, and why they decided to stay during the next hundred years rather than moving on. Did those decisions, for example, give the last two arrivals better political, economic, and social opportunities than were available back on the Isle of Coll on the west coast of Scotland and the small towns of Inverness County, Nova Scotia?

I started by developing family trees for these people noting birth, baptism, marriage, and death records for those who were newly married and for their children in order to learn more about the historical context of their lives before and after they settled in Massachusetts. Some records for the mini-family trees in each chapter, such as births or baptism records, were easy to find in the public domain and could be backed up, as needed, by other evidence, such as land records, wills, and census records. It was also sometimes possible to find DNA matches from among my own generation of cousins descended from particular persons in a particular family tree by using Ancestry.com's common ancestor matching service. Also, accounts from books and periodicals helped place some people in these families as they went about raising children, caring for relatives, working in an economy of evolving work, and sometimes preparing for new types of occupations.

Combining family tree-making with a social history perspective also prepares readers for additional information about someone's family lines, which I present in a sixth chapter whose subject is the gendering of family and work life in the Massachusetts Bay Colony (MBC) from 1630 until the period when Massachusetts, New Hampshire, and Maine became separate US states. Using a social history lens also supported a way to follow girls and women in my maternal line going back in time to their departure from the Salisbury area in the west of England and their arrival in Salisbury, MBC. That line may be of special interest to genealogists, students of American family history, and generalist readers as evidence of how the experiences of a person's maternal-line families can corroborate much of the recorded economic, social, and family history that happened in Essex County during the first three hundred years of English settlement from the run-up to the Cromwellian period in the 1650s, which profoundly influenced national and local political life in England, Scotland, Ireland, and the English colony of Massachusetts Bay, as we will see in this chapter's maternal tree.

The Life and Times of Ethel Bradstreet and John MacLean Maney

The remainder of this chapter is in two parts. First, a mini-family tree for the author's parents, Ethel Bradstreet and John MacLean Maney, is presented and the reader meets Ethel's parents' families: Alvah Bradstreet and Bertha Lovett, as well as those of John Maney, his mother, Ruth MacLean Maney, and his father, John Joseph Maney. In addition, a Spotlight feature focuses on significant research issues as well as possible solutions that may be useful to the reader. The first Spotlight has to do with some conventions that parents born into different cultures use in choosing names for their children. The second of the book's Spotlight sections highlights the role that DNA analysis is now playing in deciding who our ancestors are, since now family trees can be checked against DNA test results.

We first meet my future parents in the side garden of Ethel Bradstreet's childhood home in Danvers, Massachusetts, on the day that the couple married, August 31, 1940. The information is based on a list which survives of those who attended this wedding and a longer list of those who didn't come but later sent presents. Among those who did attend were at least two of John's Irish-American aunts, Marie Maney Stiner and Leontine Maney Subatch, plus Flora MacLean Roberts, the sister of John's Scottish-Canadian mother, Ruth MacLean Maney, who had lived with Flora and her family during the time Ruth was working at McLean Hospital near Boston.

We start with mini-family trees using the same format that will be used in the following chapters to tease out information about the Bradstreets and Lovetts, which were Ethel Bradstreet Maney's main families; and the MacDonalds and MacLeans from Scotland, as well as Maneys, Dalys, and Reillys from Ireland who were the ancestors of John MacLean Maney. The trees in this chapter start with Ethel and John's grandmothers and grandfathers while the trees in the family chapters go back further. Like the trees in the chapters to come, the ones included here are public trees that the reader can access on Ancestry.com to find out what can be known about the location and birth year for the mother and father in each generation. They also show the names and birthdates of all the other children in their direct lines. The direct ancestors in each tree are shown in **bold** and *italics*.

John MacLean Maney's Irish Family Mini-Tree

John Patrick Meany 1849-1932, who was born in Moyne, Tipperary, Ireland, and died in Lawrence, MA, married ***Bridget Ellen Reilly*** 1850-1933, who was baptized in Bohermeen parish, Meath, Ireland. They married in Providence, Rhode Island (RI), in 1874. Both John and Ellen died in Lawrence, MA.

Their children: ***John Joseph 1875-1942***, William 1877-1878, Marie 1878-1948, Thomas 1879-1957, Edward 1882-1956, Helen 1883-1922, Hugh 1885-1885, Annie 1886-1887, Joseph 1887-1969, Leontine 1888-1963, Anna 1889-1952, Teresa 1892-1893, and Matthew 1896-1978, all of whom were born in Lawrence or Methuen, MA.

John Joseph Maney 1875-1942, who was born and died in Lawrence, MA, married ***Sarah Harriet "Ruth" MacLean*** 1876-1939, who was born in Dundas, Prince Edward Island, Canada, and died in Lawrence, MA. They were married in Boston, MA, in 1909.

Their surviving child: ***John MacLean Maney 1914-1985*** was also born in Lawrence, MA.

John MacLean Maney 1914-1985, born in Lawrence, MA, died in Amesbury, MA. On August 31, 1940, he married **_Ethel Louise Bradstreet_** 1917-2005, who was born in Danvers, MA, and died in Milwaukee, Wisconsin.

John MacLean Maney's grandfather, another John Maney, had probably been born in Tipperary County, Ireland, and baptized on 10 June 1849 in the Roman Catholic parish of Moyne and Templetouhy, which is part of County Tipperary's Roman Catholic diocese of Cashel & Emly. That John was taken to live with his mother and his sisters in Stockport, England, near Manchester, when he was about one year old, and the family was counted in the English census for Stockport in 1851. In that census, there is also a record showing that a woman known as Ann Maney was running a boarding house for mill workers in her apartment and that three of her daughters worked in the local mills. All evidence found so far suggests that John's father may have stayed in Ireland with one of his sons while the rest of the family lived out the worst of the Irish Famine times working in mills in Stockport, as many other Irish people were doing. When John's mother, Anastasia or Ann Meany, moved back to Ireland before the English census of 1861 was complete, she brought back the couple's two youngest sons, John (1849-1932) and William Joseph (1854-1935) with her. William had been born while the family lived in Stockport. Two daughters, Mary and Katherine, married Irishmen living in England and are known to have come later to Providence, RI, and New Haven, CT, respectively. It is likely, but not yet proven, that the oldest sister, Ellen, may have come to Philadelphia, PA, with her grandmother, Margaret Eustace Maney.

John Patrick Maney (1849-1932), the future immigrant, came to the U.S. from Ireland in 1873, and shortly thereafter married Ellen Reilly, another Irish immigrant, in Providence, RI. Ellen was born in County Meath, Ireland, which is located north of Dublin. They had met in New York City. After their marriage, the couple settled in Lawrence, MA, where their first son, John Joseph, was born in 1875. All of their other children were born in either Lawrence or Methuen, MA, whose town boundaries meet around two cemeteries located across the street from one another. One, Immaculate Conception Cemetery, is where John Patrick Maney and his wife, Ellen Reilly, are buried in the same plot with four of their infant children: William, Hugh, Annie, and Theresa. Across the street, John Joseph Maney, and his wife, Ruth MacLean, are buried in the city cemetery, Belleview, along with two of their children who died in infancy.

On his mother's side, John MacLean Maney's grandparents, Charles MacLean and Flora MacLean MacLean, were born after their parents moved from the Isle of Coll in the Western Hebrides to Cape Breton, Nova Scotia, Canada. The couple's fathers were brothers who had arrived in Nova Scotia in a group migration of several families on the same ship. Christy Ann, the eldest child of Charles and Flora, was born in Maine in 1863, where the family lived for the first year of their marriage. Her sister Mary was born in Nova Scotia in 1864, and all the other children in that family were born in the neighboring province of Prince Edward Island, PE. Why the family moved so much is not explained by the written record. It is also unclear why Flora died at such an early age. To answer that question, we need to know more about the incidence of deaths among mothers as a side effect of childbirth in Nova Scotia and PE. One child was born to Flora MacLean and the other to Christy Campbell MacLean. Perhaps the early deaths of both her mother, Flora, and grandmother, Christy, contributed to Ruth's decision to become a nurse.

John MacLean's Scottish Mini-Tree

Charles H MacLean 1826-1890, who was born in Malagawatch, NS, Canada, and died in Dundas, PE, Canada, married **Flora MacLean** 1843-1884, who was born in Nova Scotia and died in Dundas, PE. They married in Malagawatch, NS, in November 1862.

Their children: Christy Ann 1863-1925, Mary Margaret 1864-1901, Hector Charles 1867-, Edward 1868-, Neil 1869-1942, Daniel Donald 1871-, Flora 1872-1941, Catherine "Cassie" 1875-1933, **Sarah Harriet "Ruth"** 1876-1939, John A 1878-, Elizabeth Louisa 1880-1906, and James Lauchlin 1881-1942.

Sarah Harriet Ruth MacLean married **John Joseph Maney.**
Their surviving child: **John MacLean Maney** 1914-1985, who was born in Lawrence, Essex County, MA, and died in Amesbury, MA.

The reader may recall that my parents were John MacLean Maney and Ethel Bradstreet. The mini-tree below depicts the relationships among the Bradstreet children and their parents over multiple generations. Ethel's paternal grandfather, William Bradstreet, Jr., was born in Topsfield, which is located about ten miles from Danvers, MA. The mini-tree shows the relationships between and among Ethel Bradstreet and the family of her grandmother, Judith Morrill Fullerton, on her maternal side. The mini-tree also shows that Ethel's father, Alvah, married again after the death of his first wife. From his first family with Cordelia Staples, six children grew to adulthood but one, Ina Louise 1894-1896, lived for only two years. Later, Alvah and his second wife, Bertha F. Lovett, adopted two children whom they named Ina Louise Bradstreet and Lydia Staples Bradstreet. The formal records show that the oldest child from Alvah's first marriage was born twenty-seven years before the birth of Ethel Bradstreet, the last child. As a result, the maid of honor at Ethel's wedding, Barbara Bradstreet Kimball, was almost exactly Ethel Bradstreet's age. Technically, though, Barbara was Ethel's half-niece since Florence Bradstreet Kimball, Barbara's mother, was Ethel's half-sister from her father's first marriage.

Ethel Bradstreet's Paternal Family Tree

William Bradstreet, Jr. 1823-1904, who was born in Topsfield, MA and died in Danvers, MA, married **Judith Morrill Fullerton** 1823-1898, who was born in Moultonboro, NH, and died in Danvers, MA. They were married in 1845.

Their children: Anna 1846-, Sarah 1848-, William 1849-, Marietta 1853-, Henry 1861-, and **Alvah** 1862-1961.

Alvah J Bradstreet 1862-1961, who was born in Danvers, MA, married Cordelia Staples, whose dates are 1860-1897. They married in 1882.

Their children: Emma 1882-1932, Olive 1883-1906, Cora 1884-1968, Florence 1886-1986, Sarah 1888-1892, William 1891-1959, and Ina Louise 1894-1896.

Alvah J Bradstreet 1862-1961, who was born in Danvers, MA, married **Bertha F. Lovett** 1883-1971, who was born in Beverly, MA. They married in 1908, the second marriage for Alvah.

Their children: Dudley 1909-1971, Alvah 1911-1912, and **Ethel** 1917-2005, were born in Danvers, MA, and Lydia Foster Staples, 1892-1975, was adopted.

Ethel Bradstreet 1917-2005 married **John MacLean Maney** 1914-1985, in Danvers on August 31, 1940.

As shown below, Ethel's mother, Bertha Lovett, was born and grew up in Beverly, MA, which had been the hometown of her Lovett family since they arrived in British North America (BNA) in the mid-1630s. We know from written records that Ethel's grandfather, Eben Lovett, had seven brothers and sisters and, coincidentally, that he may have been the first person in his family line to have been divorced. Census records show that he was a shoemaker and that, later on, he worked as a foreman in a shoe shop, i.e., factory. Bertha's mother, Maria Guild, came from Wrentham, a town west of Boston. The 1880 census for Beverly, MA, shows Maria operating a dressmaking business in an apartment in downtown Beverly before her marriage. After she married Eben Lovett, her business continued, as can be seen in local city directories.

An Excerpt of Ethel Bradstreet's Maternal Family Tree

Eben Francis Lovett 1848-1923, who was born and died in Beverly, MA, married **Maria Louisa Guild** 1852-1935, who was born in Wrentham, MA, and died in Beverly, MA.
Their children: **Bertha** 1883-1971, Ethel 1885-1974.

Bertha Lovett 1883-1971 who was born in Beverly, MA, and died in Danvers, MA, married **Alvah Bradstreet** 1862-1961 in 1908. Alvah was born and died in Danvers, MA.
Their children: Lydia Foster Staples 1892-1975 (adopted), Dudley 1909-1971, Alva 1911-1912, and **Ethel** 1917-2005.

Ethel Louise Bradstreet 1917-2005 married **John MacLean Maney** 1914-1985 in Danvers on August 31, 1940.

Ethel's grandmother on her mother's side, Maria Guild, had nine siblings, three of whom moved to Beverly from Wrentham, where their parents continued to live. Maria's father, Thomas Nelson Guild, is variously listed in US census records as a blacksmith and a farmer. Louisa Colbath Guild, Thomas' wife and Maria's mother, was born in Boston, MA, to a family from New Hampshire. We will learn more about this family in the book's final chapter, which traces Ethel Bradstreet's maternal line back to England. This line leads back from her mother, Bertha Lovett, a daughter of Maria Guild, and then to Maria Guild herself, daughter of Louisa Colbath, and back in time from there to people from England in Ethel's maternal line.

Ethel Bradstreet was born in Danvers about one year before the Spanish flu epidemic struck all over the United States. We can only guess at the parents' worry to protect her from being infected and the precautions they must have taken. As shown above, Ethel was the last child and only daughter of the marriage of Alvah Bradstreet and Bertha Lovett. Ethel Bradstreet and John MacLean Maney met when participating in extra-curricular activities while they both were in high school. After graduating in the spring of 1938 from Colby College in Waterville, Maine, Ethel worked as a teacher in the Brimfield, MA, public schools for two years before their marriage. Although the births, education, and families of the couple are well documented in public records, seeing their parents' wedding film in color always fascinated their daughters. However, after they watched the ceremony repeatedly as children, the film later was lost. So, like much of the content of this book, what was lost — or never written down and preserved — had to be supplemented by available records, family stories, and other means.

John MacLean Maney was born on December 4, 1914, in Lawrence, MA, the only child of John Joseph Maney and Ruth MacLean Maney to have survived infancy. John's grandfather had worked in Lawrence's textile mills while his grandmother, Ellen Reilly, kept a boarding house for mill workers from before 1900 until sometime after 1915, which we know about from the Lawrence city directory. The couple's oldest son, John Joseph, was born in 1875, educated as a doctor, and had his medical practice at Lawrence General Hospital. His wife, Sarah Harriet (Ruth) MacLean, emigrated from Nova Scotia to Boston around 1896. While she worked at a private hospital nearby, Ruth lived with her sister, Flora MacLean Roberts, and shared good times with two other sisters, Christy MacLean MacKinnon and Catherine

MacLean Logan, who also emigrated from Prince Edward Island and lived nearby in Massachusetts. Then, Ruth moved from Newton, MA, to Lawrence, MA, in order to attend nursing school. In addition to her job at Lawrence General Hospital, Ruth also started up and operated a private practice in industrial nursing.

Their son, the above-mentioned John MacLean Maney, graduated from Lawrence High School and then attended Bates College in Lewiston, Maine, but left before graduation in order to support his mother whose declining health made it difficult to continue pursuing her professional work. During the late 1940s and the early part of the 1950s, John continued taking bachelor-level courses at Boston University and Northeastern. He did not serve in the military during World War II, as most of his friends and workmates did. That was because one of his hands had had to be amputated after a childhood fireworks accident. He told his friends and family members that he had tried to enlist in the American, Canadian, and British military forces but did not manage to convince the recruitment officers to change their minds. Instead, records show that he spent his war years working the night shift at the naval shipyard in nearby Salem, MA, and, duties allowing, studying what he needed to know for the next day's classes in Boston.

Ethel Bradstreet's father, Alvah, never completed high school, while Bertha Lovett graduated from the teachers' training program at Salem State College and taught in public schools in Massachusetts and Rhode Island before she married and again when she had finished having children. After Ethel and John married, Ethel had multiple short-term or part-time jobs before getting a full-time teaching job in the French department at Danvers High School in the late 1950s. Before their children were born, the couple briefly lived in Lawrence and Malden, MA, but mostly they lived in Beverly, where Ethel had attended high school before going off to live with her aunt, Lydia Foster Staples, and attend college in Waterville, ME. John had various jobs in Boston in the early

1950s and for some time operated a backyard farm before getting permanent employment as an industrial engineer for the research department of the United Shoe Machinery Corporation (USM), which was headquartered in Beverly. John worked at the "Shoe," which was the largest employer in the city, as a technical writer. He worked with the people who wrote the instructions for technical manuals while also working closely with the staff of artists and draftsmen who illustrated the information needed by the company's corporate customers.

Before 1950, Ethel and John had a house built in North Beverly that never seemed completely finished. One of John's most-used quips was that "you don't build a house; you marry a house." They jointly worked on a present for Ethel's father on the occasion of his ninetieth birthday, which was celebrated in 1952. Their gift was the book of Alvah Bradstreet's stories and reminiscences referred to earlier that covered his long and busy life as a farmer, milkman, carpenter, housebuilder, grocery store owner, and sometime representative in the Massachusetts state legislature. His family lived at the eastern end of Danvers, just across the street from Beverly. At one hundred and thirty-five pages in length, including drawings, photos, and transcriptions of official records, his book touched on many of the same topics included in this book. It included a list of people in Alvah's direct line going back to his Bradstreet ancestors who came to British North America from near Boston, England, in 1630. Besides their jobs and raising their family, Ethel and John were active members of the Second Congregational Church located in a rapidly expanding part of the city that became a "baby boom" neighborhood after the end of World War II. In addition, John was a Boy Scout leader and Ethel was the adviser to Danvers High School French Club students. Another highlight for her was the opportunity to bring her daughters along in 1960 when she took an advanced summer course in the French language at the university in Grenoble, France.

As their children finished high school and started college, the couple built a retirement home near the Merrimac and Amesbury town lines in the northwestern part of Essex County. John had always wanted to return to the Merrimac Valley to be near his childhood friends in Lawrence. The couple enjoyed retirement together there until his death in 1985. They also enjoyed travel together in Canada and in the places where their children settled. After the death of her husband, Ethel moved back to North Beverly and later to Milwaukee, Wisconsin, where one of her children lived. She continued to travel in the U.S. and Europe until her death in 2005.

Spotlighting Important Issues in a Family's History

Before ending this chapter, a section will be devoted to a feature designed to cast a spotlight on additional information that can be important for understanding my four families, as well as yours, perhaps. Such spotlight sections highlight a combination of people, records, and other artifacts oriented around *family and community traditions, events in individual people's lives*, and *how to use records* that may be useful to readers interested in adding some context to the research they want to do about their own families' lives and times. The first category, *family and community traditions*, offers several subtopics that are useful to spotlight, such as:

The significance of names;
Likely professions and occupations;
Working conditions, such as indenture, imprisonment, and enslavement;
Religion and religious ferment;
Impacts of government and politics on the family and/or community;
Conditions of health, disease and epidemics;
Conditions of war, police, militia, and military service;

Rituals and rules for birth, marriage, and death;
Pastimes, amusements, and sports;
Formal and informal education and the role of teachers;
The importance of keepsakes and family stories; and
Gendering of family life related to any or all of the above topics.

A second category for spotlighting focuses on *events from an individual person's life*. For example, a spotlight might direct attention to a particular person who is a missing link in one of the family chapters. Or it could also illuminate someone who "got away," that is, ended up missing or unaccounted for in the usual records. Or it could be someone who reinvented himself or herself for better or for worse. Another category for spotlighting might explore a particular *role that records can play* in understanding the beliefs and actions of particular ancestors. Below, the focus is on naming conventions and the growing importance of DNA in supplementing traditional types of records that genealogists and family historians use to decide if a person is part of the main line of someone's family tree.

Spotlight: How Do Families Decide on Names for Their Children?

Some cultures and religious traditions have special conventions or traditions for choosing first names for their children. For example, MacLean, MacDonald, MacKinnon, and related families from the Western Isles of Scotland were familiar with a Scottish *Gaelic naming convention* used for choosing the first names of both girls and boys. According to this convention, the first girl child would be named for her maternal grandmother and the first boy named for his paternal grandfather. The second girl would be named for her paternal grandmother and the third daughter would be named for the mother, and vice versa for the boys. Then there were two options. One option was to keep going back along the main paternal line to find names for the boys and along the main maternal line for names for additional girl children. The second option was to keep going with the names of the mother's sisters or the father's brothers after acknowledging the child's grandmothers, grandfathers, fathers, and mothers. One of the functions of putting the aunts and uncles into the naming pattern may have been that one or more of them was usually expected to take responsibility for raising any children in the family in case one or both of the parents died.

So, if we knew which convention was practiced in a particular Scottish highland or island community, could we perhaps know why a person was given a particular name? The answer seems to be — sometimes yes but sometimes no. For example, sometimes a girl or boy may have been given the name of a sibling who had died in childhood, a practice which would throw off the birth order in assigning names. Or the parents might have decided to name the child after somebody important in the family or community. Other factors surrounding naming may also make the job of the family historian more complicated. For example, when there are no birth records, baptism records became more important for both the Scots, as shown above, and also for the Irish, where the baptism names might be written in Latin for use in Roman Catholic parishes.

Finally, the names of children might show up differently in Irish and Scottish records than how these children were addressed inside the family or among close friends, where nicknames were often used. John MacLean Maney's Irish family seems to have had a tradition that the first male child got the grandfather's name; e.g., both John Maney (1849-1932) and his brother, William J. Maney (1854-1935), named their oldest sons John. Naming the first son after the grandfather was a practice that John MacLean Maney told his children went back many generations in this Maney family. You will hear more about the author's attempts to prove or disprove this story in the Maney chapter. Second, third, etc., sons also were expected to give their own first sons the name John.

Among the Scots parish records kept on the Isle of Coll from 1776 to 1821, last names are also important but often complicated for the historian to get hold of. In this oral culture, most people did not have last names as we know them today. Everyone knew one another in any particular Scottish highland or island community, and the person might be referred to locally by a combination of a first name added to the name of the mother or father and often some kind of descriptor. The last name was often the same as that of the laird or clan, but not always. And sometimes married Scottish women in this study used their father's last name on official records in Scotland but changed to the surname of their husband after they arrived in Nova Scotia. The Irish women, on the other hand, usually were listed under their husband's name after marriage. The families from the Bradstreet and Lovett groups followed the tradition of their home country, England; so, women assumed their husband's last name, as did the Scots in Canada, the Irish living in England, and both if they settled in the United States.

Sometimes, also, which name was used depended on where the person lived over time. For example, Anastasia Doran was born in Ireland in 1809 but temporarily became Ann Maney — rather than Meany — when she lived in Stockport, England, during the Famine times of the 1850s, according to the 1851 census entry for the family. Then, after she took her two sons back to Ireland with her, she became Anastasia Meany again before she spent the last three years of her life in Rhode Island under the name of Anastasia Maney.

Spotlight: Was James A. Maney Part of Our Maney Family Tree?

Records on Ancestry.com suggest that a certain James A. Maney and his daughter Sarah, both of whom were born more than two hundred years ago, are connected through DNA with one of my siblings. Their lives in North Carolina suggest that this man and his daughter may be our earliest Irish common ancestors living in North America to have yet been identified. Irish baptism records show that this James Maney was probably born in County Wexford in Ireland. In 1755 James was living in the colony of Virginia. There he married a woman named Faye Scellos Bruce after which a daughter, Sarah, was born. Irish baptism records show a James Maney born in about 1725 in County Wexford, Ireland, which is not far from where the main line of Meanys and Meaneys had settled in a neighboring county, Tipperary.

The marriage of James Maney and Faye Scellos Bruce, as well as the later marriage of their daughter, Sarah Maney, to a man named James Metcalf, both resulted in big families. One of my siblings has DNA evidence showing that Sarah and James might be common ancestors with her and that there are descendants of at least two children of Sarah and her husband currently living who are DNA matches to two of my siblings. Indeed, a quick look at www.googlemaps.com shows that the heartland of the Maneys in Tipperary is only sixty-seven kilometers from the place in Wexford where James was baptized in 1725, and information from the 1901 Irish census showed that there were still Meanys living in Wexford then. Why these Wexford Maneys came to settle in Virginia and North Carolina is not yet clear, but the context might be that they came to North America as indentured servants and were able to buy land after paying off their indentures.

Alternatively, Sarah and her family may have received land granted for James' service in the American War for Independence. Still another possibility is that James Maney may have been a soldier in the British army when he first came to North America. Or he may have been sent to the British colony in Virginia as a convict laborer, such as happened to at least one other person in our Irish family tree. Finally, and sadly, James' name may have come from documented records of British and Scottish children being sent by the British Navy and its contractors to North American colonies starting in the early part of the eighteenth century. Long story short, we don't know yet why or how James got to North America, but he is definitely a DNA match with our Maneys.

Returning to the use of DNA to suggest location and confirm existing family connections, there are some other points to consider. I have tried to search for DNA matches systematically, not just using alternative spellings like Meany, Maney, and Mooney, but have also looked for — and found — matches with the last names of known Maney marriage partners from the eighteenth and nineteenth centuries, such as Doran, Eustace, McGrath, and Heffernan, which I already had worked on to build the main Maney family tree. I also have used DNA information to find connections between Maneys, Reillys, and Dalys, assuming that these connections would flow through to the descendants of my great-grandparents, John Maney and Ellen Reilly. The most important fact to keep in mind is that, while Ellen's father and his ancestors were Reillys, Ellen's mother and many of the women and men in her maternal line were Dalys.

That means that most, if not all, of the Dalys whom I know to be connected to us are most likely Ellen's Daly relatives, and the children of John MacLean Maney and Ethel Bradstreet are among their descendants. Most of the Reilly common ancestors came from Meath or nearby counties such as Cavan and Westmeath, both of which are located near the Ulster plantation, which includes the six counties on the Irish mainland that are still part of the United Kingdom. In the DNA matches that my siblings and I already know about, there are more than 150 people who are likely Daly DNA matches. And the number will probably continue to grow. More information about DNA connections will appear in the family chapters of this book and also in the footnotes to show some of these connections.

Looking Ahead to the Other Family
Chapters in This Book

This chapter has introduced the main topics for the other chapters and provided mini-trees for some of the generations of people who would come to the United States or other parts of British America, such as Nova Scotia or the Carolinas. The Lovett and Bradstreet families who settled in the new Massachusetts Bay Colony (MBC) in the 1630s came from England, and many of their members seem to have been content to stay near where their ancestors settled upon their arrival in the part of the MBC that included all parts of what would later become Essex County. On the other hand, the urge to keep moving, rather than staying put, definitely shows up among the families that moved from the western islands of Scotland to rural Cape Breton in Nova Scotia and then to other parts of Canada, from which they quickly began filtering into the United States. After arriving in Inverness County, Nova Scotia, in the 1820s, family elders saw some of their children start new migration journeys as soon as they reached adulthood there in the 1840s.

And we will see different emigration patterns among John MacLean Maney's grandfather's Irish families from County Tipperary, compared with those of the Dalys and Reillys from County Meath, Ireland. In 1851, John MacLean Maney's great-grandparents left Ireland for Stockport, England, which is located next to the industrial hubs of Manchester and Liverpool, England, but the two youngest sons returned with their mother to Ireland before they left separately for the United States as adults within about ten years. Accordingly, the reader should expect to see that people sometimes came to America alone and other times in family groups. After the main group came from England to the MBC in the 1660s, they were followed by families who spent short times in the original parts of the MBC before moving to towns being set up in New Hampshire, Massachusetts, and Maine. Also, it was the case that some people made their first move to New England towns such as Beverly and Salem and then moved to other English colonies, like a family of Cornings who kept up their friendship and commercial ties with people in Beverly and Salem, MA, even after they were settled in Nova Scotia. As the reader will see, the Cornings moved to Yarmouth, a maritime town like Salem in the MBC that also attracted other families who left the New England colonies because of their loyalty to Britain before the American colonies broke their ties to England and launched their war for independence.

More on this topic will be shown in the chapter about the Lovetts of Salem and Beverly. Readers will notice that a significant portion of the people who came to the area that was the heart of the Massachusetts Bay Colony (MBC) in New England during the first hundred years were Puritans who had fled the extremes of the English government's conflicts with religious and other leaders in the 1600s. The information given here allows the reader to notice some of the issues that were being contested by the inhabitants of larger cities like Boston and Salem at that time. Among those were the establishment of small farming systems designed to support the food needs of the owners, their families, and the people working for them, including children and laborers. These families also needed to adapt agriculture to the different crops growing on the new lands that had to be cleared for farming after the newcomers started building on their new MBC property.[4] There are also photographs of important buildings and images to see in the

---

[4] These issues are extensively covered in Daniel Vickers, *Farmers & Fishermen: Two Centuries of Work in Essex County, Massachusetts, 1630-1850*. Williamsburg, VA: University of North Carolina Press, 1994. You can also dip into the book's bibliography and find Phillip H. Round's, *By Nature and By Custom Cursed. Transatlantic Civil Discourse and New England Cultural Production, 1620-1660*. Hanover, NH: The University Press of New England, 1999, especially his chapter about the making of an American poet, Anne Bradstreet, part of whose story is told in the Bradstreet and Maternal chapters.

countries back home. Other images show some of the dangers of weather which sometimes caught travelers in the dangerous Atlantic sea lanes during the times when the people in this book moved to their "new" home countries during the period from the seventeenth to twentieth centuries.

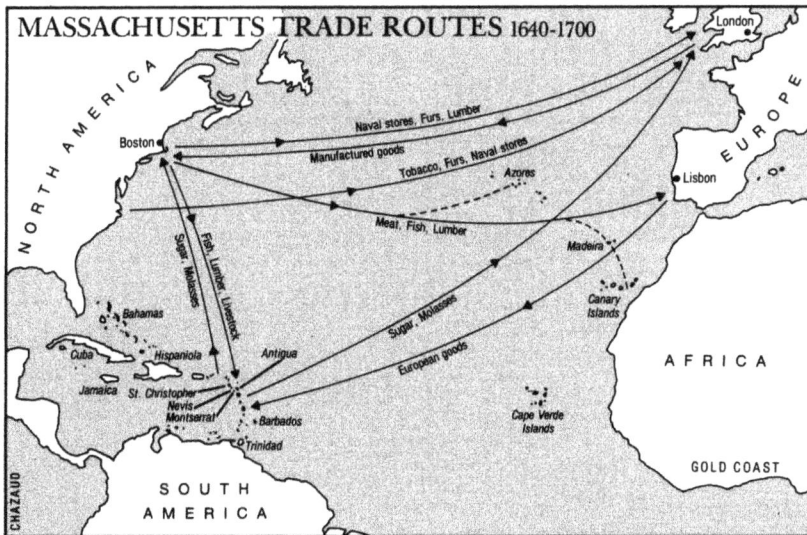

MASSACHUSETTS TRADE ROUTES 1640-1700

Innes, *Creating the Commonwealth*, New York: Norton, 1995, p. 4

Bayeaux tapestry detail

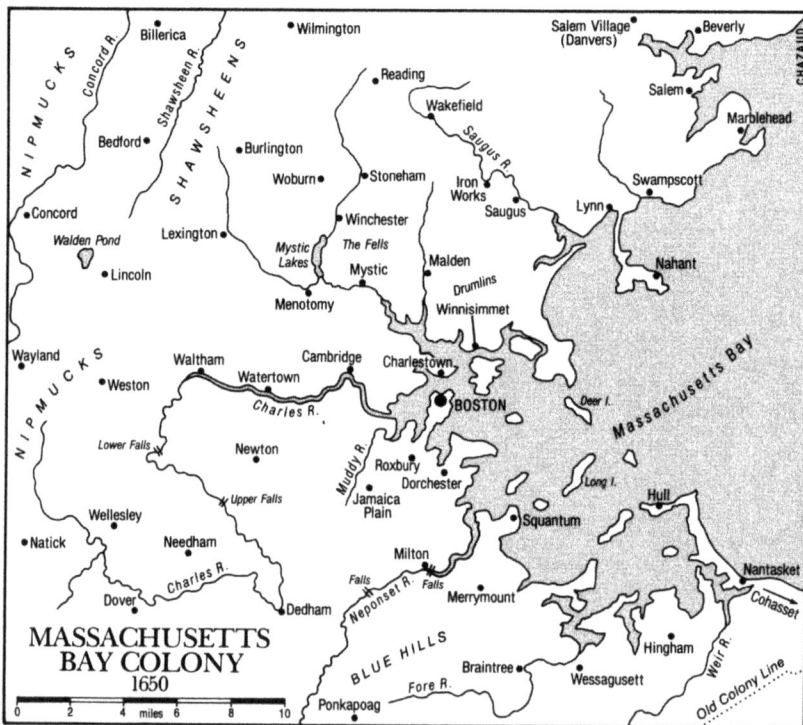

Massachusetts Bay Colony 1650, Innes, p. 4

John MacLean Maney & Ethel Bradstreet

John and Ethel preparing the cake for their guests

This is what John said to his work colleagues

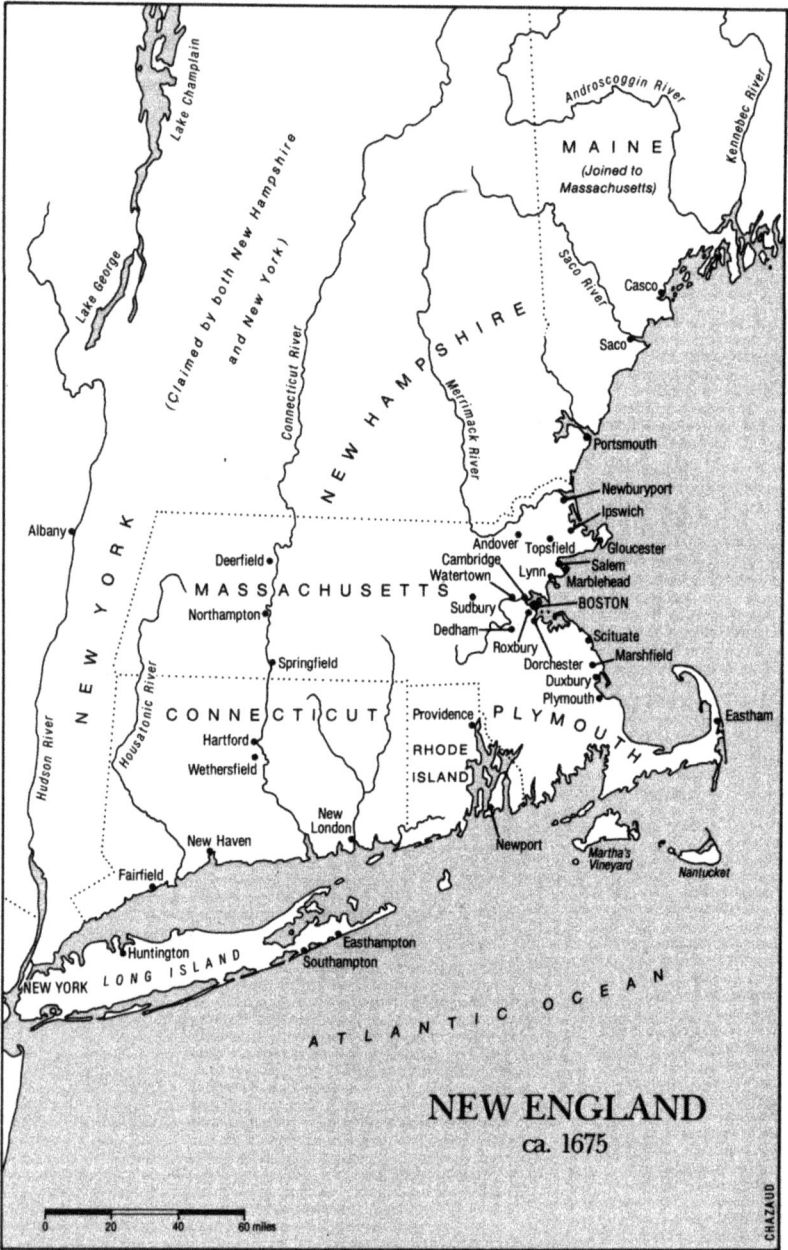

NEW ENGLAND
ca. 1675

Innes, p. 2

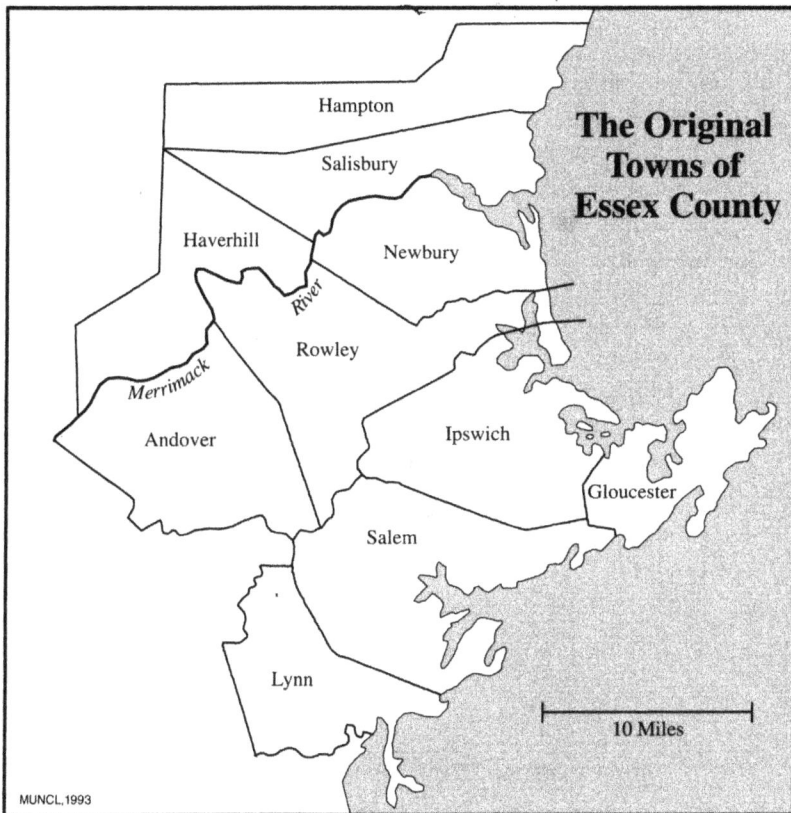

The Original Towns of Essex County

Hampton
Salisbury
Haverhill
Newbury
River
Rowley
Merrimack
Andover
Ipswich
Gloucester
Salem
Lynn
10 Miles

MUNCL,1993

From *Farmers and Fisherman*, Vickers, p. 3

02

Bradstreets Leave England for British America and British Ireland

One of the main findings of this chapter is the role that English gentry families played in the development of British North America during the 1600s, especially in the Massachusetts Bay Colony (MBC), by developing close contacts with senior leaders in the British government in London whose work required them to keep track of what was going on in New England. Like in New England, Ireland also needed English businesspeople with effective gentry connections if British efforts there were to result in the creation of a successful colony. Accordingly, families such as the Bradstreets and Dudleys living in the MBC, developed excellent connections with people in London seeking to do business in the new North American colonies and provided assistance from the British government during the Cromwellian period because of their common commitment to Puritan values. As a result, many companies were able to get governmental support for business ventures in such British colonies and dependencies as Ireland and the MBC.[1]

---

[1] It is important to understand differences in what Puritans in Boston and Salem sought for the towns they were starting up in the MBC and what roles were played by officials in Boston, the capital, on the one hand, and Salem, another

In the U.S., the connections between American business and governmental leaders in London are better understood, which is why this chapter takes a broader look at some Irish Bradstreet gentry who received military pay from government officials in London to spend money that they received from the government to buy land in the MBC or Ireland at low prices as entrepreneurs, especially in areas where the Irish Confederacy had, until Cromwell's invasion and occupation of Ireland, gained control over large swaths of land confiscated by the English government. In Massachusetts, government leaders like Simon Bradstreet invested their monetary gains in land and also launched speculative business enterprises. Many of the best-known Puritans who took part in the early stages of the Great Migration were both pious Puritans and clever business leaders. Some of the women, for example, Anne Hutchison and Anne Bradstreet, were models of Puritan piety also and were working hard to keep friends and family members still in England knowledgeable about what New England Puritans were doing in the fields of religion and culture.[2]

Most MBC Bradstreets were active Puritans, including Simon Bradstreet and Anne Dudley (1612-1672), who had left their home in Lincolnshire, England, in 1629 bound for the MBC. After that couple arrived in British North America along with members of their households including relatives and servants, they quickly put down roots in the new MBC. Both the influence of the birth family

---

large town supported by fishing, timber, and shipbuilding industries. As the next chapter suggests, Salem was the home of the second Puritan family, the Lovetts, whose stories are covered in this book. For more information about the urbanization of Salem, see Stephen Innes. *Creating the Commonwealth: The Economic Culture of Puritan New England.* NY: Norton, 1995, especially chapters 1 and 7.

[2] Both Anne Bradstreet and Anne Hutchinson are considered at length in Phillip H. Round's *By Nature and By Custom Cursed. Transatlantic Civil Discourse and New England Cultural Production, 1620-1660.* Dartmouth, NH: University Press of New England, 1999.

of Simon's wife, Anne Dudley, and her married life with Simon Bradstreet would have ensured that the couple could have flourished where they had been living near Horbling, England, nearly as well as they did near the Atlantic coast of the MBC in British North America.[3] Others among Simon's cousins, such as Humphrey Bradstreet and Anne's own parents, Thomas Dudley, his wife, and their children, left England just before the time that Anne and Simon did and with the same destination in mind. After his arrival, Simon served the New England colony as a magistrate and also played an important role in the establishment and administration of local government in the new town of Ipswich. At the same time, it is clear that, as much as those two men were capable leaders for Puritan interests in Massachusetts, a close look at other people in Simon's family shows that England's politics concerning Ireland helped ensure that members of the Bradstreet family would also do well during the second half of the seventeenth century. An example is Simon's younger brother, John Bradstreet, who also left England but chose Ireland instead of Massachusetts as his destination. John Bradstreet's project for the British government turned out to be as significant as Simon's work in British North America in general and in the MBC in particular.

Comparing Two Bradstreet "Adventurers"

Simon and his younger brother John (1606 - abt. 1688) left England separately and headed to different destinations. More is known about Simon Bradstreet's activities, especially what he did during the multiple times he served as governor of the Massachusetts

---

[3] Simon's title in the MBC was magistrate, which was like a justice of the peace. That title allowed him to hold additional appointments, such as governor of the MBC, or take up specific appointments made by the head of the executive branch of government in London, i.e., by the king and receive pay for having performed certain specified tasks. This definition was given in the *Compact Edition of the Oxford English Dictionary*, volume 1, A-O, p. 1692, Oxford University Press, 1971.

Bay Colony (MBC), as well as his work as a diplomatic representative of MBC officials working for the government in London. What little we know about John Bradstreet's early career was different from Simon's. John may have served in Cromwell's army in Ireland or moved about in parts of England, Scotland, and Ireland as a former soldier and/or businessman.

Probably he would have been paid in land grants or other benefits by the British government for his work in the turbulent times of the mid-1640s until later in that century as what was called an "adventurer." Whichever the combination of reasons was, Simon's brother, John Bradstreet, concentrated his efforts on behalf of his family as well as the English government in Ireland. The result was that he was awarded the title of baronet in Ireland by the government in England, an honor granted also to whomever would be the eldest son in each future generation. As it turned out, a baronetcy was held by this Anglo-Irish Bradstreet family until Ireland finally overthrew its colonial status and became an independent nation in 1922.

So, both brothers prospered in their new homelands under the sponsorship of government officials in London and private business partners and other investors. Besides grants of land in the MBC and later in NH and CT, Gov. Simon, like other senior governmental officials in the MBC, got licenses to start up business partnerships deemed useful by officials in London for the economic development of the colony. Simon was also sometimes paid what he was owed from his government jobs in the form of land instead of taking a salary during his terms as governor or for conduct of diplomatic negotiations on behalf of the Colony. It is very likely that Simon's brother John also received grants of land as remuneration in his capacity as an "adventurer," another title that Simon also used. That designation allowed Simon and his business partners to pursue trade and secure capital for the startup of economic activities like ironworks, sawmills, and businesses needed for the shipbuilding industry which they hoped would operate at a profit in towns such as Boston and Salem.

The most likely times for Simon's brother, John Bradstreet, to have come to Ireland are either: 1) in the 1640s as a soldier in Oliver Cromwell's army fighting the native Irish armed forces who had banded together under the name of the Irish Confederacy; 2) around the same time period but serving in the capacity of an "adventurer," who sought to benefit financially from the act which the Parliament in London passed in 1642 and which Simon took advantage of when he secured capital for infrastructure projects in the Puritan MBC; or 3) as someone who hoped to participate in the British government's activities aimed at taking more control of Ireland and areas within Kilkenny and Tipperary Counties, specifically. These plans were similar to what Cromwell's English government wanted to do after they had finished defeating the Irish Confederacy.

In sum, John Bradstreet's family prospered inside the ruling class of the British Empire in Ireland and his descendants included a long line of jurists, magistrates, and governmental leaders working for the governing class of the British occupation of Ireland. We will come back to John's family after Simon's career in Massachusetts is further described and evaluated, especially the work that a cousin, Humphrey Bradstreet, who was an early settler of the town of Ipswich, MBC, was doing at the same time. Humphrey led a quieter life but also one in which he took on the full range of community responsibilities expected of a Puritan "paterfamilias" in the Essex County town of Ipswich.[4]

---

[4] Members of Humphrey Bradstreet's family still lived in Ipswich and other nearby places in Essex County at the time when historians and others were celebrating the four hundredth anniversary of Anne Bradstreet's birth in England at events held in Ipswich, Andover, and other nearby places. At these events, the main focus was Anne Bradstreet's poetry and her influence on American women writers. However, there were also panels describing the role that she played in keeping a conversation or discourse open between the MBC and senior officials

Simon Bradstreet and Anne Dudley's
Family Flourishes in the MBC

Although Simon was frequently on call during his long working life for business, these governmental and diplomatic trips within the New England colony and to London meant that he got a close-up opportunity to assess governmental decision-making at the highest levels in London, while his wife and growing family were not able to benefit from his presence for long stretches of time because the homes that the family had in Ipswich and, later, in Andover, were out of range of one-day travel to and from the MBC capital in Boston. Anne's father, Thomas Dudley, who was Simon's first employer in England, became governor of the MBC after the colony's establishment in 1630. Anne Dudley Bradstreet was an important influence on Puritan thought in both the MBC and back home in England, partly because she had a ready audience in England of senior governmental officials of the Puritan persuasion both before and after Cromwell led the Parliamentary armies into battle in Scotland, England, and Ireland during the period from 1640 to 1660.[5] Although Anne and Simon had four sons and four daughters, I will concentrate on the family lines of two of their children, Hannah Bradstreet Wiggin and another John Bradstreet, as examples of how the family and the Puritan experiment fared from the mid-seventeenth century to the mid-twentieth century.

---

inside the London metropole, made up of a range of officials interested in Anne's poetry but also included the cultural connections she kept knitted together.

[5] See Charlotte Gordon. *Mistress Bradstreet.*" *The Untold Life of America's First Poet.* Boston: Little Brown. 1980 and Christopher Hill. *The World Turned Upside Down: Radical Ideas During the English Revolution.* N.Y. Penguin, 1991. Another view is put forward by Mary Beth Norton in *Founding Mothers and Fathers: Gendered Power and the Forming of American Society.* NY. Knopf, 1996. Anne Bradstreet is an important figure in these debates because she had the opportunity – and used it – to address different audiences who, like her, were depressed by the social changes that were loosening the bonds that Puritans held with other English people. See "Come Over and Help Us" which is chapter five of Round's already-cited work, 205-254.

Another set of Puritan parents, Mary Grant and John Lovett, who were forebears of my maternal grandmother, Bertha Lovett, will be shown in the next chapter living with their family in Salem, MBC, in the mid-1630s.

All of the Bradstreet children in Ethel Bradstreet's line were born in what is now Essex County, Massachusetts, as were most of her direct ancestors in this book's Lovett line. The lives that these two families pursued illustrate important similarities and some differences among the families who came from England to British North America in the 1630s. Members of the Lovett and Bradstreet families considered themselves Puritans, and both couples fervently believed that they were building towns and communities that would grow in size and stay active over time. The Bradstreet families focused on small-scale agriculture set in rural towns such as Ipswich, Topsfield, and North Andover in the northern part of the MBC, while members of the Lovett family played a strong role in what soon became Salem and Beverly, two bustling towns on the sea coast which quickly developed strong maritime ties throughout the world, but specifically within maritime America focused on economic activities on behalf of the British Empire in British North America, such as shipbuilding and trade between Massachusetts and the East Indies, on the one hand, and in Newfoundland, England, and with Scotland, on the other.

Bradstreet Families Living Near Boston, England, in the Early 1600s

People in the maternal and paternal families of Simon and John Bradstreet had lived in the eastern part of England bordering the North Sea coast for several generations before Simon and Anne's births early in the seventeenth century. At that time, Simon's family lived in the village of Horbling, where Rev. Simon Bradstreet (1580-1621) was the minister of a church located not far from Gislingham and Ipswich. Rev. Simon's eldest son, the future Governor Simon (1604-1697), also grew up near Boston, England, and his future wife, Anne Dudley, grew up in Northhampton, which is inside the area of the English North Sea coast known as East Anglia.

After they made their decision to emigrate, Simon and Anne joined a larger group including Anne's parents, the Dudleys, who arrived in the new Massachusetts colony in 1629 before their son and daughter-in-law arrived. The group received financial support from the British government and some London-based private investors to start up the MBC in North America. Instead of breaking ties completely with the mother country, however, the members of the colony-in-waiting had continuing support from the British government, including protection flowing from Britain's control of the high seas during their journey from England to British North America and financial support to start up the MBC through the assistance of land grants to prospective settlers who shared their commitment to Puritan goals and values.

Understanding decisions that individuals and families make in the course of breaking away from a known geography has received attention from historians, sociologists, economists, and other researchers. Recent studies show how Simon and Anne and their co-religionists prepared for life in the Massachusetts colony and how they expected their new communities to function. Their preparations were on the mark in some areas but not in others, as we shall see. More difficult to know is how individual family members saw these issues. First, we will consider factors influencing the decisions that Simon and Anne and one of Simon's cousins, Humphrey Bradstreet (1594-1655) and his family, made to leave England for the MBC. Then later in this chapter, I will explain a different decision made by Simon's younger brother, John Bradstreet, who decided to leave England for British Ireland instead, a decision that was actively supported by the British government as senior governmental officials desperately wanted English people to settle in Ireland after the Catholic military forces under the auspices of the Irish Confederacy had been defeated by Cromwell's army. British officials knew that it would be harder to govern Ireland than it had been to defeat the Irish Confederacy and needed people who had – and knew how to exercise – military and leadership skills.

This chapter uses the mini-tree approach to show the English Bradstreet families at home in the MBC. As in the other chapters, the names of the people in the main line of descent to Ethel Bradstreet (1917-2005) are indicated in the mini-trees using **bold** and *italics*. How Simon and Humphrey, two Bradstreet heads of household and their families, settled in the MBC is not the usual story of emigration and immigration for northern Europeans during the last several hundred years, i.e., these people did not decide to leave England when their situation or their economic and/or social situation became precarious because of some combination of war, political oppression by the governments of their home countries, or economic distress. Recent historiography does, however, stress that many other people and families went to British North America under indenture than what historians used to believe, including people coming under indenture on ships that were part of the Puritan fleet.

The Bradstreet and Dudley families were able to pay the full cost of their own trips to British America, however. Shortly after their marriage, Simon and Anne arrived as part of what historians call the Winthrop fleet, which was bound for the MBC with official papers under the seal of the British government and with financial backing from private English investors who saw financial and other benefits to England's establishment of a second colony near the one in Plymouth, which had been established in 1620 by an earlier group of religious dissenters. All of Simon and Anne's children were born after the couple reached their destination in North America.

A Short Version of the Bradstreet Family Tree in England

Symond Bradstreet, 1491-1556, married **Eleanor _____,** 1493-1556.

Their children: **John** born in 1518, Johane born in 1522, Rychard born in 1525, Cecilie born in 1534, Robert born in 1535, and Thomas born in 1537.

John Bradstreet, 1518-1559, married **Johane Wade Smythe,** 1522-?

Their children: Humfrey born in 1540, **Symond** born in 1542, Thomas born in 1544, Marie born in 1522, Dorothy born in 1556.

Symond Bradstreet, 1542-1620, married **Margaret Norman** -1623.

Their child: **Simon** born in 1580.

Rev. Simon Bradstreet 1580-1621 married **Margaret Sawyer 1584-1631.**

Their children born in Horbling: Samuel born in 1602, **Simon** born in 1604, John born in 1606, Mercy born in abt. 1606.

Anne Dudley's English Tree

Roger Dudley, born in 1550, married **Susanna Thorne,** 1559-1588.

Their children: **Thomas** born in 1576, Richard born in 1579, David born in 1579, Mary born in 1580, Richard born in 1583, Dorothy born in 1585, Joseph born in 1587.

Thomas Dudley, 1576-1653, who was born in Yardley Hastings, Northhamptonshire, England and died in Roxbury, Suffolk, MBC, married **Dorothy Yorke,** 1582-

1643, who was born in Northamptonshire, and died in Roxbury, MBC.

Their children: Patience born in 1598, Joseph born in 1602, Thomas born in 1605, Samuel born in 1608, **Anne** born in 1612, John born in 1616, Patience born in 1617, Sarah born in 1620, Mercy born in 1621, Dorothy born in 1622, Joseph born in 1627, Paul born in 1630, Samuel born in 1637.

Thomas Dudley, 1576-1653, married **Catherine Deighton**, after the death of his first wife.

Their children born in the Massachusetts Bay Colony: Deborah 1645, Joseph 1647, Paul 1650.

Thomas Dudley, Anne's father, and her husband, Simon Bradstreet, quickly emerged as business and governmental leaders of the MBC, with both serving as governors of the colony as well as occupying multiple local government offices. The following mini-tree shows Ethel Bradstreet's descent from Simon and Anne via their youngest son, another John Bradstreet (1652-1718). Again, the main line of Ethel Bradstreet's ancestors in each generation is shown in bold and italics.

Simon Bradstreet and Anne Dudley's Line in Massachusetts

Simon Bradstreet, 1604-1697, was born in Horbling, Lincolnshire, England and married **Anne Dudley,** 1612-1672, who was born in Northampton Borough. The couple married in Horbling, Lincolnshire in 1628.

Their children born in the Massachusetts Bay Colony (MBC): Dorothy 1633-1672, who was born in Salem, MBC, and died in Hampton, Rockingham, NH; Sarah, 1838-1691; Simon, 1640-1684, who was born in Ipswich and died in New London, CT; Hannah Anne,

1642-1707; Samuel, 1643-1682; Mercy, 1647-1715; Dudley, 1648-1706; and **John**, 1652-1718.

John Bradstreet, 1652-1718, who was born in Andover, MBC, and died in Topsfield, MBC, married **Sarah Perkins**, 1657-1745 in 1677.
Their children were all born in Topsfield: Simon, 1682-1738, Mercy, 1689-1725, John, 1693-1740, Margaret born in 1696-? and **Samuel**, 1699-1762.

Samuel Bradstreet, 1699-1762, who was born in Topsfield, married **Sarah Clarke,** 1705-1736, in Rowley, MBC in 1722.
Their children born in Topsfield: Ann born in 1724, Sarah born in 1727, **Samuel**, 1729-1777, Elijah, 1731-1760, Eunice, 1733-1811, Asa, 1736-?

Samuel Bradstreet, 1729-1777, married **Ruth Lamson,** 1733-1777, in Topsfield, MA in 1762.
Their children born in Topsfield: Samuel, 1764-1816, Ruth, 1766-? Elijah, 1767-? **Asa**, 1769-1793? 1771-? Moses, 1773-?

Asa Bradstreet, 1769-1793, married **Abagail Balch,** 1772-1861, in Topsfield in 1790.
Their children born in Topsfield: **William**, 1792-1873, Asa, 1793-1863.

William Bradstreet, 1792-1873, married **Eunice Perkins,** 1795-1879, in Ipswich in 1814.
Their children born in Topsfield: Abigail, 1814-1850, Asa, 1816-1851, Marietta 1818-1834, Lydia, 1820-1848, **William Jr,** 1823-1904, Fanny,1825-?, Moses, 1827-1832, Elijah, 1829-1913, Louisa,1832-? Moses, 1834-1906, Alonzo, 1839-1884.

William Bradstreet, Jr, 1823-1904, married ***Judith Morrill Fullerton***, 1823-1898, in Topsfield in 1845.
Their children born in Topsfield: Anna, 1846-1936, Sarah, 1848-1934, William, 1849-1925, and Marietta, 1853-1858. Their children born in Danvers: Henry, 1861-1939, ***Alvah J.,*** 1862-1961.

Alvah J. Bradstreet, 1862-1961, married Cordelia Staples, 1860-1897, in Danvers, MA in 1882.
Their children were all born in Danvers: Emma, 1882-1932, Olive, 1883-1906, Cora, 1884-1968, Florence, 1886-1986, Sarah, 1888-1892, William, 1891-1959, Ina, 1894-1896.

Alvah J. Bradstreet, 1862-1961, after Cordelia's death married ***Bertha F. Lovett,*** 1883-1971, in Beverly, MA in 1908.
Their children were all born in Danvers: Dudley, 1909-1971, Alva C, 1911-1912, ***Ethel***, 1917-2005.

Ethel Bradstreet, 1917-2005, who was born in Danvers, MA, married ***John MacLean Maney,*** 1914-1985, who was born in Lawrence, MA. The couple married in Danvers in 1940.

John Bradstreet (1652-1718) and his wife, Sarah Perkins (1657-1745), got land in Topsfield from John's father, Simon Bradstreet. This land was located not far from Ipswich and Andover, where Simon and Anne had lived. Once the paperwork was completed for the land grants that Simon organized, one or more sons in John's family in each generation farmed land in Topsfield until about 1860, when John's descendant, William Bradstreet, Jr (1823-1904), sold his farm there, bought land for a new farm in nearby Danvers, and moved his family to East Danvers near the border with the town of Beverly, which is located along the Atlantic coast. This picture of how Simon provided for his family is consistent with what other Puritan heads of household were doing to establish their families in the mid-seventeenth century after the decade of arrivals of Puritans from England known as the Great Migration.

Another of Simon's cousins, Humphrey Bradstreet, had also come to the MBC. Born in the town of Ipswich, in the county of Suffolk, England, in 1594, Humphrey died in Ipswich, MBC, in 1655. He came to British America in 1634 from Ipswich, England, with his wife and three children, four years after Simon and Anne arrived in Salem. Humphrey and his family were among the first settlers of a new town in Massachusetts which was also called Ipswich when it was established in 1636. Humphrey and his family also came to the MBC intent on creating a more godly community in which they would live and raise their own families. Puritan planners considered success would follow if they could get competent migrants to settle in small homogeneous communities united by goals and objectives inspired by their families' religious beliefs.

How they fared in these goals can be evaluated by comparing the towns of Ipswich and Topsfield, where the Bradstreet families settled, with Beverly and Salem, the towns where the second Puritan family of Lovetts settled in the 1630s. Puritan town planners also tried to understand why the English colony in Jamestown, Virginia, had failed and hoped that they would be able to establish a "new" England that borrowed what was good from the "old" country and purified what they considered as negative influences back home.[6] We can imagine some of the tasks

---

[6] According to an interesting study by Virginia DeJohn Anderson, *New England's Generation: The Great Migration and the Formation of Society and Culture in the Seventeenth Century*, Cambridge, UK: Cambridge University Press, 1991, it is helpful to compare why people came in the early years, i.e., how and why a decision was made to leave England; what happened during the ocean passage; how the Puritan settlers decided where in the MBC they would settle; and how

facing a person such as John, the youngest of Simon and Anne Dudley Bradstreet's children, as he sought to establish a farm in Topsfield on land given to him by his father in the 1650s-1670s. John's commitment to his community included playing an active role in local government and providing land to his sons to carry the experiment into the next generation.

By the middle of the nineteenth century, census records showed some of the effects that industrialization was having on the agricultural world of Topsfield, including on the land held by John's descendants. In response, Simon and Anne Bradstreet's descendants had to make changes as they understood that the agricultural model of community-building was starting to face an increasingly urban and industrializing Essex County during the mid-nineteenth century. Important parts of this story are told later in this chapter in the person of John's great-grandson, Asa Bradstreet, and also in the next chapter which describes the increasingly urban world of Beverly, the city inhabited by most of the Lovett families.

Meanwhile, What About the Bradstreets in Ireland?

What is still not understood is exactly what John – or members of his family in Ireland – did to accumulate the property that he and his male descendants held there for nearly three hundred years. John may have served in Cromwell's army in England and received land grants in Ireland as a result; or he may have come to Ireland as part of a company of investors with similar business interests to those that his brother had in Massachusetts. Another possibility was that John may have started out in one role and continued in another. For certain, this John Bradstreet was awarded land that the army had taken from Roman Catholic landowners and tenants, mostly in Counties Kilkenny and Tipperary, after open hostilities between the English and the Irish Confederacy ended in the 1660s.

---

they could develop the competencies needed to successfully work the land and work together with their neighbors, 1991, 131-177.

It seems that the success of the Irish Bradstreet brothers, sons, nephews, cousins, and their families was due in part to the connections that they had with how the British Empire was being run outside of England. Some brief information about Simon's brother, John Bradstreet, was included in the genealogical work about Bradstreets written by Ethel Bradstreet's father, Alvah Bradstreet (1862-1961), on the occasion of his ninetieth birthday. Alvah was the youngest son in the Bradstreet family of Topsfield where his father had continued to farm until he moved the family to Danvers, MA, in 1860. In his book, Alvah recollected that he first heard about Bradstreets living in Ireland when he talked with an Irish-American woman to whom he sold milk on his daily route from Danvers to Salem, Mass. and back. Did he know, this woman asked him one day, that he had a Bradstreet relative living in Stacumni, in county Kildare, Ireland, near Dublin? He also remembered that this woman told him that she knew that this Bradstreet family in Ireland had a big house and land there, and that the head of the family had the title of baronet.[7]

The Samuel Bradstreet that this woman heard about was probably one of the descendants of the John Bradstreet who started his family in Ireland at approximately the same time that his brother, Gov. Simon, was pursuing his governmental and diplomatic career in Boston, the capital of the new Massachusetts Bay Colony. The will of Sir Simon Bradstreet, 2nd baronet, dated 2 Nov 1760 in Dublin, can probably answer the question of who in the family was the next Bradstreet baronet in Ireland. In the will it is noted that this Simon's father was a Simon who had his residence at one time at Portland, Tipperary, Ireland, and his grandfather was

---

[7] In his book published in 1949, *The Life and Times of Alvah J. Bradstreet,* edited by John M. Maney and Ethel Bradstreet Maney, Alvah noted that a baronetcy had been awarded to Gov. Simon's grandfather. Maybe there was such a baronetcy which could have gone to Simon's brother, John, or John's son for work that one or the other did in Ireland in the late seventeenth century and was carried on by their descendants.

John Bradstreet, who had lived in Blanchevilles Park, Kilkenny, Ireland. A nephew, Lt. Col John Bradstreet, governor of St. Johns, Newfoundland, is also mentioned.[8]

As can be seen in the mini-trees, Simon and his brother John were both sons of Simon Bradstreet of Horbling, Lincolnshire. Anglo-Irish wills and probate records available on the internet show a John Bradstreet, Esq., dying in Ireland in about 1688. His main property was located in Blanchevilles Park, Kilkenny, Ireland. Will and probate records show family properties in Kildare and Dublin counties, where descendants in this line later lived, including Stacumni. The probate records mention a will for a Sir Simon Bradstreet, Baronet (1688-1762), living in Kilmainham, which at that time was just outside of Dublin proper. Next to inherit the title of Baronet was Sir Simon's brother, Sir Samuel Bradstreet (1695-1791), who was born at one of the Bradstreet family properties, Blanchevilles Park, in Kilkenny.

The reader may have already noted that the first names given to Bradstreet sons in each generation in Ireland are mostly the same as those given to Bradstreet sons living in the MBC, that is, Simon, John, and Samuel among others. Also, a will from 1773 records the death of Dudley Bradstreet (1711-1763), another brother of Sir Simon. Dudley had tried his hand at spying for the British during the wars with the Stewarts in the first half of the eighteenth century. This Dudley later became a writer of racy novels and for some time also ran a distillery in County Westmeath, Ireland. Dudley did not inherit the land and titles, however. Instead, Sir Simon's title was granted to his brother, Sir Samuel Bradstreet, (1738-1791), Justice of the King's Bench in Dublin. This Samuel lived in Dublin and seems to have been the person who had the country house in Stacumni that Alvah Bradstreet heard about from his milk route customer.

---

[8] See Godfrey, William. *Pursuit of Profit and Preferment in Colonial North America: John Bradstreet's Quest*. Waterloo, Ontario: Wilfrid Laurier University Press, 2006.

The line might have ended in the early twentieth century anyway because one result of the battles at Gallipoli during World War I was the death in military service of the only known son in a generation of the Irish Bradstreet line, Gerald Edmund Bradstreet, (1891-1915). However, because of the successful rising by the Irish Revolutionary Army against the British government after World War I ended, Ireland was able to win its independence from Great Britain in 1922. As a consequence, Edward Simon, the last of the line of Bradstreet baronets in Ireland, re-settled in Australia. There had been some black sheep in the Irish Bradstreet line, but most of the heads of families in Ireland seem to have been as sober and hard-working as their Massachusetts counterparts. However, it is clear that they came to Ireland to support the English government in wartime and continued enjoying benefits of that English conquest and the direct – and active – rule over the Irish people that the United Kingdom enjoyed for more than three centuries.

Before we follow another member of Simon and Anne's extended family to the near present, here is a quick update on the life of another member of this Anglo-Irish family, John Valentine Bradstreet, Baronet, who was in some respects an outlier in the Bradstreet Irish family tree. The following information is listed on the entry for John Valentine Bradstreet's gravesite at the Find-a-Grave website, which summarized his life and death in Ireland. It comes in the form of a notice from the Dublin Cemeteries Committee, which was included in the entry for him after his body was interred in Glasnevin Cemetery in Dublin in 1890.[9]

"Sir John Bradstreet, the fourth Baronet, became as strong a champion for Catholic interests as his grandfather had been on behalf of the opposing creed. For nearly thirty years he gave his toil and time to the management of Glasnevin Cemetery, and was an active member as well as being President of the Society of

---

[9] At: https://images.findagrave.com/photos/2019/306/81215746_3215e777-587e-4966-88b9-7af3714bbeb9.jpeg

St. Vincent de Paul. He died November 21, 1889. His funeral, followed by the orphans he had sheltered, and the poor whom he had long visited and relieved, was a touching spectacle."

By the time of his death, it seems, John Valentine Bradstreet, one of the most prominent among the Bradstreets from England who had ruled Ireland and gotten rich from its bounty, had become a family outlier through his conversion to the Roman Catholic faith and also could be characterized as a nearly-native son of Ireland before British rule came to an end. At the same time, in 1889, many of the Massachusetts Bradstreets were transitioning away from the small holdings that their ancestors in Essex County had hoped would support and benefit them in perpetuity.

Both the seventeenth-century Bradstreets in Essex County and generations of their children who continued living in rural places like Topsfield, MA, had pursued a more simple lifestyle than their wealthy cousins in Stacumni, Kilmainham, and Dublin. During two centuries after their coming to the MBC, most male descendants of Anne and Simon Bradstreet continued to play roles in both state and local government and in the activities of the small churches to which they belonged. Moreover, besides the heads of household, it is important to understand the contributions to community-building made by women, children, indentured farm workers, and others living in Topsfield and similar places in northern Essex County.

In England and under English rule in Ireland, the first son inherited any titles his father may have had, and the father's will apportioned land and other property to the various sons as he saw fit. In the Massachusetts colony, no titles were given or passed to the next generation. Nor, as in the mother country, did Bradstreet heads of household pass land directly to their marriage partners or their daughters. The MBC's Simon Bradstreet gave land to his sons, and probate records showed that no land was provided to his daughters, but money was instead given to the daughters' husbands. In colonial Massachusetts, especially in rural Puritan communities such as Topsfield, parents in successive generations increasingly felt pressure to acquire more land or subdivide the land which the family held in order to allow sons, grandsons, and their families to continue living nearby.

When all local land in a town was thus apportioned, the local government might add land outside the village border as long as that option remained available. In a few years, municipal leaders of the original villages had no more land to grant inside their boundaries; that meant that there was an increased burden on young men to buy expensive land some distance away from the original town boundaries. This burden was often felt especially by middle sons, who sometimes reacted by migrating to locations further away whose land cost much less than land in the older towns. At the same time, caring for the home farm and elderly parents often fell to the youngest sons and their wives. Thus, Alvah Bradstreet moved with his parents and siblings to Danvers in the second half of the nineteenth century. Alvah was the youngest son in his own family, but none of his sons worked in their traditional family agricultural businesses in Danvers during the twentieth century after they completed school.

Spotlight on Hannah Bradstreet Wiggin's Great-granddaughter from Hawaii, Mary Pukui

This section follows up the information already given about the lives of three male cousins – Simon and Humphrey Bradstreet in North America, and John Bradstreet in Ireland – with information about the lives of three Bradstreet women. Hannah's mother, Anne Dudley, will play a Spotlight role as a guest in the Maternal chapter. Anne Dudley Bradstreet is best known by historians and literary scholars as the first female poet who wrote in British North America. Her daughter, Hannah Bradstreet, was the oldest of Anne and Simon's female children. Hannah led a life heading up a household for the man she married, Andrew Wiggin (1635-1710), and had responsibility for the children and the couple's household.

Her husband served as governor of another British colony that was started up on the northern border of Essex County and became the state of New Hampshire. Gov. Simon was a good friend of Andrew Wiggin, and they were partners and "adventurers" in various joint business schemes paid for by the acquisition of public land and its subsequent sale to interested landowners; they also used the profits of the sale of land to entrepreneurs seeking to build sawmills and other needed infrastructure.

Besides Anne and her daughter Hannah, a third woman of interest, who lived and died much more recently, is another of Hannah's direct descendants. This woman, Mary Abigail Wiggin (1895-1986), is also known by her Hawaiian name, Mary Pukui, and deserves to join the ranks of those whose activities should be spotlighted. In correspondence with Alvah Bradstreet before his death in 1860, Mary declared herself proud that she was a direct descendant of Simon and Anne Bradstreet from Hannah Bradstreet Wiggin's line through to her own father, Henry Nathaniel Wiggin (1861-1930) of Salem, MA. Mary's correspondence with the Massachusetts Bradstreets, a copy of which is held by the author, gives meaning to stories about the women profiled in this chapter.

Mary Abigail Wiggin was born in the territory of Hawaii in 1895 and died in 1986, after Hawaii had become a U.S. state. Mary's contributions to Hawaiian cultural life celebrate the scope of her professional and scholarly works about Hawaii's peoples and their languages, songs, customs, and literature. In correspondence with Alvah Bradstreet's son, William, in the mid-twentieth century, Mary stressed how her life had been influenced by Anne Bradstreet and how highly she regarded her ancestor as an icon of American culture because of Anne's poetry. Mary also appreciated that many of Anne's poems were about daily life, including how she took care of her large family in Ipswich and Andover while her husband was serving in high positions in the colonial government in Boston or traveling on diplomatic trips to London.

Mary Wiggin's mother, Mary Pa'ahana Kanako'ole (1878-1941), had married Henry Wiggin, who was born in Salem, MA and lived in Hawaii for most of his life. Their daughter, who called herself Mary Pakui in letters to American friends and relatives, was a great-granddaughter seven times removed from Anne Bradstreet. Here is how Mary put it in a letter dated 23 July 1959 to her cousin, William Bradstreet (1891-1959), and his wife, another cousin of Mary's, Anne Dudley Dunford (1903-1971):

I appreciate your writing me very much and do want to write to you myself. I am slow in answering, I know, but it isn't for lack of interest. I receive many letters from many parts of our U.S.A. and Japan but they are mostly request letters... information on our music, dances, customs, and so forth... which I answer as they come.[10]
Your letter is different. It is what we call an OHANA letter... a letter of interest in being offshoots of the same root stock. Even if I am an old shoot in the group, I want to thank you for the pictures you sent of your father, self, son and grandson... a living branch we islanders call it.

This story connecting Mary, Hannah, and Anne shows the importance of letters, photos, and other family materials through which it is possible to unearth important details about the lives of family members for a genealogical memoir such as this one. Unfortunately, as with so many other people in the families at the center of this book, we do not know how Anne or her daughter Hannah managed their busy family lives. In the Maternal chapter, we will assess how women's roles changed at the household and

---

[10] This and others among Mary Pukui's letters to Alvah Bradstreet are in the possession of the author and form a part of the *Maney Family Archive*. Unfortunately, the wiki for Mary at Wikipedia.org, has been taken down but, hopefully, it will return at this online site in the future.

community levels from 1650 to 1950 in England, Scotland, Canada, Ireland, and the USA, including not only places in New England but also in Hawaii.

Spotlighting Asa Bradstreet and the Dangers of Farming in Essex County

In this part of the Bradstreet chapter, we focus on the challenge of whether agriculture could be a stable profession for descendants of the Puritans living in Essex County in the eighteenth century and beyond. This section shows how hard and dangerous the work was for a man to keep a family farm productive in northern Massachusetts in the late 1700s and 1800s, and the resulting reliance that most families placed on having the men and boys involved in two or more different kinds of work at the same time by the middle of the nineteenth century. The story told here focuses on land that Simon and Anne's son, John Bradstreet (1652-1718), had inherited from Simon and, in turn, had passed along to his own sons. Anne and Simon had raised their children in various places in the northern part of the MBC.

In each place, Simon was able to support the family household through income from his governmental service, the businesses that he and his partners set up, and the land grants that he received in lieu of cash. Simon and Anne's children lived in several northern Essex County towns, notably Ipswich, Andover, and Topsfield, and the main work that these families relied on was small-scale or subsistence agriculture. During his career Simon stayed for long periods in the Boston area since the house that he had built for Anne and the children in Andover was too far away to travel to and from the capital on a daily basis. As a result, no available evidence suggests that Gov. Simon spent much time in the kind of frontier agricultural communities that Topsfield and Andover were during his long lifetime.

An interesting set of records provides information, however, about how a farm operated during the short life of Asa Bradstreet

(1769-1793), who was a great-grandson of Anne and Simon's son, John Bradstreet, in the line running to Ethel Bradstreet through her father, Alvah Bradstreet. Asa's marriage to Abigail Balch (1772-1861) was recorded in November, 1790, and soon thereafter, a son, William (1792-1873), was born at the family home in Topsfield, followed by a second son, Asa (1793-1863). See the mini-tree for Simon and Anne above. The death record showed that Asa, the father, died a month later during October of 1793 at the age of twenty-four. Probate records subsequently showed that Asa did not have a will and had died intestate. The cause of death was an accident, either while he was taking produce from his farm to market in Boston or while returning from doing so. Alvah Bradstreet, who was one of Asa's great-grandsons, wrote in his memoir that Asa would frequently fall asleep while driving a team of oxen from Topsfield to Boston. On one particular trip, he was instantly killed when the wagon wheels ran over his head.[11]

Alvah reported that it was typical for farmers in Topsfield and other communities to work on the home farm most days and then drive a fully loaded oxcart to Boston and back overnight multiple times during the harvest season. Sometimes, farmers also went from Topsfield to Boston, Charlestown, or other nearby towns towing trees to be made into masts for sea-going vessels bound for trans-oceanic trips from ports such as Salem and Beverly or for ships outfitted for fishing on the Grand Banks of Newfoundland. William Bradstreet (1792-1873), Alvah's grandfather, continued making the same treacherous trips to Boston and back by oxcart even though his own father had died doing the same trips. The

---

[11] An account of Asa Bradstreet's trips bringing produce and other goods to market by oxcart is provided in Alvah Bradstreet's book on pp. 13-14, as is Alvah's commentary on how differently he managed the same job when his turn came to run the farm and allied milk business. Also told about in Alvah's book at p. 105, was the shoe shop which his father had created among the farm's outbuildings. See *The Life and Times of Alvah J. Bradstreet*. Danvers, MA: 1949.

manner of Asa's death shows how differently the Bradstreets and their fellow Puritans lived in North America compared with how their Bradstreet cousins were living at the same time in Ireland. After Asa Bradstreet's death, the family continued to farm in Topsfield for another sixty-five years before leaving Topsfield to set up a new farm in the nearby town of Danvers in 1860.

Alvah also noted that when he started to manage the new farm, he preferred delivering milk to taking produce to market in Boston because the horse knew the way and would stop the milk cart at each customer's home along the route and wait for Alvah to wake up and leave off the milk for each of his customers. In the late 1850s, however, Alvah's father, William Bradstreet, Jr. (1823-1904), and his family did leave Topsfield but did not go west, as other friends or relatives had done. Instead, they adopted a different model of farming, which required that they move closer to towns and cities that were gaining population in eastern Massachusetts during the U.S. Civil War and needed the agricultural produce that a re-tooled Bradstreet farm could provide. Accordingly, in 1860, William Bradstreet, Jr. sold the family's Topsfield farm and bought a chunk of land nearly one mile square, which included land fronting on both sides of one of the main streets running from the center of Danvers to the center of Beverly.

Step by step, William, Jr., with help from his sons still living on the farm, Alvah and Henry (1861-1939), improved pasture land for their milk cows and added land along the Danvers River on which they planned to build houses and cottages near the shore for summer visitors from nearby cities. William concentrated his farming in Danvers in two ways: one was to operate a milk business, and the other was to continue the practice of taking agricultural produce to market in Boston. In the twentieth century, Alvah Bradstreet further diversified the family's agricultural businesses by selling off part of the land, constructing houses on other parts of it, operating his milk business, and opening a neighborhood grocery store.

Farming and Shoemaking in MA in
the mid-Nineteenth Century

Changes were also coming to the people who continued to keep farms in Topsfield, as census documents from the mid-1800s show. The first clue can be seen in the pages of the Massachusetts state census, showing that in Topsfield in 1855 agriculture was still at the top of the list in terms of sheer manpower needed. In these records, we can see Alvah's father, William, still living in Topsfield with his wife, Judith Morrill Fullerton Bradstreet (1823-1898), and three of the couple's young children. William's occupation is given as farmer, but his son, Alvah, wrote that his father also worked as a shoemaker in the winter. In the census, three hundred and thirty-four men were listed. Sixty-five heads of household worked as farmers. In addition, twenty-nine men described their occupations as laborers, eighteen as carpenters, and one hundred and fifty-six men and boys are listed as shoemakers.

Who could be buying that many shoes made in one small rural community? Part of the answer is that farmers had been engaged in shoemaking and boot-making for their own families in Essex and other Massachusetts counties ever since settlers from England started farming there in the 1600s. Traditionally, it was a job done by farmers and their children during winter months when there was not much work that could be done outside of the house and barn. The second part of the answer to the same question is that many of these shoes were destined to be sold to people in larger-populated towns and cities. Topsfield farmers and members of their families were already contributing to an expanding regional shoemaking economy that was becoming a key factor in Essex County's growing prosperity. We will hear more about shoemaking in the next chapter, as it was also a stable second occupation for many men and boys in more populous places like Beverly and an occupation in which women and girls participated, as well as men who were not away on maritime trading trips or fishing on the Grand Banks of Newfoundland.

There were other stories told by Alvah Bradstreet about the strategies that he learned from his father to supplement the viability of their farm in Danvers. Alvah still was taking some produce – but not timber – to Boston markets in the late nineteenth century. Also, in Alvah's time the roads were better and, as his business in Danvers prospered, he took only vegetables to Boston and surrounding cities and towns. By the end of the nineteenth century, Alvah wrote, he started taking the train to Boston on market day to meet up with his wagon when it made the rounds of the merchants he dealt with there. Alvah also devoted a lot of time and energy to his milk route. He wrote in his memoir that he was able to learn enough of their native language to be able to converse with some of his French-speaking customers. After the Civil War, he wrote, Irish immigrants and later French people from Canada came to work in the mills in Danvers, Salem, and other nearby towns, and he wanted to actively vie for their business.

Increasing economic opportunities were presenting themselves in some of the leading towns and cities of Essex County by the second half of the nineteenth century. Suppliers distributed materials for the shoes that people were making at home, then bought up the finished products, and also managed the sales of these shoes and boots to urban people in nearby cities and towns. The rapidly expanding town of Lynn, which was located near the southern edge of the county, was becoming one of the major centers of shoemaking in the U.S. during the mid-1800s. By the time that the national census was conducted in Topsfield in 1860, William Bradstreet and his family had departed for Danvers, but shoemaking was still the other job listed by men and their sons in Topsfield, where many families continued to farm the land that their ancestors had passed down to them. In the Lovett chapter, we will have an opportunity to compare Topsfield and Beverly to get a better picture of who worked in Essex County's sprawling shoe industry and what the jobs were in that industry for girls and women in those two places. First, though, we need to have one more spotlight session.

Spotlight on the *Surf City* Disaster of 1898

This is an exciting story featuring my grandmother, Bertha Lovett, and her sister, Ethel. It also has Alvah Bradstreet and some of the children from his first marriage in supporting roles. It is of interest in spotlight form because it described an important event in the lives of both of our Bradstreet grandparents as well as a traditional feature of coastal regions. The story shows a popular summertime activity in Salem, Beverly, and Danvers from two perspectives. One is taken from a local newspaper account of what actually happened at the event when it was held in 1898, and also shows how people involved in it talked about it later at family gatherings. The main topic in the newspaper coverage was how a holiday excursion went terribly wrong.[12] The story was later re-told in the annual holiday card sent out in December 1955 by Bertha Lovett Bradstreet and her husband, Alvah. Both accounts stress that there was a day-time shipwreck off the joint harbor of Salem and Beverly that took place so close to the shore that it could almost be seen by people on the shore searching for their loved ones.

The excursion boat left from Beverly in good weather on the morning of 4 July 1898, and everyone expected that it would have returned to Salem on time later in the afternoon. The destination was to be Salem Willows, a city park that was a popular summer amusement destination with restaurants and a beach that attracted families, especially on weekends and holidays. The trip featured a harbor tour and a stop at Baker's Island, just off the coast of Salem and Beverly. The name of the vessel that made the trip was the *Surf City*. The account on the holiday card was written from the perspective of Alvah Bradstreet, whose teen-aged daughters Emma, Olive, and Cora were on the excursion along with their high school friends, Bertha Lovett, and her younger sister, Ethel.

---

[12] This story was reprised on p. 8 of the *Beverly Times* on 2 Jul 1966 and written by Robert E. Campbell under the title "July 4th Brings Memories of 'Surf City' Sinking."

Alvah's job that day had been to drive the party to Beverly in the morning and pick everyone up when they arrived back at the appointed time at Salem Willows in the afternoon. What no one expected was the violent thunderstorm that hit Salem with hurricane-force winds and a downpour of rain. The only person in Alvah's group to be seriously affected was his future wife, Bertha Lovett, who, when asked by her grandchildren to tell the harrowing story one more time, always started by giving thanks to her sister, Ethel, who held onto Bertha's hair to keep her head above water until rescuers arrived. Much more fun was usually derived by the grandchildren from participating in summer outings, such as spending time at a local beach or going blueberry picking somewhere in nearby Wenham or Topsfield.

Whenever Bertha Lovett Bradstreet organized a day of blueberry picking, our grandmother always used a different location that only she knew had more blueberry bushes than anywhere else. On those outings, all of the children had pans attached to their waists by strong belts. Grandpa Alvah would be seated near a big blueberry bush with instructions not to miss a single berry. His grandchildren remembered those hot summer days when we were eating the fruits of our summertime labor during the fall and winter holidays in the form of the pies that were baked.

What's Missing From this Picture of Bradstreet Families in Essex County?

Now, we come to the last section of this profile of the Bradstreets. It has to be said that not all the researchers included in the bibliography spent time asking questions and getting answers about the original Native residents of Essex County, who may have opposed the arrival of Europeans in their lands during the seventeenth century and later. And we know that the growing towns and cities like Salem and Beverly began to have small populations of "others" who had been brought to Essex County as slaves from the Caribbean as well as from Maryland, Virginia, the Carolinas and other colonies. However, towns to the north and west of Boston sometimes did experience armed clashes with Native American populations during the first century of white settlers on these Indian lands.

Nor did female Puritan children have anything like an equal chance as boys to contribute to the intellectual, community, or faith-based innovation developed by men who were full citizens in the seventeenth century. So, unfortunately, while some records exist about Simon and Anne's male children, much less information is available about the roles that the daughters of Puritan grandees played as adults in their own families' lives, save for exceptions to this rule by women like Anne Hutchison and Anne Dudley Bradstreet. Sometimes, the former Anne Dudley detailed her own household activities in the classical-style poems she wrote while she was keeping house and taking care of her children during Simon's absences from Andover on governmental business in Boston and/or diplomatic trips to England. Anne was recognized for her writing by the city of Boston, England, and its cathedral church in their depiction of her as part of a stained-glass window put up after the original had been destroyed by a German air attack on that city during World War II.[13]

Based on knowledge gained in writing this book, I believe that Gov. Simon Bradstreet deserves new attention from historians so that the full canvas of his life in Massachusetts can be compared with the life of his brother in Ireland. After the death of his wife, Simon married a widow, Ann Gardner, who was a relative of former MBC governor, John Winthrop. Simon and his second wife were buried in Salem after his death in 1697. In contrast with the tomb of her husband, we know only that his first wife, Anne Dudley Bradstreet, died in Andover in 1672 but the exact place of her interment is not known. Sadly,

---

[13] Anne is depicted wearing Puritan dress. The new window was added to the church after World War II.

there is also no known burial site to be found for Simon and Anne's daughter, Hannah Bradstreet Wiggin, who died three years before her husband in 1707, but there is a Find-a-Grave[14] record, as well as a short profile of her in Wikipedia. Happily, Mary Pukui's Wikipedia entry is more informative because she was still working when she was interviewed. Consequently, it shows some of the voluminous information that exists about her active role in the cultural life of Hawaii.[15]

Anne Bradstreet's Hannah Bradstreet and Mary Pukui deserve to be considered among the ranks of Anne and Simon's children, along with John Bradstreet of Topsfield and his great-grandson, Asa. Readers of Anne's poems, or those who hear them spoken aloud, notice her wonderful command of English literature and language and her concerns about how to live a life serving both family and community. One of her gifts was to take care of her large family according to the beliefs she had about her religious duties. She was also able to live a kind of parallel life through her writing, a life that in today's world we might consider one of self-reflection. In the next chapter we will see less interest in further migration, even locally, by the family members of Ethel Bradstreet's maternal Lovett line. However, the focus on the economic activity that sustained their lives and livelihoods only changed a little. Boston, Beverly, and Salem created their own maritime lifestyles while the rest of the newcomers from England

---

[14] Find-a-Grave.org is a nongovernmental organization for which volunteers take photos of gravesites that others interested in that person can use to compare the official records about birth baptism, death, and other records. There is a Find-a-Grave account in this chapter of the burial site of one Bradstreet baronet.

[15] The information about Mary Pukui can be found at Wikipedia under her name, Mary Kawena Pukui. It was accessed by the author online on 6 October 2023 after an earlier, more informative wiki had been taken down. That wiki was available when checked on 7 Feb 2021 at: https://en.wikipedia.g/wiki/Mary_Kawana_Pukui. A photo of Mary Pukui can be found among the images in chapter 6.

paid more attention to agriculture, industry, and community development. And another thing that large and small towns had in common was that men and women living in both kinds of towns in most of Massachusetts continued relying on shoemaking for a secondary livelihood as heavily as their fellow Puritans did throughout Essex County.

Painting of Governor Simon Bradstreet

Ethel Bradstreet and John Maney in someone's roadster

Gov. Simon Bradstreet's mansion, built by his wife, sister of Sir George Downing, about 1650.

LIFE AND TIMES

OF

ALVAH J. BRADSTREET

BY

ALVAH J. BRADSTREET

DRAWINGS BY

BARBARA CHASE PALSON

EDITED AND MIMEOGRAPHED BY

JOHN M. MANEY

AND

ETHEL (BRADSTREET) MANEY

1 9 4 9

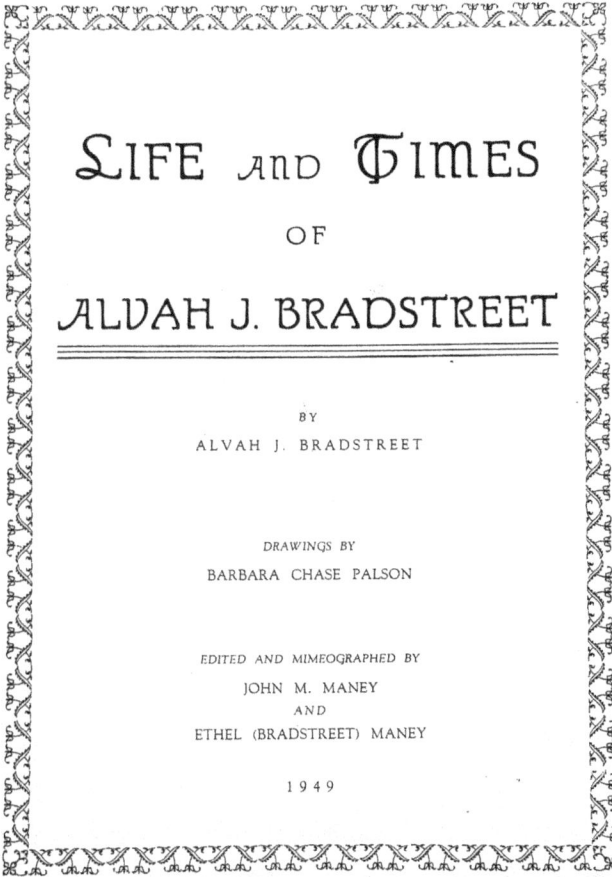

Alvah Bradstreet's book, edited by Ethel and John Maney

Ethel Maney French lesson

Seasons Greetings
from our house
to your house

Alvah J. and Bertha L. Bradstreet

Alvah Bradstreet's and Bertha Lovett's house in Danvers, MA

ANNE OF BOHEMIA   MARGARET BEAVFORT

Anne Dudley Bradstreet (third from left), stained-glass window at St. Botolph's, Boston, England. She is holding a basket of chicks that represent her children

Portrait of Thomas Dudley (1576-1653), attributed to Sir Peter Lely, was one of the first governors of the Massachusetts Bay Colony

Sir John Valentine Bradstreet (1815-1889) gravestone in Dublin

03
Lovett Families Living on Essex County's Maritime Frontier

T his chapter explores several puzzles about John Lovett and his wife, Mary Grant Lovett, who sought land in the Beverly neighborhood of Salem as Puritans in the middle of the 1630s' decade. At the time, Beverly was a neighborhood increasing its population as newcomers seeking to live in a coastal town rushed to buy land offered by the town of Salem, according to the requirements that local leaders of the Massachusetts Bay Colony (MBC) had set for settlers. One puzzle is why no record seems to exist specifying where the Lovett family came from in England or if they came from some other colony connected with British America. Consequently, researchers are still searching for where they first touched ground after sailing from England or some other stopping place in British North America. Neither the couple, nor John or his brother Daniel separately, nor Mary Grant and her mother, were listed as part the Great Migration's list of Puritans unlike other new arrivals in the Massachusetts Bay Colony (MBC) during the second half of the 1630s.

Another puzzle — or lack of information — surrounds the qualifications that John Lovett and his wife, Mary Grant, had that connected with the Puritan lifestyle. We know that John was a cooper, an occupation which produced casks and barrels; being a cooper was definitely a profession whose skills were necessary in order for the colony's multiple communities, including Salem and Beverly, to survive and flourish economically. His wife seems to have been a good fit for the church and community activism that Puritan leaders also placed at the center of the spiritual and civic life that they wanted both women and men to share in order to get their farming and community development activities done. After John and Mary were married in the town of Salem in 1637, there are many records showing information about their family life, which is why I use that year as the one when this Lovett family took up official residency in the town of Salem, MBC. Supporting that choice there is also a record of the birth of their oldest son, John, whose baptism took place at the church in Salem in 1636 to confirm their residency in the Salem area.

The next century-and-a-half shows the descendants of this big Lovett family to have been active participants in the community and its seafaring life. First, through the records shown in this chapter, the reader can see the Lovett family adapting to the local economy in Salem. Soon after their arrival, the adult Lovetts were participating in subsistence agriculture and developing the infrastructure needed to support a small seaport and businesses like cooperages. You can also follow this family as their children began contributing to the prosperity of Salem's younger partner in fishing and other maritime trading, the town of Beverly. Also, some of Mary and John's adult children and grandchildren worked as sailors on fishing trips to Nova Scotia, Newfoundland, and as officers and captains on transatlantic shipping voyages.[1] Of course, evidence of deaths at sea can be tracked for any Beverly or Salem Lovett

---

[1] See, for example, the crew listing for a certain Robert Lovett as per the requirement of February, 1803, now in the collection of the National Archives and Records Administration, Northeast Region, and included in the collection of Salem Crew Lists, 1799-1879, at https//research.mysticseaport.org/databases/crew-lists-salem/

family through numerous Find-A-Grave records and tombstones in the main cemeteries showing the manner of death of Beverly men in their twenties and thirties leaving wives, children, parents, and siblings during the seventeenth and eighteenth centuries and into the 1800s.

Nevertheless, success in maritime pursuits continued overall as Beverly became a home port for fishing trips to Newfoundland in the period before the city's transition into an industrial economy. Puritans living nearby in rural areas of the MBC, such as Simon and Ann Dudley Bradstreet's youngest children, Hannah, Dudley, and John, faced many of the same problems in the northern MBC communities as their religious brothers and sisters in the Lovett families did as active inhabitants of Salem and later of Beverly. Examples included 1) encountering native Americans in nearby frontier areas of Puritan settlement; 2) developing and implementing strategies for dealing with wealth and labor issues in areas where neither labor nor capital was extensively provided for; 3) bringing slaves from England's Barbados colony and other islands to work for New England families and businesses, including in Salem and Beverly; 4) getting involved in putting down uprisings by Native peoples in western and central Massachusetts; as well as 5) dealing with challenges posed by increased industrialization during the middle of the eighteenth and nineteenth centuries.

Daniel Vickers writes about labor issues in the coastal communities of the MBC in his *Farmers and Fishermen: Two Centuries of Work in Essex County, Massachusetts, 1630-1830*[2], in particular the two kinds of Puritans we already know something about: farmers like the Bradstreets and their descendants, on the one hand, and fishermen and other townspeople who plied the maritime frontier of the MBC, as seen in the lives of this

---

[2] Vickers was born and raised in Canada's Newfoundland province, which gives this author excellent background knowledge about the maritime economies of the state of Massachusetts and the province of Newfoundland.

chapter's Lovetts. Vickers researched his book using the libraries and museums of Essex County, Massachusetts, especially those in Salem where he found the names of prominent businessmen. In this list of merchant families Vickers includes Lovetts among other Beverly merchant families on p. 193 like Obers, Cabots, and Thorndykes. Another book which helped me better understand the outlines and fault lines of the Puritan world was Stephen Innes' *Creating the Commonwealth: The Economic Culture of Puritan New England New York: Norton, 1995,*[3]

The complexity that this Lovett family presents to historians trying to untangle records about them probably arises from a combination of circumstances. First, during the last four hundred years, descendants of John Lovett and Mary Grant married into other early settler families living in Salem and Beverly. Secondly, the same first names within the family, for example, Joseph, John, Robert, and Ebenezer, were given to male children through the generations. Thirdly, most researchers have had difficulty connecting these Massachusetts Lovetts with a wealthy and powerful family inhabiting several parts of Buckinghamshire in England with whom the British American brethren shared a last name. Knowing exactly how these MBC families did or did not connect with Lovetts in Buckinghamshire will, however, definitely depend on additional assistance from the science of DNA.

These efforts may also benefit from information shown on websites such as *www.wikitree.com,*[4] so that we can start to untangle

---

[3] All of those books are listed in the bibliography, as well as in some of this book's footnotes. Also of interest to the issues raised in this chapter is New England's connection with the Newfoundland fishery in particular, as shown in the book written by John J. McCusker and Russell R. Menard, *The Economy of British America: 1607-1789,* pp. 92-102.

[4] The website www.wikitree.com asks readers to submit information from their own family trees. The site assigns a monitor for each family's information and is particularly useful if someone's goal is to trace back a recognizable family of some prominence in a region or locality, e.g., McKinnons, McLeans, etc.,

connections that John Lovett may have had with a powerful English Lovett family whose roots go back to the Norman Conquest of England and Ireland during the middle of the eleventh century. And this chapter can help with evaluating evidence about the Lovetts of British North America and the MBC, who settled in Salem and then Beverly, and how the lives of their family members complement the picture of Puritanism drawn in the Bradstreet and Maternal chapters. Lovett family members would have satisfied the qualifications that Puritan planners hoped would attract people because they had competencies in trades and related occupations needed to assure the colony's success.

Another good research source is Virginia DeJohn Anderson's book, *New England's Generation: The Great Migration and the Formation of Society and Culture in the Seventeenth Century.* Cambridge: Cambridge University Press, 1991. This book is called by the author a 'collective biography' of nearly seven hundred English settler families who came to the MBC as part of the New England Historical Genealogical Society (NEHGS) Great Migration study.[5] It relies for evidence on passenger lists and only includes travel by people from 1629 through to the mid-1630s. Anderson found that many of these people relied for their passage on money paid by their employers, whom they had to pay back. In many cases, this was not a permanent kind of servitude according

---

with the help of the monitor who takes care of that tree. Besides the Scots in chapter four, that might include Bradstreets and Dudleys whom the reader has already met.

[5] Anderson supplies information on pp. 8-11 of her book about 693 people whom the author analyzed along five different dimensions, including 1)the reasons for that person's coming; 2)what happened to them during the passage from England to New England; 3)transplantation or the process of setting up a home, marriage, etc. after reaching Salem or Boston, MBC; 4) the competency which would strengthen the colony, e.g., a particular occupation such as being a cooper; 5) and legacy or the impact that person had on Beverly and in Essex County. See also p. 157.

to Anderson. However, I have not found any records which show John Lovett or his brother Daniel arriving by ship in Salem or Boston, and they are not included in the Great Migration series of books published by the Boston-based NEHGS.

John and Mary Lovett's Family Seeks
Membership in a New Church

In each family chapter, I show when a particular family arrived in North America and where else they lived before settling in Essex County. There is not enough information to do that for Lovetts although there is a lot of detail about their lives once they got here and records about them have been kept. Wherever they came from and however they got to Salem, John Lovett and Mary Grant sought land ownership and participation in the Salem church at some point during the mid-1630s. At first, John worked at subsistence farming while he and his neighbors built their houses and grew most of their foodstuffs in small gardens attached to these new homes. That John did well economically is demonstrated by the amount of land he was able to purchase and pass on to his sons for their families. Also important was that he had come to the MBC with a work background as a cooper, not the church or governmental office backgrounds of people like Simon Bradstreet and Thomas Dudley. His occupational competency is clear from the probate record after his death, where we can read that his will included the requirement to pass his cooper's tools to his oldest son, John Lovett, Jr. (1636-1727).

So, neither John Lovett nor any of his relatives were among the people whom Anderson included in *New England's Generation*. Nor did the couple arrive as part of the Great Migration group of prominent Puritan leaders profiled by the Boston-based New England Historical Genealogical Society (NEHGS). However, John's competency as a cooper definitely fit with occupations that Puritan leaders knew they needed to have, such as blacksmiths, joiners, locksmiths, and tanners, whose work backgrounds would assist the colony to grow and help it become permanent. At the time of their marriage, John Lovett and Mary Grant were living in the Beverly neighborhood of Salem, which was quickly gaining a population large enough for neighbors to sign on to a petition for Salem to set up a second church. Records show Mary's name on a petition asking for the Beverly neighborhood to have its own church even before Beverly was populous enough to separate from Salem and form a new town.

Their new church was set in what is now the city of Beverly where subsequent generations of Lovetts, including Ethel Bradstreet Maney's (1917-2005) mother, aunt, and maternal grandparents, were living through the early twentieth century. Beverly is also the place where Ethel Bradstreet and John MacLean Maney (1914-1985) lived when their first child was born. One reason why the town grew was because of the joint harbor which Beverly shares with Salem. The result was that both cities had opportunities to start developing transportation and commercial linkages with the world beyond the MBC even before the end of the 1650s with the help of trading and seafaring companies based in London which had a stake in financing the MBC and Salem's financial success.

In the 1630s maritime and other businesses were needed to support the various trading industries that the MBC was developing with other New England colonies, as well as with British colonies on Barbados, in Maritime Canada, Virginia, and with private companies connected with the motherland no matter where they were based. All of this maritime trade got underway in Beverly and Salem soon after the European settlers had built their first houses. Wikipedia's entry for Salem references that city's maritime history including numerous voyages to the East and West Indies that were undertaken before the end of the 1700s, as well as to Africa and Europe. For many years, seamen and master mariners living in Beverly sailed from the port of Salem before the growth of the Cape Ann fishery during the eighteenth century spurred Beverly's port to grow as well.

The economic model that the towns of Salem and Beverly were developing shows strong linkages but also some contrasts with the subsistence agriculture approach of northern MBC towns such as Ipswich, Andover and Topsfield, where the Bradstreets lived in the 1ast half of the seventeenth century. Soon after their establishment, rural Puritan settlements needed access to what the coastal towns could provide from maritime trading and local industry in places like Gloucester, Beverly, and Salem. Within just a few decades, the commerce provided by Beverly, Salem, Boston, Marblehead, and Gloucester nicely complemented the dominant Puritan rural and agricultural model and brought benefits to each side of Essex County's Puritan community. For example, local farmers in Beverly and Salem developed business relationships with rural towns so that merchants were able to stock food products as provisions for the voyages of Beverly's maritime trading ships.

Before the end of the seventeenth century, these two maritime towns were also developing somewhat different profiles in their business dealings with suppliers and customers. At first, Beverly's Puritan economy was oriented around coastal fishing in Maine, Nova Scotia, and Newfoundland while Salem began shipping raw materials and some finished products as far as the West Indies, Europe, and other foreign ports. And from quite early days, a network of merchants, like those already operating on the Salem side of the harbor, was duplicated in Beverly and included fishermen and merchants some of whom descended from the marriage between Mary and John Lovett.

Some of these voyages were organized and financed jointly by Beverly merchants and those living in Salem. See, for example, merchants such as Captain Larcom, whose family is discussed in chapter six of this book. In the second half of the eighteenth century, the China trade showed many kinds of items brought back from trips by MBC mariners trading with cities in China and the Far East. That kind of trade was possible after big ships were re-purposed after the colonists had spent the Revolutionary War years harassing British ship traffic as privateers. It is also likely that both towns were involved in the triangular trade with Britain and Barbados that involved not just the sale of sugar in North America and Great Britain but also the slave trade.

In the next section of this chapter, some of the migration and settlement decisions made by Lovett families in Beverly and Essex County are shown, and evidence is presented about why Lovetts and others in Beverly and Salem chose to pursue opportunities along New England's maritime frontier rather than migrate to areas in western Massachusetts or to other colonies before the War for American Independence had begun in 1776. Virginia de John Anderson's analysis showed that people often tried one or more towns to find the best opportunity to acquire land grants, which usually offered better terms if one's family was part of — or had connections — with the first group of settlers in that community.[6]

That could mean that people moved further away from the first settlements to places like Haverhill or Newbury in northern Essex County or to southern New Hampshire. Beverly's maritime pursuits became more complex in the 1700s, and by the early nineteenth century the city was becoming urban and industrial, as were neighboring coastal cities like Lynn and Salem. So, while the main Lovett family flourished in Beverly, it is helpful to consider alternative options that some Lovett families chose to pursue when

---

[6] Anderson calls that process the "great re-shuffling," which went on until people were more or less satisfied with the choice of land which they could afford from the land that was available. One solution was for some Lovett people to opt for migration and re-settlement elsewhere on the New England coast, such as in coastal New Hampshire, Maine, Nova Scotia, and other points easily accessible from coastal Essex County. A final focus for what follows in this chapter includes discussion about the jobs and careers available to male Lovetts and their neighbors in Beverly, the competencies of their potential marriage partners and children, and how their descendants' lives changed over time, including new roles that women and children began playing in the town economies of both Beverly and Salem.

land grew scarce and became more expensive inside the coastal towns for their sons to get enough money from the family to set up their own homes.

Who Were These Lovetts, According to the Mini-tree?

This section includes mini-trees for the Lovetts up to the birth of Ethel Bradstreet, the daughter of Bertha Lovett and Alvah Bradstreet, which took place in 1917. At the end of this chapter we will learn more from some official written records, look at family photos, and learn family stories involving people from Ethel Bradstreet's main Lovett family line, along with the variety of occupations that the heads of Beverly's Lovett households held as revealed in the U.S. census. Also important are indicators for when wives and children joined the heads of households in paid employment outside of the home. As the manufacturing economy developed in the mid-1800s, we will also look for evidence showing if, or how, these changes affected relations inside the family.

For example, we know that sons in the Bradstreet family living in Topsfield worked on their parents' farms as they waited to get land for their own farms after their fathers died or could no longer continue tending their agricultural holdings. In Beverly, however, many teen-aged boys started working as fishermen and did not expect — or want — to be farmers. However, one thing that was the same in both types of towns, whether in rural or urban settings, was that boys, as well as their fathers and grandfathers, were likely to work inside their homes during the winter making shoes and boots, no matter what other profession they may have had. Evidence will show that their sisters also developed expertise in shoemaking, especially in shoe binding which could be done in someone's home.

As discussed earlier, the origins of these Lovetts in England are not clear. No evidence convincingly names John's or Mary's parents, although some researchers believe that John may have been the youngest son of a Fraser who had a peerage title as Lord Lovat and was a British peer. The town of Chesham in Buckinghamshire is often mentioned as a home base for Lovetts in this peerage family. The town exists today at the northwest edge of the urban sprawl of Greater London. It has been supposed by other researchers that John and Daniel may have come to the MBC with their mother and perhaps a sister after their father's death.[7]

Since Daniel is not profiled in the mini-tree, it may be useful to note his birth and death years here (1608-1691). We also know the names of his children and of his wife, Joanna Blott (1620-1694) from local records. The Lovett mini-tree below shows that about eight children were born to the family of John Lovett and Mary Grant, although some probably died before reaching adulthood. The descendants of two of their sons, John, the first born, and the son they called Joseph, started the two main Lovett family branches that accounted for most of the Beverly-based heads of household with the last name of Lovett during the period from 1645 through to the mid-twentieth century. Here are the mini-tree results using **bold** and *italics* to identify the main line for Ethel Bradstreet's Lovetts.

Ethel Bradstreet's Lovett Family Mini-tree
John Lovett, 1610-1686, and ***Mary Grant***, 1610-1695 Their children born in Beverly: John, Jr. born in 1636, Symond born in 1637, Simon born in 1642, Mary born in 1646, ***Joseph*** born in 1650, Randall born in 1651, Bethiah born in 1652, Mary born in 1656.

Joseph Lovett, 1650-1734, married ***Elizabeth Solart***, 1652-1734.

---

[7] Some of my siblings and I have DNA connections with John Lovett's brother Daniel as well as with people from the main subparts of the family tree of the Beverly Lovetts. It may well be that the Buckinghamshire Lovetts received titles from the British government that included them in England's peerage in Ireland, the same process that Simon Bradstreet's brother had in the same British colony in Ireland.

Their children born in Beverly: Elizabeth born in 1673, Mary born in 1673, **Joseph** born in 1676, Mary born in 1679, Simon born in 1681, John born in 1684, Josiah born in 1687.

Joseph Lovett, 1676-1734, married **Katherine Sallows,** 1678-1735.
Their children born in Beverly: Simon Joseph born in 1696, Robert born in 1697, Katherine born in 1697, **Ebenezer** born in 1702.

Ebenezer Lovett, 1702-1778, married **Joanna Thorndike,** 1703-1775.
Their children born in Beverly: Hannah born in 1725, **Joseph** born in **1726**, Joanna born in 1728, Ebenezer Jr. born in 1729, Robert born in 1732, John born in 1734, Sarah born in 1737, Mary born in 1740, Hannah born in 1740, Joanna born in 1754.

Joseph Lovett, 1726-1819, married **Anna Woodbury,** 1726-1809.
Their children born in Beverly: Elisha born in 1750, Joseph born in 1753, Joanna born in 1755, Robert born in 1756, Thankful born in 1758, **Ebenezer** born in **1760**, Ruth born in 1761, **Rachel** born in **1763,** Anna born in 1765, Hezekiah, 1767-1840.

Ebenezer Lovett, 1760-1827, married **Molly Smith,** 1763-1804.
Their children born in Beverly: Robert born in 1784, **Ebenezer** born in 1785, Sally born in 1787, Edward S. born in 1789, Molly Thorndike born in 1792, Elisha born in 1795, Thankful born in 1797, Becca born in 1799, Edward Smith born in 1801.

Ebenezer Lovett, 1785-1827, married **Rachel Foster,** 1785-?
Their children born in Beverly: Anna born in 1812, Josiah Foster born in 1820, Rebecca born in 1820, Joseph Allen born in 1820, **Ebenezer, Jr.** born in **1822**, William born in 1825.

Ebenezer Lovett, Jr. 1822-1882, married **Sarah Trow Trask** 1827-1858.
Their children born in Beverly: **Eben Francis** born in **1848**, Sarah Lidia born in 1851, Preston born in 1852, Ariston Ward born in 1854, Solon born in 1858.

Eben Francis Lovett, 1848-1923, married **Maria Louisa Guild,** 1852-1935.
Their children born in Beverly: **Bertha Francis** born in **1883**, Ethel Louise born in 1885.

Bertha Lovett, 1883-1971, married **Alvah Bradstreet,** 1862-1960.
Their children born in Danvers: Dudley, 1909-1971, Alva C, 1911-1912, **Ethel Louise,** 1917-2005.

Ethel Louise Bradstreet (1917-2005) married **John MacLean Maney** (1914-1985).

Descendants of John (1610-1686) and Joseph Lovett (1645-1734) usually married descendants in other original settler families in Beverly during succeeding generations, including women and men with last names such as Dodge, Ober, Trask, Trow, Woodbury, Thorndike, Herrick, Conant, Corning, Barrett, Larcom, and others. Some researchers have suggested that Joseph's older brother Simon may have died, followed by the birth of another son to whom the parents gave the same name. Since that second Simon is not mentioned in his father's will, it is supposed by advocates of this view that he died as a young man, perhaps in one of the battles that the European settlers had with bands of indigenous people who lived in territory not far away in central and western Massachusetts.

As you read the names of the children of the large family of John Lovett and Mary Grant, keep in mind that after a few generations there were two main male lines, one that is known as the line of John Lovett, Jr., the oldest son of John and Mary. The second main line is the one which is known as the Joseph (1650-1734) line of Lovetts and is indicated by bold and italic letters in the mini-tree. Ethel Louise Bradstreet, the daughter of Bertha Lovett and Alvah Bradstreet, was part of the Joseph line, as are the author of this book and her siblings. Similarities and differences in how the Bradstreets and Lovetts lived their lives are also important to analyze. Some things, however, are the same in both families. For example, in each generation for the first hundred years of settlement, the number of children in both families was quite large. Another similarity is that male heads of Lovett and Bradstreet families routinely held local elective and appointive office, including election to the General Court, as the lower house of the state legislature is called in today's Commonwealth of Massachusetts.

However, the two families also show interesting differences over time. It appears that Lovett children from many successive offshoot lines were more likely to remain in Essex County than the Bradstreet children were. Another difference may be that the desire for farming lasted longer for the Bradstreets who stayed, but more of the Lovett families in the MBC illustrate what emerging research has to say about the importance of fishing and maritime business as positive forces for the economy of Essex County and the state of Massachusetts, especially in the period from 1630 through 1850. Besides attracting young men with useful occupations as colonists, leaders of the Puritan venture in British North America did not want to have a lot of single men among the colonists as had happened among the colonists who came to the Jamestown colony in Virginia in the first decade of the 1600s. Instead they wanted young men who would marry and start families in the new communities which had a bent toward either agriculture or fishing/seafaring.

Puritan leaders stepped into a situation where they found a winning combination of both independent farmers in places like Topsfield and people who became innovative merchants and resourceful maritime industry workers along the county's coastline in places such as Salem, Beverly, Marblehead, Gloucester, and Ipswich. In subsequent generations, young men in Ethel Bradstreet's big Lovett family mostly contributed useful trades like bricklayers, tailors, shoemakers, coopers, and fishermen to their communities, as well as becoming mariners, merchants, lawyers, and sea captains.

This study accepts as plausible the notion suggested by a Lovett descendent, Frank Nelson Hall, that the birthdate of John and Mary Grant's second son, Joseph, was probably 1645 and that the later date of 1650, which is used in some genealogies and also in official records, is more likely his baptism date. The reader should also make a special note about the Rachel Lovett whose name was in bold and italics in the Lovett family mini-tree shown above. She was born into the Joseph line in 1763 and married Josiah Foster of Beverly. They were the parents of a daughter, Rachel Foster, born in 1785, who married one of her Lovett cousins in the Joseph line, Ebenezer Lovett (1785-1827). This Ebenezer was born in the same year that she was and her information is also bolded and italicized. Unfortunately, the death records that I found did not show a death date for Rachel Foster Lovett.[8]

---

[8] A Seafaring Certificate was awarded to Robert Lovett, son of Joseph Lovett and Anna Woodbury, who was someone of that name who was a brother of Rachel Lovett. See Salem crew lists, 1799-1879, https://research.mysticseaport.org/satabases/crew-lists-salem/

Both Robert and Rachel were either siblings or cousins of other people in Ethel Bradstreet's Joseph Lovett line.

The mini-trees in this book focus on Ethel Bradstreet's forebears from the Joseph Lovett side. The Guild and Colbath lines on Ethel's maternal grandmother's side are discussed in the chapter about Ethel Lovett Bradstreet's maternal line. Here, however, we should note that three siblings on the Guild side of Ethel Bradstreet's tree also came to Massachusetts from England during the 1630s and lived northwest of Boston in Haverhill in Essex County at first and later moved to Wrentham in Norfolk County. John Lovett's brother, Daniel Lovett (1608-1691), who lived for a short time in Salem after John had moved there, later settled in Mendon in Worcester County, MBC. In the next section, we look closely at two Lovett-related families who decided to leave Beverly by moving along Essex County's maritime frontier to Yarmouth, Nova Scotia, another maritime and seafaring town whose economy was much the same as those in Salem and Beverly.

Settlement Along Massachusetts' Maritime Frontier

Moving to a new place was made easier because Beverly, like other Essex county coastal towns and cities such as Salem, Marblehead, and Ipswich, also became closely connected with coastal places in sister colonies easily reached by ship travel. In addition, many Lovett boys and young men had their first jobs outside of the family home and their home town as fishermen who were away for months at a time. Besides trading for commodities in the seventeenth century, Beverly, Salem, Marblehead, Gloucester, and Ipswich had active fishing fleets plying the waters off of Maine, New Brunswick, Nova Scotia, and Newfoundland. At the same time, residents in nearby rural towns began developing different economic footprints, lifestyles, and differences in daily life during the 1700s.

Not surprisingly, Puritan towns like Salem or Beverly also looked different from the rural towns nearby because the former depended mostly on fishing and other maritime industries. One example is shown in Frank Hall's online paper, which he titled

"A Lovett Genealogy."[9] Hall wrote about the migration of some Lovett families away from Beverly and Salem, which took place between 1730 and 1740. Included in the group is Simon Joseph Lovett (1696-1756), who was the eldest son in the line headed by Joseph Lovett and is an offshoot of Ethel Bradstreet Maney's line. Hall uncovered a wealth of information in deeds and other public records that he sourced with the help of local experts in Beverly and in various local history collections in Maine about the places where this group settled. The reason why Simon Lovett and his second wife, Emma Rea (1700-1735), decided to move away from Beverly is not entirely clear, but there is enough information to speculate.

Emma became Simon's second wife after his first wife died. The couple then endured the deaths of their first son, Joseph, and then quickly gave birth to four daughters and another son, all of whom were born at 1 or 1½ year intervals after 1722. All of these children died in 1730, victims of what probably was an epidemic. Some historians believe that a diphtheria outbreak took place in New England, as that disease frequently affected children in colonial America, including at the time that this Lovett family experienced the death of so many children at one time. According to Hall's genealogy, the parents reacted to the deaths of more family members in two ways: by starting up a new family with two sons and a daughter who were born by 1736; and by joining a group of people they knew from Beverly who were planning to move away together. The group's goal was to get land in what is now the state of Maine but was part of Massachusetts until 1820.[10]

Within a few years, this same Lovett family was living in another coastal town near their friends "down east" along the coast

---

[9] The online document is owned by Ancestry and has been kept since 2004 in their collection of genealogical documents in Provo, UT. The title is *John Lovett of Beverly, Massachusetts, Landed from England prior to 1639*, compiled by Frank Nelson Hall, 2041 West Oak St., Denton, TX, 806p.

[10] Additional information on this topic is in the Lovett section of the *Maney Family Archive*.

that includes northeastern Massachusetts, a small piece of NH, ME, New Brunswick, Nova Scotia, and across the open ocean to the Canadian maritime province of Newfoundland. In order to raise money for the move and to purchase land in Maine, Simon sold the land he had in Beverly to his brother, Ebenezer (1702-1778) who is a direct ancestor of Ethel Bradstreet and her children; Ebenezer continued living in Beverly. He bought out his brother's share from what would have otherwise come to Simon in their father's will.

After re-locating to what was then Cape Porpoise and is now Kennebunkport, ME, Simon set up a new tailor's shop and began to ply his trade again. It is significant that the couple had decided to move to a new location but hadn't chosen a place based on the quality of the land for farming but a place on the coast only about sixty miles as the crow flies from Beverly. It seems that these Lovetts and their friends who moved from coastal Essex County with them were used to travelling by ship and could find opportunities to shape new locations into similar communities relying on fishing and the maritime trades in the colonies of New Hampshire, Maine, and, even in New Brunswick, Nova Scotia, and other parts of maritime Canada.

A second example of a family moving from Beverly along the maritime frontier is another early settler family. Ebenezer Corning (1732-1780) was a mariner born in Beverly who owned his own ship as well as a trading company. He moved his family to Yarmouth, Nova Scotia, in 1762. One of Ethel Bradstreet's eighth great-grandmothers, Remember Corning (1630-1715), had had numerous mariners and ship owners in her family over several generations and profited from ship traffic between Nova Scotia and coastal towns in the MBC. When the likelihood of war with Britain increased during the decade of the 1760s, Ebenezer Corning, one of Remember Corning's descendants, moved his family to Yarmouth, NS, where they remained Loyalists committed against the fight for independence which was supported by many people in Beverly.

After the end of the War for Independence, however, the Corning family's economic and trading connections with Essex County quickly resumed.

This quick summary raises some interesting questions. First, should we think about the Corning's move as migration or emigration? The first term is usually applied when someone moves from one area or region to another but in the process stays under the jurisdiction of the same country. The second usually refers to a move across a boundary from one country into another. Or perhaps the extended Corning family members saw moving to Nova Scotia as a business decision because they did not believe it would be easy to continue trading with business partners in Massachusetts towns and Yarmouth, Nova Scotia, if the New England colonies became independent.

When Simon Lovett left Massachusetts for Maine, his new home was still within the MBC, which, in turn, was still inside the kingdom of England, Ireland, Scotland, and Wales. When Ebenezer Corning moved to Yarmouth, Nova Scotia, he was moving from one British colony to another British colony but his family members wanted to remain as subjects of the British Empire. And when the Lovetts and Bradstreets left England in the 1630s, they could be said to have migrated — not emigrated — because they stayed under the authority of the British government in their new homes in the MBC, Nova Scotia, New Brunswick, and Prince Edward Island. It is only when MacLeans and their McDonald, McKinnon, Kennedy, McPhaiden and Campbell ilk, as well as the Maneys, Dalys, and Reillys entered the United States after settling in Canada after 1783 that we are more likely to call their stories emigration sagas.[11]

---

[11] There is more discussion about the long-standing permeability of the border between the United States and Canada in the chapter about Nova Scotia and Prince Edward Island people emigrating from Canada to the U.S. in the nineteenth and twentieth centuries. And there is more information about a

New Occupations and a Different Workforce Needed in the 19th Century

Now it is time to take a quick look at how a manufacturing economy was taking root by 1850 in increasingly urban towns like Salem and Beverly which had been oriented on regional and international markets since the seventeenth century. New economic opportunities also came to Essex County's farming communities in the middle of the nineteenth century, as can be seen in the 1840 U.S. census. By the middle of the nineteenth century, Topsfield's agricultural economy was becoming strained and farmers were increasingly inclined to supply agricultural and forestry products, not just for their families but also for buyers in Greater Boston and in other countries. An example is hauling trees to Boston, which could be made into ship's masts at the Charlestown Naval Shipyard, as well as for numerous shipbuilding enterprises in coastal Essex County.

In this section, information is taken from different U.S. and Massachusetts censuses in order to compare the occupations recorded for men and women in Topsfield and Beverly during the same period. Also, new occupations are seen in the Beverly census records for jobs which would become even more important to that city in the second half of the nineteenth century as the economy continued to change. Let's look first at occupations in mid-nineteenth century Beverly. A complete tabulation of male occupations for Beverly that year shows census results that will not be surprising: men were working in a much larger set of occupations in the Beverly census than was the case in Topsfield in the same year. Now, let's add to the mix another set of occupations

---

woman named Sarah Corning in the chapter about Ethel Bradstreet's maternal line. Sarah's professional life, which straddled the same border between Nova Scotia and the U.S. during the twentieth century, is discussed in this book's final chapter and follows some of the main story of Ruth MacLean Maney, the mother of John MacLean Maney (1914-1985). This information is also part of the *Maney Family Archive*.

for men in Beverly which were listed in the Massachusetts state census for 1855. The number of active jobs in just the emerging shoemaking industry that year included shoe dealer, shoe cutter, and shoe manufacturer.[12]

This census information gives the reader an idea about which economic activities were taking place in Beverly. Of these, maritime and shoemaking occupations stand out. However, that of farmer is also included in the top rank in Beverly. Mariners, chandlers, fishermen, fish dealers, victuallers or food provisioners, rope makers, ship carpenters, and oystermen provided support to the supply chain for Beverly's fishing industry whose workers regularly plied the coasts of New Hampshire, Maine, Nova Scotia, and all the way to Newfoundland and back. We can also see occupations such as merchant, trader, and custom house officer, whose occupations supported the large ships that hauled both unfinished and finished goods to markets in the American south, the West Indies, the East Indies, and Europe.

There were also ships that brought timber to Salem, Boston, and other shipbuilding cities. In the Bradstreet chapter I told a story about an accident that killed Asa Bradstreet after he fell from his perch on a wagon while taking goods to Boston.[13] Indeed, tall trees were sometimes brought from elsewhere along the Essex

---

[12] The total of these occupations included *cabinetmaker, carpenter, carver, chair manufacturer, chandler, clergyman, clerk, clothier, coachman, counsellor, currier, customs house officer, daguerrotypist, editor, expressman, fancy goods dealer, farmer, fish dealer, fish merchant, fisherman, furniture polisher, gardener, hair worker, hardware dealer, hardware store, hatter, insurance agent, japanner, law student, lawyer, librarian, machinist, mariner, mason, master mariner, melodeon maker, merchant, milkman, miller, mustard manufacturer, oysterman, painter, physician, printer, railroad engineer, railroad man, ropemaker, rubber factory, rubber factory superintendent, sailmaker, salesman, ship carpenter, ship master, shoemaker, shoe cutter, shoe dealer, shoe manufacturer, stabler, storekeeper, stone cutter, tailor, tallow chandler, teacher, teamster, tollkeeper, trader, tallow chandler, treasurer, turner, varnisher, victualler, watchmaker, wheelwright, wood and coal dealer.*

[13] There is more to this story in Alvah Bradstreet's book. See pp. 13-15.

County coast and from as far away as the interior of the state of Maine where tall pine trees were being harvested in order to be turned into masts for ships trading via transoceanic sailing voyages. When Gardiner, a town in central Maine, started in 1757 on the Kennebec River to support the economic activity of shipbuilding, there was a Lovett on hand. Although no people on the 1855 Beverly census list declared that they operated a ship-building enterprise in Beverly, the explanation is probably that the various shipbuilding industries were becoming increasingly specialized and that other nearby coastal communities, such as Marblehead, Gloucester, and Ipswich, were specializing in outfitting ships while the merchants in Salem and Beverly were busy recruiting crews and master mariners and selling the goods that the ships brought back to the region.

The next logical step in Gardiner, ME, might be to try to build tall ships there, not in Massachusetts, so as to keep more of the profits in the state of Maine. From Gardiner, the trees would find their way to merchant owners in towns involved in trading via ship travel. Finally, the same 1855 state census showed occupations where men worked in or managed specialized shops and their products, employing tailors, watchmakers, wood and coal dealers, jobs related to land transportation, plus people engaged in manufacturing and education. The growing roles of merchants and industrialists in Beverly, Salem, Lawrence, Lynn, and Lowell, all of which were towns in Essex County, also directed attention to many shoe and textile manufacturing industries even though the specific occupations on offer for men and women were still quite different at that time.

Spotlighting Henry Wilson in Ethel Bradstreet's Lovett Tree

Before we compare the role of shoemaking and manufacturing in urbanizing Beverly and rural Topsfield, we need to discuss a cousin in Ethel Bradstreet Maney's maternal Colbath line who used shoemaking to jump-start a life change after growing up in difficult circumstances in rural New Hampshire away from the maritime frontier that has just been discussed. Much about how this man's life unfolded may remind readers about challenges that faced the country lawyer from Illinois who became president of the U.S. in 1860. This shoemaker's name in American history books is Henry Wilson (1812-1875). One of his many claims to fame is his service as the vice presidential candidate on the Republican Party ticket for 1872 along with the former general and new president, Ulysses S. Grant (1822-1885). Other Wilson claims to fame were his leadership of the new Republican political party in the decades before the Civil War and his selection as a Massachusetts senator in the U.S. Congress.

For our purposes here, it is important to know that at his birth in 1812, the future Henry Wilson was given the name Jeremiah Jones Colbath, and was a cousin of Louisa Colbath (1822-1891), who was Maria Guild Lovett's mother, Ethel Bradstreet's great-grandmother, and Ethel Bradstreet's children's second-great-grandmother. After serving an indenture as a teenager to a local farmer in NH, Jeremiah Jones Colbath successfully petitioned that state in 1833 to allow him to change his name. The paperwork needed in New Hampshire to adopt a new name is available online today, but we probably will never know exactly why this man was so committed to the project of changing his name or how he chose that particular name.

His next step was to study briefly at a free high school for adults in rural Strafford, NH, after having been allowed to study for only a couple of months each winter during his childhood and indenture. Next, he secured a job working for a cobbler in Natick, MA, just west of Boston and more than one hundred miles from his home in NH. He got there by walking all the way. In addition to his shoemaking work, he continued his education and worked part-time as a schoolteacher before he moved to Boston, bought and ran a newspaper, and started a political career. In what follows, we look at Henry Wilson's job of shoemaking as a window into what was going on in Essex and other Massachusetts counties during the middle decades of the nineteenth century.

Female Occupations in Beverly and Topsfield in 1860

As we dip again into governmental information, this time it will be in the form of the U.S. census for 1860 which allows us to make comparisons between the paid occupations in which Beverly women worked and those occupations of female residents living in nearby rural Topsfield where Alvah Bradstreet's relatives had farmed. In the 1860 census, Beverly women held positions in approximately twenty-five different occupations. Also interesting is that many women working outside their homes in Beverly were from recently-arrived immigrant families who had fled the severe political conditions and humanitarian disaster taking place in Ireland. At the same time that Irish women increased their numbers in Beverly's female labor force, another large job category for female employment included twenty women who described their occupations as teachers in the local schools. In addition, another Beverly woman taught future teachers at the Salem normal school, which is now part of Salem State University. As in Topsfield, women in Beverly performed jobs needed by the local shoemaking industries, predominantly as shoe binders. That job classification employed twenty-eight women in 1860.

Servants, school teachers, and shoe binders made up seventy percent of Beverly's total workforce of female paid employment that year. Shoe and boot binders stitched leather to the soles of shoes, a job that could be done at home and could be fitted into a woman's regular housekeeping schedule. Also, as in Topsfield, some men and boys listed shoemaker and its close cousin, cordwainer, as their professions, jobs that had often been done at home in cities and in New England's rural areas during the first two hundred years of European settlement. Making shoes for family members had long been a necessity that could best be done after the fishing or farming season was over. As with a trade occupation, family historians can identify a person who had a second occupation as a shoemaker from the kinds of tools that are listed in probate records as possessions to be passed along to one of that person's children.

Shoemaking also suited fishermen, who had made shoes and mended sails and nets after returning home from long fishing trips to Maine, Nova Scotia, and Newfoundland since the earliest days of European settlement in the MBC. Getting safely to all the destinations that served coastal merchants' fishing and merchant fleets meant that the town needed fish merchants, mariners, provisioners of food and supplies, ropemakers, and other occupations and trades in order to fit out and send ships on extended voyages. Over time, the most important destination for Beverly's fishery had become Nova Scotia and the Grand Banks of Newfoundland. The latter is an area which attracted fishing fleets from the U.S., Ireland, the UK, Spain, and Portugal each year.

Sometimes, ships working for various fishing enterprises spread out along the Atlantic coast and dropped anchor alongside those from European countries. The participants usually did their work in two steps: first, catching fish in the best locations, which is why American sailors were working close to fishermen from other countries. Then later, sailors from Europe and New England worked near each other on land to cure the catch before returning home. In its heyday as an international fishing destination, Newfoundland was truly an international environment for those who worked on the high seas, and Newfoundlanders developed a genetic profile that mixed together DNA from any or all countries mentioned above.

The occupations that women held in 1860 in the paid workforce in Topsfield were fewer, but the pattern was similar to the categories in which their sisters worked in Beverly. In Topsfield in 1860, sixty-five women were listed as engaged in paid employment, especially as servants, school teachers, and shoe binders. In addition, two female heads of household in Topsfield used traditional male occupations to describe their work: one called herself a shoemaker[14], and the other was listed as a cooper. Choosing this type of work has been described by Laurel Thatcher Ulrich as women claiming the role of "deputy husband," the work that widows did when they headed up the family after the death of the male breadwinner. Ulrich also used the term in several other ways, including applying it to widows who headed up and kept a family business going after their husbands died. In another application, women living in communities such as Marblehead, Gloucester, Salem, and Beverly made financial decisions, paid bills, etc., when their husbands were fishing on the Grand Banks, sailing halfway around the world to the East Indies, or not having as good a head for business as his wife may have had.

The best account of shoe binding and other tasks that female shoemakers were doing all over eastern Massachusetts in the nineteenth century comes from a book by Mary Blewett, *Men, Women, and Work, Class, Gender, and Protest in the New England Shoe Industry, 1780-1910,* which is included in this book's bibliography and which we will consider again later on in this book. Ulrich's book also featured women whose families lived in localities near those inhabited by native peoples, for example, on the western and northern frontiers of the MBC for two hundred years with a focus on settlement of colonists in the northern parts of New England. She and other authors focus on the ways that the various Puritan communities in the North American part of the British Empire benefited from using a range of human bondage systems that solved some of the labor problems they encountered by delivering convicts, indentured servants, Black Africans, and indigenous peoples native to New England and helped businesses develop multiple ways to create unfree labor systems and conditions for these and other non-free people.

Besides pursuing traditional female jobs such as boarding house operator, seamstress, coat maker, dressmaker, milliner,

---

[14] Vickers, *Farmers and Fishermen*, 318-319.

washerwoman, and nurse, some of these women had to defend their families against attacks by native peoples living nearby, especially in last half of the seventeenth century. By the middle of the nineteenth century, a few of the jobs that women were holding in Beverly previewed the city's developing shoe manufacturing economy, e.g., machinist, machine runner, machine girl, shoe machine tender, and shoe manufacturing laborer. Another useful source of information about work outside the home in the nineteenth century comes from city directories published during the second half of the 1800s in Salem, Beverly, and other nearby towns. The table below includes occupations held by all adult Lovetts who resided in Beverly and had their names included in the Salem city directory for 1886.

That year was chosen to survey because it supplements information provided in the decennial U.S. census which is conducted at the beginning of each decade. In 1886, the only woman on this list of Lovetts in Beverly was Maria Guild Lovett who was Bertha Lovett Bradstreet's mother. Both Maria Guild's business and the occupation of Maria's husband, Eben Lovett (1848-1923), are listed in successive city directory entries. Meanwhile, Eben's half-brother, Ariston Lovett (1854-1904), was listed as a shoe cutter at the Myron Woodbury shop, and his brother Solon Lovett (1858-1932) described his work as that of a shoemaker in 1886. The city directory also showed two Lovett managers, one a merchant and the other the Beverly Town Clerk. We will meet the Town Clerk again when the 1880 U.S. census results are reviewed below.

Occupations of Lovetts in Beverly in the City Directory of 1886

Allen – laborer
Ariston – shoemaker
Eben F – foreman in a shoe manufacturing company
Edward – laborer
Francis S – farmer

Francis S, jr – farmer
George F – shoe cutter
George W – painter
Israel E – shoe cutter
John D – merchant in Boston
John W – teamster
Joseph A – shoemaker
Josiah W – peddler
Maria L – dressmaker
Thomas D – consulting engineer
William D – town clerk

The jobs held by Solon Lovett are also interesting to follow as they became more complex in city directory entries during the years from 1890 to the 1920s, just as the Beverly shoemaking industry was becoming more specialized. After a while, the city directories and census records show that Solon was operating his own shoe business. At first, his shop concentrated on preparing leather for shoes, then emphasized making heels for shoes that got finished at another shop. In later city directories, Solon, a cousin of Ethel Bradstreet Maney, described his business as manufacturing leather for the soles of shoes, as well as making counters, which are the molds for the shoes, plus taps, inner soles, and other shoe parts. After retiring, he listed his business in the city directory as real estate.

In a chapter that compares paid employment for Lovett men and women in Beverly, it is also interesting that there are no family records or stories that I could find that explained how and why Maria Guild, two of her siblings, and a cousin came to be living in Beverly in 1880. These Guilds were from a family in Wrentham, a rural town in Norfolk County, located west of Boston and may have had distant Lovett family connections. In 1880, Maria, who was born in 1852, was renting a room in an apartment in downtown Beverly and her occupation is listed as dressmaker. The same record shows that she shared the apartment with three other young women. Two of them were working for shoe shops or small shoe factories and another young woman was working as a female tailor or "tailoress," as it was called in the census records. The census records for Beverly and other Massachusetts towns and cities are available for viewing in public libraries, online and a copy of the information is contained in Ancestry.com records for members and also in the *Maney Family Archive* along with copies of the photos and images that go with each chapter of this book.

By 1880 Maria's brother, William Guild (1842-1920), who was ten years older, had married and was working in another shoe shop/factory in Beverly. The owner of the house where Maria and the women lived in 1880 was an Ellen Lovett (1846-1935) who owned her family's big house in downtown Beverly and lived on one floor with two of her brothers, William and Israel Lovett, and a sister, Martha. Ellen and her siblings were relatives of Eben Lovett from the other main Beverly branch of their family. That is, they were from the line of John Lovett and Mary Grant's first child, John Lovett, Jr. (1636-1727). In the 1880 census, Eben Lovett's marital status was divorced and his home address was another big boarding house in Beverly where Maria's cousin, Ida Guild, lived while she also worked for a shoe shop.

Spotlight on Change and Continuity in Essex County's Workforce

Why and how young women came to live in Beverly from other Massachusetts towns before they married is a subject to which we will return in later chapters. For example, several of John MacLean Maney's Scottish grandaunts and cousins left Nova Scotia and Prince Edward Island for towns and cities near Boston at some point in the last half of the nineteenth century, and some of these young women plus others can be found living in Beverly and Ipswich in the 1880 census and later. Some of these young women worked as domestics and others as shoe binders. Shoe binding is especially interesting since there were many women and men in the paid workforce in Essex County in the second half of the nineteenth century who were doing jobs that are little remembered today. In addition, by the time of World War I, Lovett, MacLean, and Maney women were also entering occupations in the nursing field in Essex County and beyond, as will be shown in the Maternal chapter.

Meanwhile, three years after the 1880 census introduced us to Maria Guild and her siblings, Maria and Eben Lovett had married and begun raising two daughters while continuing their day jobs. It seems that by that date not all Lovetts could count on inheriting the land on which their Puritan ancestors had settled their families after they arrived in Beverly in the 1630s. Shared values and success were still held dear by Puritan descendants living in small rural communities and in urban and maritime economies in Essex County, Massachusetts. However, another set of Puritans will get our attention in the final chapter of this book. That group was made up of migrants from the west coast of England, some of whom began populating the northern part of the MBC in the 1660s and spilled over into what later became the states of New Hampshire and Maine.

In her book, *Good Wives*, which was published in 1991, Laurel Thatcher Ulrich wrote about families whose Puritan competencies and pocketbooks were strong enough to enable them to settle lands north of where earlier Puritans had already developed towns such as Ipswich, Salisbury, Haverhill, and Hampton, NH.[15] The towns that they founded looked more like the Puritan villages based on agriculture west of Boston in locations like Dedham

---

[15] Her book focused on what happened in northern MA and some parts of NH and Maine in the period from 1650 and 1750. In addition Ulrich pays attention to urban southern MBC towns like Salem. A major theme was the business activities of wives and mothers working with the family's sons after the husband had died or was incapacitated. See especially *Good Wives*, 1991, 13-50.

and Wrentham, not maritime towns on the coast such as Salem, Gloucester, Marblehead, Marblehead, and Beverly. Furthermore, Anderson's analysis confirms that the people who came in the 1630s tried one or more towns to find the best opportunity to get land grants. From the available information, then, it seems that the Lovett family had also followed the process of re-shuffling that Ulrich and Anderson describe.

The in-comers from the west of England included descendants of Ethel Bradstreet's maternal tree who had begun to populate towns and villages in northern Massachusetts at the same time that England, Scotland, and Ireland were roiled by Oliver Cromwell's army and his Puritan allies in the seventeenth century. Cromwell and the Puritans had won against their enemies in England first, then in Scotland, after which they had also gained control of Ireland. That would mean that if, for example, you came from the west of England after the 1650s and were seeking land in what Ulrich considered northern New England, you probably would have had to move further away from the first settlements to new places like Haverhill or Newbury in northern Essex County or even to towns in southern New Hampshire and Maine.

Helping England Build an Empire While Also Doing Their Puritan Duties

This chapter has addressed how Puritan towns such as Topsfield, Boston, Beverly, Danvers, and Salem helped build the human and community infrastructure needed for the successful operation of the British Empire far from Ireland where we have already seen Bradstreets taking active roles in repressing and governing native Roman Catholic Irish people like the Maneys of Tipperary County. I learned that residents of coastal and nearby cities and towns in Essex County in the seventeenth and eighteenth centuries participated in efforts to forcibly police Native peoples in regions nearer home. All of the Puritans featured in this book had met similar challenges where their religious teachings lacked some important topics, such as how to view and treat "others" from outside the colonists' Puritan world. Not surprisingly, conflicts erupted that were similar to what happened between Cromwellian soldiers in Ireland and the native Irish people and their allies, the Hiberno-Normans, as the native Irish sought to reclaim their own land in order to successfully govern their own people as we will see in the Irish chapter of this book.

In Massachusetts there were also "other" people, including convict laborers, indentured servants, Black slaves, female workers, Native peoples, and people from Roman Catholic Ireland who had been brought to the United States and to British North America against their will. Their presence brought additional conflict to Puritan life, including the issue of how Puritans should treat African slaves and others who were living and working for Puritan families in Massachusetts cities and towns. Sadly, these newcomers were not deemed worthy to merit the spiritual and social care that Puritans like the Bradstreets and Lovetts automatically extended to their own kind. However, by the nineteenth century leaders of coastal cities and towns like Beverly and Salem – and their counterparts in England – understood that MBC industries like fishing, shipbuilding, shoemaking, farming, and seafaring were learning how to successfully compete with their counterparts in the United Kingdom.

The presence of these "investments" over time had allowed industries in British North America to compete better with similar industrial sectors in England, Scotland, and Ireland, which constituted the heart of the British Empire at home. In the case of this research on the Lovett family, DNA matching is helping connect Lovett and Maney family descendants in the twenty-first century through the science of DNA. Specifically, that includes descendants of Lovetts living in Salem in the 1630s and the family of John's brother, Daniel, who settled in central Massachusetts at about the same time. Also in the case of Daniel Lovett, DNA matches in the Lovett family tree have provided hints about additional locations in British North America like Nova Scotia where Lovetts may have visited by ship before 1635 when John Lovett and Mary Grant settled in Salem.

Similarly, genealogy trees have confirmed the identities of people in both the John and Joseph lines who formed the backbone of the Lovett family in Salem and Beverly. In the Maternal chapter, attention will be given to Sarah Corning, who, like Mary Pukui, is a distant cousin of my siblings and me, this time on Ethel Bradstreet's Lovett side. A recommendation to anyone hoping to work on family trees is to recognize and accept that a lot of that work depends on knowing about locations since after we know where people were living and visiting, we are often able to find the vital records necessary to create a helpful family tree. For example, I learned to look in U.S. census records to confirm if William Bradstreet, Jr. was getting ready to sell his family's Topsfield land in the late 1850s. If so, then I could begin to write about why there were so many male shoemakers in Topsfield and because William Bradstreet's son, Alvah, knew that his father was planning to use an updated model for farming and getting agricultural products to market in Boston and in nearby cities such as Salem and Beverly.

By mining available records, I also came to know that among the Lovett families in the Massachusetts Bay Colony people from both the John and the Joseph lines would likely continue to live in a medium-sized coastal city that thrived on change and was already seeing newcomers to Beverly arrive from famine-wracked Ireland before the 1860 census announced their arrival. Later in this book the reader will be able to assess the work of contemporary scholars like Mary Blewett[16] who help focus our attention on women in the textile industry in the city of Lowell, as well as the city of Lynn

---

[16] See for example, *Men, Women, and Work: Class, Gender, and Protest in the New England Shoe Industry, 1780-1910.* U. of Illinois Press. Urbana and Chicago. 1989.

as a shoemaking center. What this meant for the jobs held by the last three generations of Lovetts, including Eben Lovett and Maria Guild, as well as for Bertha Lovett and Alvah Bradstreet, Ethel Bradstreet and John MacLean Maney, and others is suggested in the next three chapters of this book.

View of the Beverly-Salem Bridge from the Beverly side
From https://omeka-s.noblenet.org

FARMERS & FISHERMEN

TWO CENTURIES OF WORK IN

ESSEX COUNTY, MASSACHUSETTS,

1630–1850

Cover page of *Farmers & Fishermen*

January 23, 1980   ③

Dear Ethel:

I enclose a genealogy of my grandfather, Solon Lovett, taken from a four-volume set, <u>Genealogical and Personal Memoirs, Boston and Eastern Massachusetts,</u> Lewis Historical Publishing Co., N.Y., 1908. The line starts with Joseph, son of the John who came to Beverly sometime before 1638. This first John had another son, John, and the Lovetts in this area are all descended from either sons John or Joseph.

Dorothy reminded me that there was a Governor Curtis Guild, probably in the 1920's or earlier. There is a Curtis Guild Camp (State or National Guard) in Wakefield. I note in the genealogy that your grandfather, Eben Francis, married Maria Guild, which explains your interest.

We hope you are getting along OK; take care. Regards to Tony.

Faithfully yours,

Bob Lovett

Author's copy of a Lovett geneaology

The Beverly-Salem cruise boat that sank in a storm in 1898

Ethel Lovett, a teahouse operator and the author's grand aunt

VITAL RECORDS

OF

BEVERLY

MASSACHUSETTS

TO THE END OF THE YEAR 1849

VOLUME I — BIRTHS

PUBLISHED BY THE
TOPSFIELD HISTORICAL SOCIETY
TOPSFIELD, MASS.
1906

Cover page of official records for Beverly

The Lovitt Genealogy.

One of many Lovitt/Lovett geneaologies

United Shoe Machinery Corporation. One of Beverly's largest employers in the twentieth century

Mills on the Merrimac River, Lawrence, Mass.

A large mill on the Merrimac River in Lawrence, MA

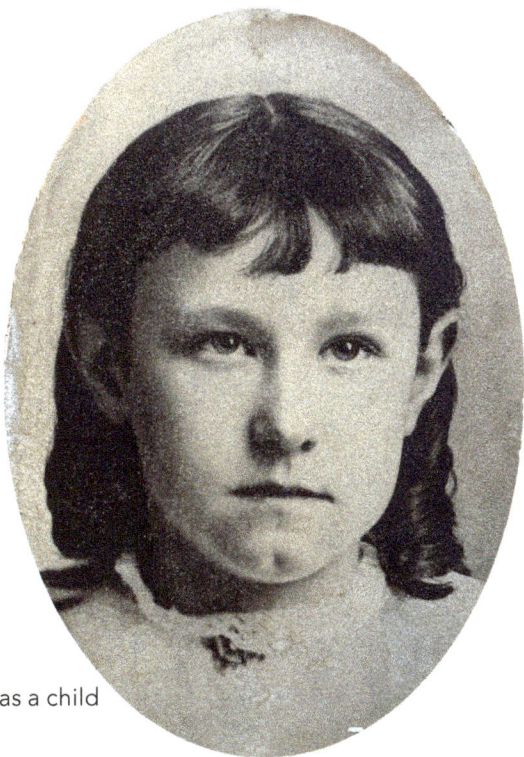

Ethel Lovett as a child

Beverly birthplace of Lucy Larcom (1824-1893), teacher, poet, mill-worker

Henry Wilson, also known as Jeremiah Jones Colbath, a cousin of Maria Guild Lovett. He served as vice president in the administration of President U.S. Grant.

Fishing ships moored in Beverly Harbor. See https://omeka-s.noblenet.org

Old Fish Wharf in Beverly Harbor. See https://omeka-s.noblenet.org

04

Scottish Families Emigrate to British America

This chapter focuses on Scottish families who had been living for centuries on islands close to the mainland of western Scotland, as well as in more remote parts of that country. Some Scottish families in the tree of my father, John MacLean Maney (1914-1985),[1] started leaving their traditional homeland before the end of the eighteenth century, at about the time that the union of Scotland and England became technically operative. People living in the Highlands and Islands of Scotland were mostly subsistence farmers and hoped that farming in British North America (BNA) would be more economically advanced and sustainable than was the case in Scotland. They also expected that there would be new economic opportunities in Scotland's governmental capital, Edinburgh, and its business center, Glasgow, as well as in the Lowlands near the border with England. However, better economic opportunities did not materialize for people living on the Isle of Coll and other small islands by the end of the eighteenth century and they did not believe that sustained

---

[1] The reader will note that most names of people living in Scotland or in North America outside of the USA begin with Mc. Some of those living in the USA are spelled with Mac, a decision explained at the end of the chapter.

economic opportunity would reach the Highlands and Islands for several more generations. Nor were they convinced that the conflicts between the Campbells and other clans would be overcome.[2]

Moreover, no one among them could know ahead of time how similar and dire the situation would be between fellow Scottish Gaels and the Irish people by the middle of the nineteenth century, when economic conditions began to deteriorate sharply, occasioned by each country's respective famines. On the other hand, being part of the British Empire made Coll people eligible for land for farming in eastern Canada. The British government was trying to fill up land in Nova Scotia that had been vacated by the French in the wake of Napoleon's defeat at the beginning of the nineteenth century. Maybe some of those leaving Coll in the first quarter of the nineteenth century had already decided to keep moving, whether westward to 1) Ontario where farming was better; 2) other nearby provinces, including Prince Edward Island (PE) where land was less expensive; or 3) locations in the newly independent United States. Many Scots sensed that with assistance in the cost of passage and with land purchases once they arrived, the British government was making them an offer they dared not refuse.

They prepared for going to Nova Scotia and not another part of British America for several reasons. First, because Scotland had been separate from England until 1707, the Scottish people had known a long history of independence before they joined the new United Kingdom. Second, Scotland's citizens were eligible for land grants in a continuing UK land grant program for Nova Scotia, an offer that was not made if Scots chose to come to live in any of the New England areas that were part of the USA. Third,

---

[2] Where necessary, information from the *Maney Family Archive* in the form of online records is used to supplement formal census records that began to be kept in from 1776 until 1821 by the Church of Scotland minister on the island by which time most of John MacLean Maney's Scottish relatives were living in Nova Scotia rather than on Coll or elsewhere in Scotland.

Scotland had had some experience managing a colonial territory of its own located in Darien, in the isthmus of Panama and had sent people educated in Scottish universities to be managers in Britain's colonies in North America and in other countries. Finally, although Scotland was a majority Protestant country, Scots who might have been candidates for emigration may not have thought that they were going to be given financial support and benefits at home from either the government in faraway London or the elected and appointed officials in Scotland's capital, Edinburgh.

Scotland's weak national economy can be seen in two stories about walking cattle to market in central Scotland and ultimately into England. The story of cattle raising on small Scottish islands is a story of the relations among the families living on the laird's land on a particular island, the ragtag groups of workers who accompanied the cattle on the droves, the people who kept track of the costs and saw that small farmers in places like Totronald, a farm on the Isle of Coll, where the laird got paid in real money by his workers for some of their workplace activities. These complicated farming activities are addressed in a book, *The Drove Roads of Scotland*[3] which showed that drovers and English consumers wanted regular access to Scottish beef and therefore farm workers continued to use poorly-cared-for roads and routes as the main means of walking the cattle to their final destinations.[4]

---

[3] The last of the jobs involved in the cross-country travel to market using drove roads in the eighteenth and nineteenth century were phased out only in the twentieth century, but the results were the same, as will soon be seen, because consumers still wanted to have access to Scottish beef.

[4] The drove roads book, which was re-published in Edinburgh by Birlinn in 2008, was written by A.R.B. Haldane. See the bibliography in this book for articles and chapters giving more information about the economic behavior of the lairds and the ways that they interacted — or didn't — with their workers. Also, famine came to Coll and other islands in the 1840s, but a lot of people were already gone by that time and soon the laird of the Isle of Coll had also left after cashing out his landholdings to live in a UK colony in Africa.

A few years ago, I had the opportunity to see the twenty-first-century equivalent of this long trip when I visited Mull, one of the McLean islands located near the Isle of Coll. There my Scottish friends and I could see the place where Coll's black cattle were still being brought by boat to the Isle of Mull even in the 21st century in order to join cattle from Mull, Tiree, and other small islands nearby. In earlier years, the next step was to walk the cattle across the Isle of Mull to board another small boat that would take them to Kerrera, an island close to Oban, one of the main transportation hubs on the Scottish mainland. From Kerrera they swam to the mainland and started their long journey along stony dirt paths up one hill and down the next.[5]

Some Collachs Arrive in North America and Begin Farming

So, in the early 1820s, people from several inter-related families on Coll started preparing to get free land in Nova Scotia and PE while there was a good offer on the table. Soon several families to whom my father, John MacLean Maney, was related on the Isle of Coll did in fact leave together for British North America along with other people from our family's main line of McLeans, McDonalds, Kennedys, Campbells, and McKinnons. They left the Western Isles after the British wars with France ended in the 1810s. Descendants of the people who came to Nova Scotia around 1820 were still living near one another at the time of the first full Canadian census for Nova Scotia's Inverness County in 1871. Because they belonged to big families in Scotland, and because famine struck in the Highlands and Islands at about the same time period as it did

---

[5] Before I left Mull a few days later, I saw a modern version of the process of droving-by-truck take place. As I watched, a big truck full of cattle was being prepared to go south to somewhere in England carrying the same type of Scottish cattle that continue to be admired and sought after for feasts and Sunday dinners. More information about the particular drove roads used in the nineteenth and twentieth centuries are shown in Haldane's book.

in Ireland, many people in the same families continued to migrate out of Scotland to Australia, New Zealand, Nova Scotia, and other parts of Canada as well as to the Scottish Lowlands and big cities in the northeastern parts of Massachusetts, including Boston and other towns and cities in Essex County.

When they finally left Coll, the ancestors in John MacLean Maney's main Scottish line settled mostly in two locations in Nova Scotia's Inverness County. Many of these people at first continued to intermarry with other Collachs in the new country. One group led by McKinnons settled near Nova Scotia's Lake Ainslee, which is located west of where the other group, which included McLeans and McDonalds, settled in the rural area of Malagawatch along the Denys River in Inverness County. More Scots from the islands came to live near their friends and relatives as economic conditions continued to worsen on the Scottish mainland and islands. We know the Canadian locations from the decennial census records which started to be kept in 1871, in land records, in local newspapers and other publications, and in communications sent back to family members and friends on Coll and other nearby Scottish islands.

Many of the topics considered in this chapter may seem familiar from earlier chapters, but there are also important differences. One is that Collachs and other Scots did not consider themselves to be Puritans. Indeed, most Collachs belonged to the Church of Scotland and a smaller number were Roman Catholics. They were also not committed to creating new types of communities when they arrived in Nova Scotia but to welcoming people from the same part of Scotland and working together in practical ways to develop towns, schools, churches, and needed community social services. At first, all spoke Scottish Gaelic, at least the adults did, which is not exactly the same as the language and Gaelic culture among the Irish. However, we do need to understand more about starting points in Scotland that show what had been happening in the islands and highland communities for the time period during the seventeenth and eighteenth centuries, the same period highlighted in the other family chapters.

The mini-tree approach is used so as not to lose John MacLean Maney's maternal McDonald family group among the stream of migrants with similar names leaving the Western Isles in the nineteenth century.[6] As in the other chapters, the availability of farmland and employment in growing cities influenced decisions that people made about what occupations they would pursue as the power of the clans weakened over time. And as in Ireland, England, and British North America, people emigrating from the Scottish Highlands and Islands had an easier time making the move if they could get land grants before they needed to have them.

Origin Points Show Big Changes for the Western Isles

Most researchers quickly learn that no official baptism records are available today to show who lived where on the small island of Coll, far away from the mainland of Scotland, in the mid-1700s. This genealogical memoir focuses on Coll and two other islands close by, Tiree and Mull. All three were in the territory of Clan McLean, which had taken over from the McDonalds as one of the strongest clans in the Western Isles. Until the middle of the seventeenth century, the main McLean clan leader had his castle on the Isle of Mull, which was not far from Coll. However, this McLean laird was toppled from power during a period of prolonged inter-clan conflict that engulfed the region during the

---

[6] Recent research about the Scottish clearances in the nineteenth century suggests there was a change in the behavior of lairds and other landowners since the last serious attempt to install a Scottish king failed in the 1740s. A good account is R. H. Campbell, "The First Phase of Clearances," 91-108, in T.M. Devine and Rosalind Mitchison, eds., *People and Society in Scotland*, Edinburgh: John Donald., vol. 1, 1988. Most of this information also comes from a listserv that incorporates records generated on Coll and nearby islands, which is included in the *Maney Family Archive*.

seventeenth century. By 1674, the McLean clan chief had lost most of the land he owned on the neighboring islands of Mull and Tiree after his debts had been bought up by the McLeans' archenemy, the Campbell Duke of Argyll County, who was the informal leader of governmental forces in the highlands and islands on behalf of the Scottish and English governments.

Clan histories and research by modern Scottish historians agree that before the 1600s most Scottish clans had multiple branches whose leaders worked together in wartime but reverted to frequent feuding with each other whenever there was no common enemy. Over the centuries, clan chiefs had given parcels of land — or sometimes whole islands to their sons, much as the Puritan Bradstreets and Lovetts, as well as migrants from the west of England, had passed land to their sons. Thus, the McLean laird of the small island of Coll used land to keep his supporters nearby as well as to recruit followers and allies to live on the island in order to protect himself, his close lieutenants, family members, and others. Successive lairds of Coll especially wanted to protect their own interests against the growing power of the Campbell clan and also remain relatively independent from their distant relative, the weakened McLean chief on Mull.

Strong Coll clan chiefs played important roles leading their people into conflicts with traditional enemies including the Campbells, as well as through joint efforts to return the Stuart monarchy to power during the 1700s. When the tide began to turn after the Campbells had taken possession of the neighboring islands of Mull and Tiree in the second half of the 1600s, successive Coll lairds managed to keep hold of many of their farms on Coll, but they could see the handwriting on the wall and so could tenant farmers and people who were relatively well-off. Accordingly, small farmers began to get ready to leave for North America whenever an opportunity appeared to procure land grants anywhere in British North America. After 1776 there were opportunities to go to the newly independent American states as well as to those parts of eastern Canada in which the French still held sway. After the wars with France ended in the second decade of the nineteenth century, the British government wanted to have English and Scottish people go to Nova Scotia rather than those places held by the USA which were no longer under the sway of the British Empire.

It is against this backdrop that we examine information gathered in 1776 when the incoming Church of Scotland minister on the Isle of Coll conducted an unofficial census of his parishioners. After that, succeeding ministers made sure that baptism and marriage records were kept in the joint parish of Coll and Tiree until 1841 when the United Kingdom began taking an official census every ten years. Thus, in 1776, a semi-official paper trail of baptisms and marriages on the island began to be created, showing which families and individuals were actually living on Coll at that time. These same documents, which have been updated and are now kept online, allow family members of Collachs to learn exactly where their families lived on the island in 1776 and later on. From the 1776 church records it can be said with certainty that most of the people living on Coll after 1674 were descended from those who had continued to owe allegiance to the Coll laird during the turbulent 1660s. So, it does not matter if someone living on Coll in 1776 had been born on nearly islands such as Mull or Tiree or had intermarried with husbands or wives who had different clan names. If their allegiance was to the laird of Coll in 1776, we should consider them Collachs.

The reader should also know that into the nineteenth century people living in the Highlands and Islands still used Gaelic as their main common language. Among other things, this means that on official occasions a last name might be used, but that was not how someone usually described someone else who lived in the same community. For example, you could summarize John MacLean Maney's paternal Scottish grandfather by identifying him as follows: he was Charles, son of Hector — or Eachunn Ruardh, which is

"Red-haired Hector" in Gaelic — and grandson of another Charles — Tearlach mac Ailean, or Charles the son of Allan — McLean. Such a red-haired Charles seems to have been the informal leader of the group that left for Canada in 1820. He also managed the process of getting land grants in Canada for the group from Coll. However, in practice it would have been more complicated to describe John MacLean Maney's relationship to people on both sides of his family since his mother's father, the red-haired Charles and John's grandmother, Flora, were cousins. One option was to add some particular personal features to a given person's first name. For example, people might add information suggesting that the person had fair hair, a reddish complexion, or had lost a hand in an accident. That would help people use the Gaelic language to share a long story about the person with neighbors and relatives under the guise of saying someone's name.

The clan system had been under acute stress since the mid-to late 1600s because there were new players from the mainland like the Campbells, who held the position of Duke of Argyll, engaged in the usual inter-clan fights. Finally, everyone on Coll and Tiree could sense that important political and social forces were working to leave the Western Isles further behind in political, social, and economic trends that were benefiting Glasgow, Edinburgh, and the southern part, or Lowlands of Scotland. Chief among the changes taking place had been the move to unite the kingdoms of Scotland and England. The first step of this process had occurred in 1603, and a stipulation had been agreed between the two kingdoms that the union would not be complete until one hundred years had passed. First, the Scottish king, James VI, the son of Queen Mary, was invited to become King James I of England in addition to keeping his title as Scotland's king. Additionally, each kingdom would get to keep its own parliament and legal system.

The union of the two countries' parliaments offered some opportunities for economic growth, especially for people in high governmental circles and for business and industry in Glasgow, the country's unofficial business capital. However, there were few economic opportunities for people in the Highlands and Islands region unless the head of household, or one or more of his sons, joined the military or the family moved to another part of Scotland or emigrated to another part of the British Empire. Instead, the joint government in Edinburgh and London seemed content to leave the faraway parts of the Scottish Highlands and Islands to the tender mercies of England's closest and most powerful ally in the west of Scotland, the Duke of Argyll and other leaders of Clan Campbell.

Mini-Tree Information Collected by the Coll Minister in 1776

Most of the information about the families on Coll, whether they emigrated from Scotland to Canada or decided to stay, can be seen from the records kept by the Coll minister starting in 1776. (More information about the survey of Coll's inhabitants in 1776 can be found at www.collgenealogy.com and a sister site, www.tireegenealogy.com). The information in the mini-tree was taken from the Coll baptismal records and allows readers to focus on one key McLean family, adding people with other last names as needed. In the minister's survey, Allan McLean's (abt. 1725-?) name is easy to find in the list for Totronald, as is that of Allan's wife, Catherine McKinnon (1836-?). Both were documented in 1776 as living on a farm in Totronald with three children: Red-haired Charles (abt. 1761-1845), Mary (abt. 1765-?), and Angus (1776-abt. 1841). All are ancestors of John MacLean Maney and his mother, Sarah Harriet Ruth MacLean Maney. The people listed in bold print in each generation are in John MacLean Maney's direct line starting with his third-great-grandparents and ending with his mother and her big family of siblings who grew up on Prince Edward Island in the last quarter of the nineteenth century. Dates and locations for births and baptisms for Coll are included.

Mini-tree for John MacLean Maney's Scottish Line

Allan McLean, who was born about 1725 in Scotland and died in Scotland after 1813, married **Catherine McKinnon,** who was born about 1740 in Scotland and died after 1813 on Coll.

Their children: **Red-haired Charles McLean,** who was born about 1761 and died about 1836 in Malagawatch, NS; Mary, who was born in about 1767 and died in Nova Scotia (date unknown); and Angus, who was born about 1771 and died in Scotland.

Charles McLean had two children by **Ann McLean**, who died in about 1787. No marriage record has been found for the couple.

Their children: Marion, who was born on Coll in 1784, and Flory, who was born on Coll in 1786.

Charles McLean then married **Mary McKinnon**, who was probably born on Coll about 1765 and died in Grimisary, Coll, in 1789.

Their children: Roderick McLean, who was baptized in 1787 on Coll, and died abt. 1868 in NS; and Mary McLean, who was baptized in Grimisary, Coll, in 1790.

Charles McLean next married **Mary McDonald**, who probably was born in about 1768 on Coll, and died in 1840 in Nova Scotia. They married on 25 Feb 1790 in Grimisary, Coll, and both died in Inverness County, NS. Their children: **Hector**, who was born in Grimisary, Coll, in 1791 and died in NS before 1881; James, who was born in 1792; Neil who was born in 1792 in Grimisary, Coll and died in 1865 in Whycocomagh, Inverness, NS; Mary, who was born in 1794 in Grimisary, Coll, and died in 1884 in East Lake Ainslee, Inverness, NS;

Lachlan, who was born in 1795 in Grimisary, Coll, and died in 1855 in NS; Alexander who was born in 1798 in Kilbride, Coll, and died in 1845 in River Denys, Inverness, NS; Margaret, who was born in 1799 in Kilbride, Coll; Christian, who was born in 1801 in Kilbride, Coll; Hugh, who was born in 1803 in Kilbride, Coll; Allan, who was born in 1805 in Kilbride, Coll, and died in 1891 in Grand Narrows, NS, and **Donald,** who was born in 1809 or 1813 in Kilbride, Coll, and died in 1890 in Sydney, NS.[7]

Hector McLean, who was born in Grimisary, Coll in 1791 and died in NS in 1881, married **Christy McDonald**, who was born on Coll and died after 1881 in Nova Scotia.

Their children, all born in Malagawatch, NS: Mary, who was born in 1829 and died in 1905 in East Lake Ainslee, Inverness, NS; Flora, who was born in 1831; Christy A. McLean, who was born in 1834; **Charles Hector**, who was born in 1836 and died in 1890 in Dundas, PE; Neil, who was born in 1840 and died in 1927 in River Denys, NS; Catherine, who was born in 1841 and died in Valley Mills, NS; John, who was born in 1845 and died in 1895 in NS; Hector, who was born in 1849 and died in South Side, River Denys Basin, NS, in 1921; Christy who was born in 1852 and died in Valley Mills, NS in 1889; and Margaret, who was born in 1854 and died in 1886.

---

[7] There may have been two Donald McLeans, one born in 1809 and the second born in 1813. Donald always used the second date which was also the one inscribed on his tombstone in Sydney, NS. Perhaps the first Donald died and the parents named the second child Donald to take his place.

Donald McLean, a son of Charles McLean and Mary McDonald (see above), who was born in 1809 or 1813 on Coll and died in Sydney, NS in 1890, married **Christian Campbell** in NS, who was born in 1817 in Grishipoll, Coll, and died after 1844 in NS.

Their children, all born in Nova Scotia: Neil, who was born abt. 1833; Hector George, who was born in 1833 and died in 1910 in Massachusetts; Roderick, who was born in 1834 and died in Quincy, MA, in 1890; Catherine, who was born 1838 and died after 1921 in NS; **Flora**, who was born in 1842 and died in 1883 in Dundas, PE; Christiana, who was born in. 1843 and died in 1905 in the town of Chelsea in Suffolk, MA; and Mary who was born in 1844 and died in 1891 in the town of Ipswich, Essex, MA.

Donald McLean then married **Catherine McPhaiden**, also from Coll, who was born in 1837 and died in 1862 in Sydney, NS.

Their child: John Charles was born in Sydney, NS in 1861 and died in Palm Beach, FL in 1943.

Donald McLean then married **Louise A. Irish**, who was born in 1836 in NS and died in 1902 in Sydney, NS. Their children, all born in Sydney, NS: Amelia Augusta, who was born in1870 and died in Sydney in 1871, and Bessie J., who was born in 1872 and died in Sydney in 1921.

Charles H. McLean married Flora McLean

Their children: Christy Ann, who was born in Bath, Maine, in 1863, died in 1925 in Medford, MA; Mary Margaret, who was born in 1864 in NS, died after 1901 in Inverness County, NS; Hector Charles, who was born in 1867 in PE; Edward, who was born in PE in 1868 and died before 1881; Neil, who was born in De Sable, PE, in 1869 and died in 1942 in MA; Daniel Donald, who was born in 1871 in De Sable, PE, and died in Esmeralda, Nevada; Flora, who was born in De Sable, PE, in 1872 and died in Newton, MA, in 1941; Catherine (Cassie) who was born in Dundas, PE, in 1875 and died in Concord, Middlesex, MA, in 1933; **Sarah Harriet Ruth,** who was born in Dundas in 1876 and died in Lawrence, Essex, MA, in 1939; John A., who was born in 1878 in Dundas, PE; Elizabeth Louisa, who was born in 1880 in Dundas, PE, and died in Bridgetown, PE, in1906; and James Lauchlin, who was born in 1881 in Dundas and died in 1942 in Idaho, USA.

Sarah Harriet Ruth McLean married **John Joseph Maney, MD.**
Their surviving child: **John MacLean Maney,** who was born in Lawrence, Essex, MA, on 4 Dec1914 died in Amesbury, Essex, MA, on 21 Dec 1985.

In 1776, the minister's census showed one hundred ninety-seven farms on the island with a total population of 677 adults and unmarried adult children living at home. There also were 261 younger children who had not yet started religious training under the minister's supervision. The minister did not have in his remit to check on Roman Catholics living on Coll and, indeed, there were probably few or none from that faith to be counted although some could be found on nearby islands. Indeed, when people migrated to Canada, some came along from islands near Coll whose populations were nearly or completely Catholic. This enumeration in 1776 did not include information about the occupations of heads of families which might have helped readers today estimate the island's economic conditions and capacity to support a population of that size. For other information we need to read accounts from visitors to the island like Samuel Johnson and James Boswell, who had a meeting with the laird of Coll. In the 1792 report on Coll from the Scottish Old Statistical Accounts, the local minister reported that thirty-six Collachs had emigrated from Coll to North America in 1790-91 after a bad harvest.

These governmental reports done at the end of the eighteenth century described agricultural and economic activities, such as boat-building, fishing, kelping, and other economic activities going on in each parish. They show two main cash crops: money paid for cattle sent to market in central Scotland each year, as we have seen, and for kelp harvested from seaweed and used for medicinal purposes. In addition, some local men and women worked in the Lowlands at harvest time and brought back cash money from that economic activity, as they also did if they participated in the annual droving and sales of Scotland's black cattle.[8] In the 1600s and 1700s, Collachs lived in small settlements that they rented from whichever laird was the landlord. Relatives of the clan chief often served as factors (or farm managers) and might get special living conditions, like not having to pay rent. As in the British royal family, the role of primogeniture operated to settle most disputes about who would become laird or a junior laird in charge of one or more of the main laird's properties.

At a time when big families were the rule, the laird often had second, third, and fourth sons and each would want his share of land. People whose fathers and grandfathers had been close relatives

---

[8] There is information in the *Maney Family Archive* and the Irish chapter in this book which shows that it was not unusual that young women and their brothers worked to bring home cash money in the Lowlands of Scotland each year for their families, a practice which Irish historian, R.F. Foster, writes about in his *Modern Ireland, 1600-1972*, London: Allen Lane Penguin Press, 1989. According to Foster, Irish women were also working to do what they could to support their families in the perpetually uncertain times, especially in agriculture and in millwork.

of the laird might use part of their land to grow a few cattle to sell in the Scottish Lowlands each year, and part of the cash received was expected to go back to the laird or factor, i.e., the farm manager for the laird. Under this system, a lot of bartering could and did go on. Among the 197 separate family units on Coll in 1776, McLean was the name of the head of household for the most. However, more than one hundred families included no one at all with the McLean name.

A similar picture appears when we look at the eighty-two people whom the minister counted in Totronald that year, a location with a reputation for having some of the best agricultural land on the island. In 1776, Totronald was the second-most-populated place on Coll. Of Totronald's eighteen families, only four were headed by McLeans. However, the most common arrangement was the island's version of what might be thought of as a "mixed marriage." In such cases, a Kennedy might be married to a McMillan, a Campbell married to a McLean, or a McLean married to a McDonald or McKinnon. Totronald is also important because it was in the center of the island, which had remained under the control of the Coll laird after more than one hundred years of conflict with clan Campbell. By 1776, the Duke of Argyll, the head of the Campbells, had added to his domain some farms at the eastern and western ends of Coll. There were four McLean heads of households in Totronald that year while there are seven McDonald families, two Campbell families, two McKinnon families, and one family each in which the head of household was a Kennedy, McInnes, or a McPhaiden. So, it was not unlikely that the current McLean laird — or perhaps his father or grandfather — had given some of his McLean allies, as well as various McDonalds, McKinnons, and others, incentives to live in Totronald, Grishipoll, and other places in the center of the island in exchange for their loyalty in the next fight with the laird's enemies.

The family described at household #70 in Totronald in 1776 was headed by Allan McLean and Catherine McKinnon. However, we cannot tell from the list whether either or both parents might have been married before or whether all three children were the offspring of both of the listed parents. Nor can we know from the information provided if there were any older children from this family who had already married and were raising their own families separately in Totronald or elsewhere on Coll. Some other people born on Coll might have been living elsewhere in Scotland, serving on military assignment including as British soldiers fighting against the people seeking independence from England in the American states, or might have already emigrated from Scotland.

We can see from the baptism and marriage records that were kept after 1776 that the older son in this particular family, Red-haired Charles, fathered children with at least three different women. The name of the first was Anne MacLean (1765-1786), but we do not have any records showing where or if a marriage was performed. We also have records for Charles' marriage with his second wife, Mary McKinnon (1765-1789), but not the names of her parents or where she was baptized. One the children of this marriage was Charles' first son, Roderick, (1787-1868), who later had a big family of his own including people who are DNA matches with John MacLean Maney's children. The second child, Mary, was baptized in Grimisary, Coll, on 6 Oct 1789 after Mary McKinnon's death,

This Red-haired Charles then married one of the daughters of his family's neighbors, Lachlane McDonald and Mary McLean, living in household #73 in Totronald in the minister's census. A daughter, Mary McDonald, of this couple was born a McLean and was a second great-grandmother of Sarah Harriet "Ruth" McLean Maney. This Mary was born in approximately 1768 and died in Cape Breton about 1840. Similarly, we can see in the baptismal records from 1776 to 1820 the names of the children who accompanied Mary McDonald and her husband, Red-haired Charles, to Cape Breton, Nova Scotia, as well as those who remained behind or came later with their own families. John and

Mary, the couple just described, had at least eleven children, and John MacLean Maney's (1914-1985) children have DNA matches with multiple descendants of the marriage of Charles and Mary McDonald, as well as to descendants of Charles' sister, Mary, and to the children of Charles' eldest son, Hector McLean, and his wife, Christy McDonald.

Coll Families Leave Scotland in 1820 for Nova Scotia

The Coll baptism and marriage lists from 1776 to1821 also help us see how people in the family of Charles McLean and Mary McLean McDonald intermarried with other Totronald families both before and after coming to Nova Scotia in 1820. As mentioned above, the first full census for Nova Scotia was not taken until 1871 which was after Charles and Mary had died. It shows that some of their children married Kennedys, McKinnons, McPhaidens, McDonalds, Campbells, and McLeans whose families were from Coll during the first generation after their migration to Canada. Since we now know that so many Collachs left Coll in the first half of the nineteenth century and ended up living quite close to one another in Canada, the information in the minister's census of 1776 may suggest a false sense of stability and normality of life on Coll during 1776 until 1820. Recent findings by Scottish historians suggest, however, that several important factors were at play in small Highland and Island communities like Coll during the period from 1700 to 1820.

First, successive dukes of Argyll and other wealthy landowners were developing different interests among themselves than the ones they shared with their tenant farmers. Also, they had deeper pockets and could usually count on support from the government of the United Kingdom during inter-clan conflicts in the eighteenth and nineteenth centuries. The UK government's increased focus on "improving" the Highlands and Islands may also have been payback for support that McLeans and related clans had given to Charles Stuart, also known as Bonnie Prince

Charlie, in his rebellions against the British during the eighteenth century. The clan chiefs' movement away from the traditional obligations that had bound them to their clan members' and tenants' needs suggested that lairds had begun thinking more like landlords than clan chiefs who understood the traditional responsibilities that lairds – or their representatives – should have felt for their tenants and followers.

Finally, increased opportunities for tenants to migrate from Argyll County to industrial jobs in Glasgow or work as agricultural laborers in the Scottish Lowlands were making it likely that many who left Coll were probably not going to be coming back. From this perspective, it looks like the McLean landlord on Coll and the families of many Collachs were already trying out coping strategies in 1776 when the minister's census of Coll was taken. Both landlords and tenants were struggling to keep their heads above water. Migration to North America may have been hastened because leaders of most clans had cut themselves off more and more from their tenants. By the 1840s, when the Scottish potato crop began to fail — as was happening also in nearby Ireland — large numbers of people faced desperate conditions and had to decide whether to leave for jobs available in Glasgow or in the Lowlands.

A third option, depending on the family's contacts and financial situation, was migration to Australia, British North America, or the United States in order to escape famine conditions, the same choice which faced the Irish in the second half of the nineteenth century. By the time that the famine was taking hold on Mull and Tiree in the 1840s, the Coll laird had sold his land and had left Scotland for South Africa. Researchers have sought to convey what life was like on Coll during the period from 1776 until many of these people on Coll began leaving for Canada and other countries. Gaelic society had a rich oral culture that poets and bards used to tell stories that reflected values that people held dear. New initiatives aiming at "improvement" coming from the government in Edinburgh or from landlords were met with a kind of passive resistance, the same strategy that Collachs applied to the Campbell lairds' leading role in the introduction of "improvements" in agriculture. Attacks on sheriffs, the appearance of illicit distilleries, and glorification of smugglers were celebrated in poetry, songs, and stories of the time that fit this picture.[9]

Life in Nova Scotia Was Significantly Different

For the first generation after their arrival in Nova Scotia, former Collachs may have sought to continue conducting their everyday lives using the Gaelic language. For example, a certain Neil McDonald authored occasional columns about the daily lives of the transplants to Inverness County, Nova Scotia, that appeared in a Gaelic language newspaper, "MacTalla," which was based in Sydney, NS. Neil was probably a son of Neil McDonald (1787-?) and Flora Kennedy (1792-1814) and was likely a younger brother of John MacLean Maney's great-grandmother, Christy McDonald McLean (1808-1881). Neil (1818-1899) had become blind as a result of an accident and was living in Malagawatch in Inverness County when the first full census of Nova Scotia was conducted in 1871. In one of his newspaper columns, he described the first year the Collachs spent in Cape Breton. Similarly, a book, *The History of Inverness County*, authored by J. L. McDougall in 1922, described the people who had lived in the same River Denis voting district in 1871. McDougall used an oral history format when he published the stories that people told him about what Malagawatch was like in the "old days" and which people used to live in each place.

McDougall's writing is detailed enough that it can be compared with the land grant maps that the migrants received from Nova Scotia's provincial government. There are also numerous official

---

[9] See Cregeen, Eric R. and D.W. McKenzie. *Tiree Bards and Their Bardacht. The Poets in a Hebridean Community.* Coll, 1978.

records including censuses, birth records, marriages, deaths, and others that fill in details about this community whose population had spread out from the original settlements at Malagawatch and Valley Mills. For example, a Nova Scotia archivist provided helpful information when she recommended that I carefully read McDougall's book, paying close attention to a family whom McDougall referred to as the carpenters. Sure enough, I found three brothers, or a mix of brothers and cousins cited in this chapter's mini-trees, who had been living together at a home site included in the census.

Here is what McDougall wrote about these male children and grandchildren of Red-haired Charles McLean and Mary McDonald: "Next to these last-mentioned McLeans another family of McLeans settled, including Donald, Rory and Neil, known collectively as the 'carpenters'." McDougall was able to persuade people to tell him about who lived in each neighborhood in a manner that conveys respect for the oral tradition that these people brought with them from the Western Isles. The story published in *Mac Talla* written by Neil McDonald, as well as McDougall's account of an extended neighborhood or village, drew on the format that had been used by storytellers in Scotland over the centuries when they recounted news of the community, its scandals and triumphs, and the results of the most recent inter-clan battles.

More Migrations Coming

Before 1871, Christy Campbell McLean had died, leaving her husband, Donald, the carpenter, with six children most of whom were born in Canada during the early 1840s. According to family stories, the oldest, Neil McLean (abt. 1833-?), probably left for Ontario as a young man and never returned home. Hector, the second child, married a McLeod woman, and they lived near Sydney, NS, before moving to Greater Boston, MA. This Hector worked as a carpenter in both Nova Scotia and Massachusetts, and his descendants are proven DNA matches for John MacLean

Maney's descendants. Roderick Mac Lean, another son of Donald and Christy, was born in Nova Scotia and moved to Gloucester, MA. He married an Irish emigrant, and they had a big family of children born in MA and NY, some of whom are DNA matches for John MacLean Maney's children.

Another of Donald's daughters, Flora (1842-1883), and her husband, Charles Hector McLean, were the parents of John MacLean Maney's mother, Ruth, who was born in Prince Edward Island. One of Donald and Christy's daughters, Christiana or Christy, had left NS for Massachusetts where she worked as a domestic in Boston before she married Charles Spiller, a farmer from Ipswich, Essex County, MA, in 1873. And still another of Donald and Christy's daughters, Mary, married James Greenleaf in 1862. James was a fisherman with family connections in Ipswich and other coastal towns in Massachusetts and Maine. Like many of the Lovetts, he worked up and down New England's maritime frontier. Greenleaf and his wife, Mary, married in the same year as Flora and Charles, according to marriage records from Nova Scotia's vital statistics office. For a few years, the two couples lived in Edgecomb, ME, during the U.S. civil war. Edgecomb was James' and Mary's home until Flora and Charles went back to Nova Scotia with their first child, Christy, who might have been named for one of her grandmothers from Coll.

By 1903, they are sharing another address in the city directory for Beverly, Essex county. Viola and Izora's descendants also show up as DNA matches for John Maney and Ethel Bradstreet's children.[10] During visits he made to Cape Breton with his mother

---

[10] Per research shown in the 1900 U.S. census records and the *Maney Family Archive*, Mary and James Greenleaf and their children later moved from Maine to Ipswich in Essex County, MA, where they lived until Mary died in 1891. They raised a big family, and I found two of their daughters, Viola and Izora Greenleaf, whose occupations are listed in the 1890 US census for Beverly, MA. They were working at various shoe industry jobs like shoe binding in that and other years that could be done at home. After their mother's death in 1891, both

in the early 1930s, John MacLean Maney developed a friendship with some of the children of Bessie MacLean Morrison (1872-1921), the surviving daughter from Donald McLean's marriage to Louisa Irish (1836-1902). John also enjoyed collaborating with Bessie's daughter, Leila MacLean Morrison (1902-1994), about the common history of their families. This history of Donald's life and that of the children of his several marriages would not have been possible to untangle if the two cousins, Leila and John, had not written down what they found out about their own descendants and also left a copy of their joint work in the Beaton Institute archives at Cape Breton University, which was where I was surprised to find it.

Spotlighting Ruth MacLean Maney and Her Parents

Here are two stories spotlighting John MacLean Maney's Scottish-Canadian grandparents, whom he had never met. The first is about a Japanese kimono which was passed from one generation to another in this big MacLean family. John received it from his mother, Ruth MacLean Maney, and passed it along to one of his children. After her mother's death in PE, Ruth lived for several years with her mother's sister, Kate McLean Campbell, in Sydney, NS. During that time, Ruth may have been the first in her generation to have a high school degree which she earned at Sydney Academy. One summer when Ruth was living in Sydney, her aunt received a request sent by a French naval officer visiting Sydney inviting Kate and her niece, Ruth, to tour his ship and have afternoon tea. This naval officer, Commodore LeClerc, told his guests when he greeted them with great ceremony that he had often visited Sydney as a young midshipman because his job in the French naval quartermaster corps involved buying poultry from the MacLean farm while the French fleet was in the city.

---

sisters lived on Hale St. in Beverly's ward 1 with their father and an older sister, who is listed as head of household.

On one of his first visits, in about 1860, when Ruth's mother, Flora, was about twenty years old, Commodore LeClerc had met Flora and her sister Kate while doing his job of provisioning the French fleet. So, Aunt Kate, Ruth, and one of Ruth's cousins had their own visit on the commodore's ship after which Ruth and the commodore entered into a long-distance correspondence that continued after she left Sydney to live in Massachusetts. Later, he sent her the kimono as a present from a trip that he had made to Japan. In the photos for this chapter, you can see a framed section of the kimono, which her grandchildren have kept in memory of Ruth's mother and her friend, this French naval officer.

Other records are also useful in documenting the life of Ruth MacLean when she was living in Sydney, N.S. Numerous train and ship records, for example, showed her trips between Boston and Nova Scotia via Halifax, Sydney, Yarmouth, and other NS ports in the first decade of the 20th century. She sometimes used the train, crossing into the US at Vanceboro, Maine. Later, we find her as an adult working at McLean Hospital in Belmont, MA, while living near Boston with her sister, Flora MacLean Roberts. There is also a photo of Ruth, with two of her older sisters, Flora and Christy, as well as Christy's daughter, which is shown in the images for this chapter. By 1906, records show Ruth living in Lawrence, MA, where she was working as a nurse and studying to get a diploma from Lawrence General Hospital's nurses' training program. In 1912, she married a colleague at the same hospital, John Joseph Maney, MD. Before her marriage, we know from a postcard collection that Ruth enjoyed "working vacations" with nursing school friends at Huggins Hospital in Wolfeboro, NH, which is located on the coast of Lake Winnipesaukee, a much-loved summer destination for vacationers fleeing hot New England cities. Another photo taken around 1930 includes a trip that Ruth made with her son and my father, John MacLean Maney, so he could meet relatives in Sydney and Inverness County.

In sum, research into the Scottish families in our tree benefited from several big advantages, including the ready accessibility of census, land grant, sales, and baptismal records, which quickly had become normal in Canada, as well as postcards sent to family and friends and continuing connections among families whose members lived on both sides of border between New England and Nova Scotia. However, I could not make good use of such records until I knew that my grandmother was born on Prince Edward Island and that one of her Scottish grandfathers had lived in Sydney. On the strength of that information, I was able to find some documents that suggested to the Beaton Center's archivist that Ruth MacLean Maney's (1876-1939) grandfather, Donald "Carpenter" McLean, was likely buried in Sydney's Hardwood Hill Cemetery. The best news of all was that when I visited the cemetery and read what was written on Donald's tombstone, I learned where and when he had been born on the Isle of Coll in 1813. That breakthrough enabled me to go back in time to the lives of ancestors who had been living in Coll and the Western Isles of Scotland before leaving for Canada.

The second advantage in my search for relatives on my grandmother Ruth's side of the family was finding information written on small white index cards that my father and his cousin, Leila MacLean Morrison (1902-1994), had deposited in the archives of the Beaton Center. With that information, I was able to find the correct Donald in the Coll baptismal records which, in turn, suggested that his parents were Charles "Tearlach Ruardh" McLean and Mary McDonald. At that point, I could start working on when the family had left Coll and where they lived on Cape Breton before moving to Sydney. In sum, I learned several important lessons from this complicated search. First is how useful it is to consult archives and archivists for family history information and learn what else they have in their collections that may be equally useful. Second, I was reminded how important the Find-A-Grave website can be.

My siblings and I have many DNA matches with people who share common Scottish ancestors with the main McLean, McKinnon, McDonald, Kennedy, and Campbell families under study in this chapter. These former Collachs had big families while living on that island and continued to do so during the first fifty years of living near one another in Nova Scotia and Prince Edward Island. I hope that I will find more DNA match results for fifth-great-grandparents for our *Maney Family Archive*. Also, information showing possible DNA matches with Campbell common ancestors has helped me set an agenda to search for Scots DNA matches in North and South Carolina that might match with the McLeans living in what had also been part of British North America at approximately the same time as the American Revolutionary War with England.

After finding records for someone named Malcom Campbell living in Cumberland County, North Carolina, around 1800, I will be interested to learn if he was one of Christy Campbell's relatives and also one of my ancestors from Coll. At the same time, analysis of DNA matches also points a way to discover if ancestors from our family's main Scottish lines had been living on islands in the Outer Hebrides, such as Harris and Lewis, before moving to Coll long before the people in this chapter had lived there and when that earlier move might have taken place. The DNA matches I am finding with Coll people now include surnames that usually belonged to clans active on the Isles of Skye, Harris, and Lewis, as well as the county of Inverness in mainland Scotland. If the connections go back longer in time I might learn how long ago other people, such as the McDonald, Kennedy, and McKinnon families had lived together on Coll.

Drawing Conclusions About These Coll Families

First, however, we should sum up information about the Coll families who came to Nova Scotia in 1820. These were primarily multi-generational families who wanted to own land and farm.

That they were successful in doing so can be seen in the 1871 and 1881 census records for the River Denys voting precinct in Inverness County as well as in records of marriages, land sales and other Canadian government documents. While most of the heads of families emigrating in 1820 had died by 1871, several of the children and grandchildren of McLeans and McDonalds from Coll were still living next to one another in the census of that year and later when they got land to farm on Prince Edward Island. And as in censuses done in Essex County, MA, we are able to learn more about these Scots by seeing the occupations they claimed to pursue as described in the Canadian censuses. By 1881 in Sydney, there was a wider range of occupations that they were pursuing than had been the case in the 1871 census. And by 1900 most of "Carpenter" Donald McLean's children had moved to Massachusetts or other parts of New England.

In the process, some male McLeans, McKinnons, and McDonalds left behind an unexpected record trail that has turned out to be a useful resource which I hope to expand upon in the future with additional information housed in the *Maney Family Archive*. This useful set of documents, which is available at Ancestry.com's online card catalog, is a list of members of Masonic lodges in Massachusetts. That is where I can see that some of the Scots-Canadian men had changed the spelling of their family names from "Mc" to "Mac" in the Canadian censuses after 1881 or when they moved to New England. A decision like joining the Masons when a Scots-Canadian moved to the Boston area may have signaled to others who were interested that they were of Scottish heritage and not Irish, and probably Protestants, not Roman Catholics. Why such a signal would be needed is a story about the various groups inhabiting urbanizing Massachusetts cities during the late nineteenth and early twentieth centuries.

My father, John MacLean Maney (1914-1985), who did join the Masons and had been brought up by his mother and other Collachs as a Presbyterian, surprised me when I found that my own baptism record was part of Ancestry's online card catalog. Although my siblings and I were raised as Congregationalists in the faith of my mother's Bradstreet and Lovett families, apparently my father had made sure that I was baptized first into the Presbyterian church of Ruth MacLean Maney, my Scots-Canadian grandmother. Why that occurred is more interesting when you know what happened after baby John MacLean Maney had been taken home by his mother from the hospital after his birth. Soon after their arrival at home, some of his Irish aunts appeared and offered to take care of the baby for the afternoon so that his mother, Ruth, could do some errands. What Ruth found out later was that the aunts had taken the baby to a Catholic priest that afternoon so that he could baptize baby John into the Roman Catholic faith. One generation later after his mother had died, her son, John, had the satisfaction of doing his mother a return favor by having me baptized as a Presbyterian before I could get into any significant trouble.

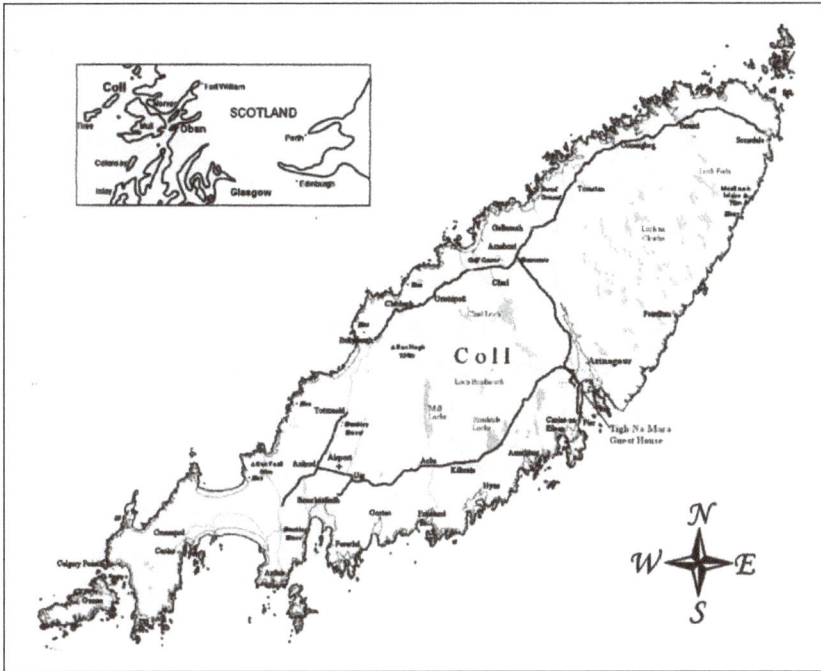

Isle of Coll where emigrants from the McLean's region of Scotland left for North America

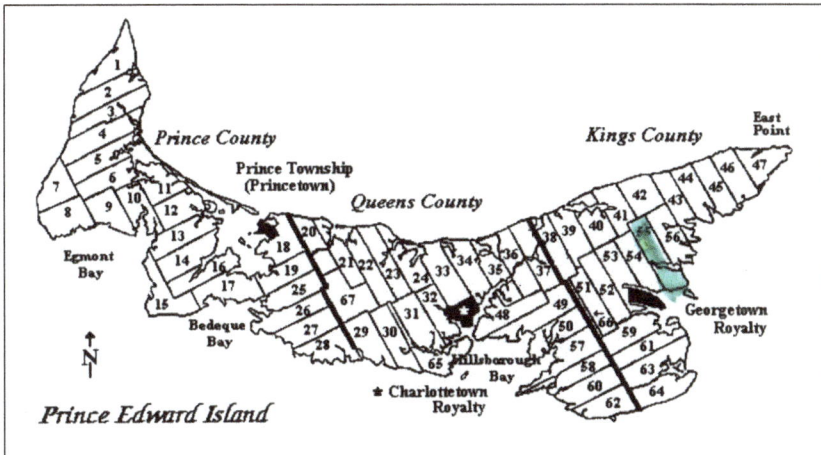

The author's family lived in the shaded region of Kings County shown in the map above

Maclean, Donald   (Came from Scotland at 12 yrs age)   b. 1810-12
  1. Mrs. _ _ _ _ _ _ _ _ _
      Hector G (m. Mary Maclean) to U.S.
      Neil (died young)
      Christine (m. Charles Spiller) to U.S.
      Mary (m. Charles Greenleaf) to U.S. T/C
      Flora (m. Charles Maclean) to PEI (Dundas – 10 children)
      Kate (m. Alexander Campbell) adopted "Maggie" who married "Peavey"
  2. Mrs _ _ _ _ _ _ _ _
        John (Furniture Store in Somerville – deceased) to U.S.
  3 Mrs Louise (Irish) of Mabou, C.B.
        Bessie J. (m. John B. Morrison – Wreck Cove C.B.)

Maclean, Mr. Hector George   (Carpenter – Builder)
    Mrs Mary (MacLeod)   of Big Glace Bay, or Mira
    Charles (m. Julia - - - -)
    John died unmarried
    Daniel died at 18 yrs
    Neil (m. Julia Tucker)
    Christine Hannah (m. Nathaniel Treadwell Lowe)
    Margaret (b. 7/1/1872) (m. Charles A. Earle)
    Katie (d. single)
    Sarah (Sadie) (m. George Wilson – no children)

Index cards from John Maney's research into his McLean family

MAC-TALLA.

"An ni nach cluinn mi an diugh cha 'n aithris mi maireach."

From the Isle of Coll to Inverness County: A Pioneer's Account

For the Scottish Highlander old-world material life was based in a familiar climate and ancient agricultural practices. Their thatch or sod-roofed dwellings were commonly built of stones gathered up from surrounding landscape largely bare of tree cover. In a time-worn landscape knowing settlement beyond memory, daily routine remained little altered for centuries. A dramatic change in environment awaited the Highlander immigrating to pioneer Canada.

Eastern Nova Scotia's trackless forests presented great challenges to Gaels inexperienced with clearing land, confronting wild animals and constructing houses framed with wood. Eyewitness reports of early historical circumstances supply us with a sense of the Highlanders' demanding task of founding new homesteads on unacquainted shores. One such description of emigration and settlement is provided by a Coll man identifying himself as Bartimoss and writing from Malagawatch, Cape Breton in the 1890s. The following is translated from Mac-Talla: July 7, 1894 and July 14, 1894.

At the end of July 1820 my father, with eight of his family and many others, left the Isle of Coll to immigrate to America. The vessel boarding the exiles lay in Tobarnory Bay (Isle of Mull). It was a pathetic sight to see relations parting with little expectation of meeting again.

The weather was clear as the sails were hoisted and the *Dunlop* of *Greenock* left Tobarmory under the command of John Brown, setting a course from the west side of Barra for Cape Breton (although the settlers were landed in Pictou). We were fortunate as we endured only one storm during the voyage. Five children were born aboard the ship: John MacLean, Lachlan MacKenzie, Ebenezer MacMillan, John Rankin and a MacNiven. All were of Coll stock. Three came out to Cape Breton and two went on to Prince Edward Island.

Five weeks after departure, at 10 o'clock on a sunny morning, we got our first glimpse of Cape Breton. Since there was a favorable breeze, every yard of sail cloth was unfurled and in a short while we entered the Strait of Canso with the wind and current. Settlers turned out to greet us from both sides of the strait and before nightfall we reached Cape George (Antigonish County). A pilot was taken on board who guided us into Pictou Harbour where the immigrants and their belongings were put ashore. The passengers dispersed, some going to Cape Breton and others to Cape John. The *Dunlop* of *Greenock* continued on to Richibucto (New Brunswick) picking up a cargo of pine lumber for the return trip to the Old Country.

My father and a number of others chartered a small vessel from one Angus MacDonald to bring us to Cape Breton. The weather was fair leaving Pictou, but reaching Cape George we were overtaken by a storm from the northwest. The boat was tossed to and fro until the top rigging was destroyed by the fury of the waves. It was the passengers' opinion that if not for the presence of an adept Harraman accustomed to such situations we wouldn't have made port. As Alasdair Mac Mhuighstir Alasdair said in his poem to Clan Ranald's Galley, "The navigator called to the helmsman and another took from her what was needed…" And so, we safely reached the Canso Strait where we were met by a kindly man from Long Point, Judique. He advised us to spend the winter and five families accepted the offer.

Over the winter we received generosity from two men, a MacDonald and a Chisholm, and also from the parish priest Reverend Alexander MacDonald. When summer arrived, the charitable folks of Long Point gave us seed and advised us to plant it on their land so we would have it for the next winter.

My father heard a report on the great Bras d'Or Lake. After the planting, a party of us with a guide went in a small boat to St. Peter's. There we hauled the boat over the "Crossing" and onto the Bras d'Or where we were met by a magnificent view on that calm, sunny day. The south side of West Bay was already taken up by those who came before us, but North Mountain (Marble Mountain) was unoccupied. We passed many lovely islands and went through the Boom Narrows to Malagawatch Lake – named by the Mi' kmaq and meaning "Lake of Abundant Islands." Here was the headquarters of the Mi' kmaq tribe and its chief, John Denny, from whom the River Denys derives its name. He was a brave and benevolent man but very wild when angry. The Mi' kmaq retained their territory here, and although few live in the area today, a thousand acres of the best land was reserved for them.

The River Denys empties into Malagawatch Lake. When we arrived in 1821 there wasn't a single European living on the lake's shores.

We began to clear the forest where we intended to settle; all near to each other. After that, we communally built moss-caulked log houses covered with bark. Slender, adze-hewn trees served as flooring.

At the end of a month's time we went back to Judique for the winter. In the first month of summer, 1822, we returned to Malagawatch with seed from the previous summer's crop and made our homes there. In the way we had learned from our Judique friends, we made our first planting. Fences were unnecessary as there were no animals to bother the crops other then bears that came at night to chew on sprout tops. Squirrels stealing seed from the barns to store for winter were troublesome after the harvest.

Once we acquired livestock, a cow would often come home mangled by a bear. When we got sheep, the women made every type of clothing from their wool. Since we had potatoes and the lake was full of fish, we envied no one under the sun. Those were happy days, although modern folk think they were mindless. I must confess, however, that there were dark days, lacking as they did a school and teacher inside the Bras d'Or region. What's more, there wasn't a doctor in the territory we now call Inverness County. In 1823 a neighbour's legs were frozen and it was necessary to take him 60 miles by small boat to Dr. MacDonald in Antigonish.

Dr. Noble arrived around 1824, and many readers of *Mac-Talla* are familiar with the lament made for his wife by Bard MacLean. In the year 1824 William Compton, from Prince Edward Island, built a saw mill on the north side of Malagawatch Lake; something that was a great service to the area's people. There was no road from Judique to River Denys around Malagawatch or to West Bay. A track ran from West Bay through River Inhabitants to the Strait of Canso.

A person had to follow the shore, going around every point and cove. Fear of bears kept travellers out of the woods.

In 1825 John Lewis was commissioned by the government to establish property boundaries for the settlers. He opened the first road running from Malagawatch through Judique Mountain and on to Long Point. In the same year the Kavanaughs arrived in St. Peters. They were in business on the Boom Strait (Alba) buying lumber and shipping it to Europe. I remember once seeing four great three masted schooners loading lumber at the same time and very often three.

In 1827 the ship called *James and Tom* was built for a company out of Liverpool, England. John MacNeil, one of our neighbours and a good scholar, sailed aboard her to England. He obtained finances from the Home Mission to open a school here which was done upon his return in 1831. After a few years he relocated to Prince Edward Island where he remained. By this time River Denys had become well populated and was famous for its lumber.

Donald MacDonald from Glengarry, Scotland was the first minister to come out to Cape Breton. He served for two years between Whycocomagh, West Bay and Malagawatch. From here he went to Prince Edward Island where he died. In 1826 the Free Church of Scotland sent the Reverend John MacLennan to Cape Breton as a missionary. He advised the people of this area to build a church in which visiting clergy could preach. The community began this work with a single purpose in 1828. The church measured 20 feet by 30 feet, was three stories high and gabled at both ends. It had a spacious capacity and was the first Presbyterian Church built in Cape Breton. Among those contributing to its building was a young lad who made spruce shingles. I saw him preaching in that church after he had received an education from the Free Church in Edinburgh. The church heard its first sermon in the summer of 1829, delivered by the Reverend Dougal MacKeigan. In 1832 the Reverend John Stewart was posted in West Bay. From him we received a service ice every fifth Sunday. Following that in 1837, the Reverend Peter MacLean was appointed to Whycocomagh and the congregation was provided with a service by him every fifth Sunday as well.

Great changes have occurred since my first memories of coming to Malagawatch. Fine homes have taken the place of humble shanties, and the old church has been replaced by a new one including a manse a few yards away. Regular schools and a Sunday school have been established along with wide, horse and coach travelled roads. The mail is delivered regularly, and there are many other improvements which I needn't waste time mentioning. The proverb is true that says, "He who lives a long life sees many things."

Mac-Talla translations and editing by Jim Watson of Cape Gael Co-op

Nova Scotia, indeed Canada, can take exceptional pride in the fact that the longest-running weekly (terminating as a bi-weekly) Gaelic newspaper was Sydney-based Mac-Talla, in print from 1892-1904. We are pleased to print excerpts in translation and the original from Mac-Talla in this on-going column. Readers should find the Mac-Talla legacy as stimulating now as it was then.

Reprint of Gaelic-language newspaper published in Sidney, Nova Scotia during the first half of the nineteenth century

The Last Will and Testament of Charles McLean (-1890, Dundas)

By the Grace of God Amen

I Charles McLean of Dundas Lot or Township Number Fifty-five Kings County in the Province of Prince Edward Island Farmer being of sound mind and judgement do make this my last Will and Testament as follows

1st I give and bequeath to my wife Jessie Louisa Two Hundred and Twenty dollars

2nd I give and bequeath to my Daughter Christy Two dollars

3rd I give and bequeath to my Daughter Mary Two dollars

4th I give and bequeath to my son Charles Two dollars

5th I give and bequeath to my Son Neil Two dollars

6th I give and bequeath to my Daughter Ruth Two dollars

7th I give and bequeath to my Son Donald Twenty five cents

8th I give and bequeath to my Son John Alexander Twenty five cents

9th I give and bequeath to my Daughter Flossy Two Cows and Three Sheep and to have them on the place as long as she remains on the place and to have the good of them all along.

10th I give and bequeath to my Daughter Catherine One Cow and Two Sheep and to have them on the place as long as she remains on the place and to have the good of them all along.

11th I give and bequeath to my daughter Elizabeth Louisa Two Dollars

12th I give and bequeath to my son James Lauchlin Sixty five acres of land that I reside on now and bounded on the West by Grand River – on the North land in the possession of John _____ McLean. On the East by Cumberland Hill Road and on the South by land in the possession of Donald McLean.

I also give and bequeath to him all the farming implements that will be on the place and all the stock namely horses, cows, sheep, pigs and hens clear of what I have give the other girls.

13th I appoint Samuel McDonald and William Hunter my executors.

Signed Sealed and Delivered in the presence of   (Signed) Charles McLean
Having been first read over and explained

(Signed) E. Hodgson McDonald (") Edgar L. Burdett

Taken and acknowledged before the above names
This twenty first day of May A.D. 1890

This will was proved on the 11th July 1890,
on the oath of E. Hodgson McDonald a subscribing witness before ____McDonald,
and was filed on the 25th July 1890,
all certified by Charles Young

The Ruth MacLean highlighted in the text was the author's grandmother

Pictured, second from the left, is the author's grandmother Ruth MacLean

Massachusetts death certificate for Donald MacLean's son, Hector

PROVINCE OF NOVA SCOTIA.

Marriage solemnized at	*Sydney*
In the County of	*Cape Breton*
Date and place of Marriage...	*Nov. 29. 1868 - Sydney*
How married; by License or Banns	*By License*
Full name of Groom	*Donald McLean*
His age.........	*Fifty five years*
Condition (Bachelor or Widower).........	*Widower*
Profession or Trade............	*Carpenter*
Residence. ...	*Sydney C.B.*
Where born	*Argile (Scotland)*
Parents names.........	*Charles & Mary McLean*
Their profession	*Farmers*
Full name of Bride............	*Louisa Matilda Irish*
Her place of residence.........	*Maben, C.B.*
Age.........	*Thirty two years*
Condition (Spinster or Widow)	*Spinster*
Parents names.........	*Augustus & Mary Irish*
Their profession	*Farmer*
	Will Turnbull

Excerpts from voluminous records of Donald MacLean's family

Remnants of a kimono given to Ruth MacLean by a French naval officer

.

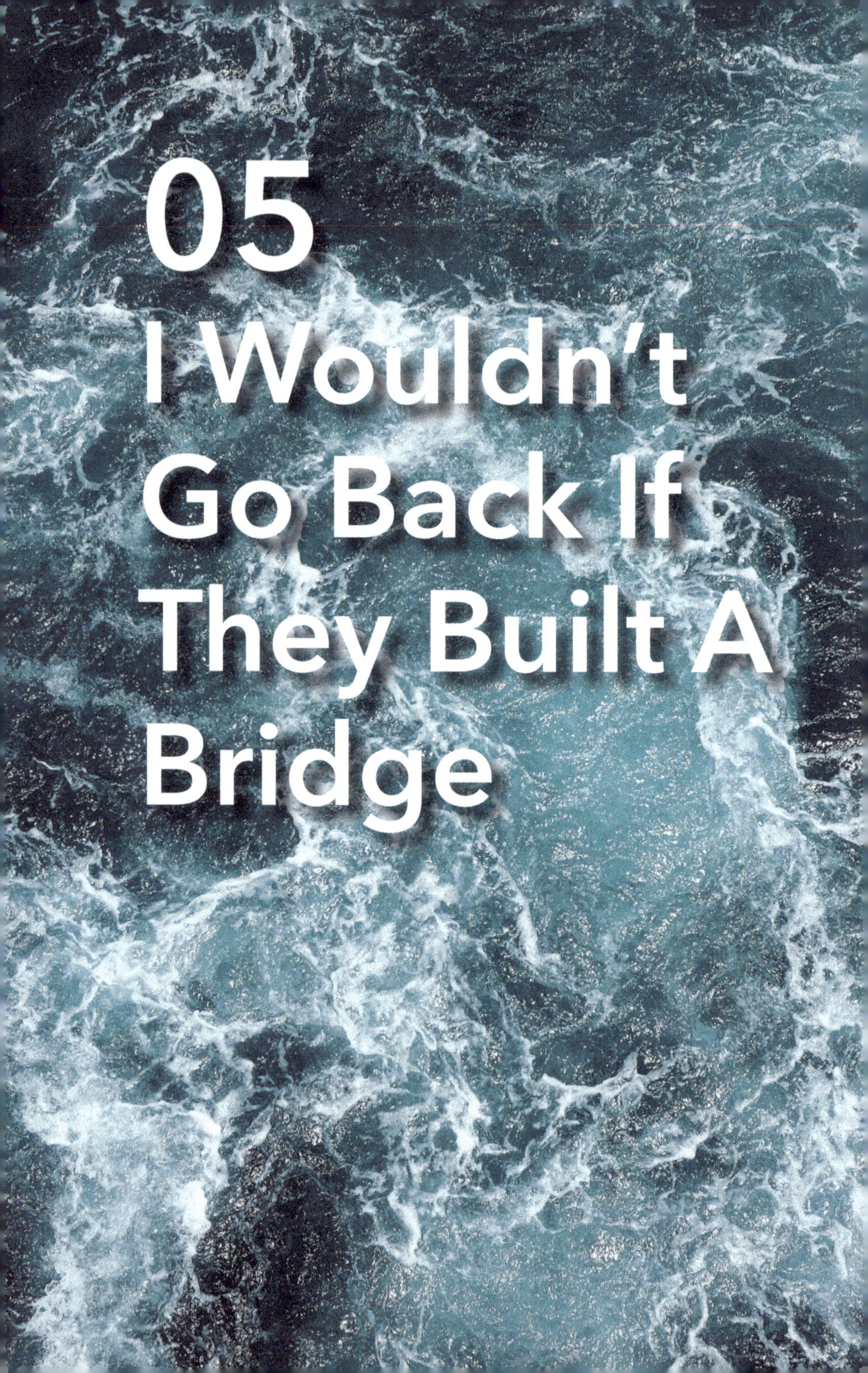

05

I Wouldn't Go Back If They Built A Bridge

T his chapter addresses problems that native Roman Catholic Irish people had had to face after the mid-1500s and provides some interesting comparisons between how Britain treated one of its first colonies, Ireland, and how they treated Ireland's Scottish and Gaelic neighbors. Since the 1850s, millions of Irish emigrants from the time of the Famine to the present day left what has now become an independent country. These comparisons have prompted a great deal of scholarly research which this chapter combines with stories told about Ireland, some by Irish people themselves. Let's start by acknowledging that "never going back" to Ireland was probably the firmest resolve that my great-grandfather, John *Meany* (1849-1932) held about the homeland that he left at about twenty-four years of age in 1873. As our Irish mini-tree shows, my great-grandfather was probably born in or near Cashel, County Tipperary.

There *Meany*, *Meaney* and sometimes even *Mooney* baptisms, marriages, and deaths were carefully recorded in Roman Catholic church records which show families with those last names living in Tipperary County since at least the beginning of the eighteenth century when the keeping of Roman Catholic church records had improved. Baptism records show that this John's grandmother was named Margaret Eustace.[1] Her family likely came from Norman ancestors some of whom had held important roles in Irish governmental affairs after coming to Ireland from Normandy in France. Because most Normans were Roman Catholics like the native-born Irish, it will not be surprising to find that Norman-Irish people supported the native Irish in government, business, and foreign relations with officials of other Catholic countries both before and after the Protestant English aristocracy took a harder line against working with the Irish people during the sixteenth century.[2]

Also a quick note may be useful. Because so many Meanys and Meaneys had sons with the same first names, e.g., the Johns cited in this chapter, etc., I will provide birth and death years for the main male family members in the text to make it easier for the reader to be sure which John I am focusing on at a particular time. For the same reason, I also continue to use MacLean, my father's middle name, when the text refers to this particular John in order to remind readers that John MacLean Maney was Irish on his father's side and Scottish on his mother's side. Some of the brothers of John MacLean Maney's Irish grandfather, John Meany (1849-1932), including his youngest

---

[1] Margaret Eustace was born about 1793, according to Catholic baptism records. Her baptism took place in Cashel, County Tipperary, as did her marriage to John Meany or Meaney (1780-abt. 1830). See https://www.ancestry.com/family-tree/person/tree/24430911/person/172004605374/facts

[2] Margaret Eustace married three times. It is possible that Margaret Eustace Maney died in Philadelphia, PA, in about 1870. Information that the author has seen suggests that is the year when a woman having that name was buried in Philadelphia's New Cathedral Cemetery. Her age is given as seventy-nine. If this was Margaret Eustache Maney, she was probably accompanied to Pennsylvania by one of her children in order to leave Ireland after her husband, John Maney (1780-) died in County Tipperary. The name on the death papers was Margaret Meany and date of burial was 8 Apr 1870. If she is that person, it is not known which of her children organized her move to Pennsylvania, but it may have been her eldest daughter, Ellen.

brother, William (1854-1935), came to America on their own, while most of their sisters came with their Irish husbands and sometimes were accompanied by their children. The last of John Maney's (1849-1932) close relatives to come to the USA was his mother, Anastasia Doran, who arrived in Providence, RI, in 1886, soon after her husband John, (1809-1886), died in Thurles, Tipperary, earlier in the same year. There were still Meanys and Meaneys in Ireland after that, but the sprawling family that had included direct descendants of each generation's first sons named John had cleared out.

Can Maneys be Traced Using Hearth Tax Records?

How best to use Ireland's hearth tax records is still an open question. We know it is possible, as I will try to show below. Information about exactly where Meanys were living in County Tipperary in the eighteenth century is easier to come by now that Roman Catholic baptism and marriage records have been put online by the Irish government and made available to members of Ancestry.com, as well as to people working with other search engines. We also can see that there are certain kinds of British property tax records from the seventeenth century that showed that people with the names of Meany and Meaney were paying this property tax required by the English government in County Tipperary, as well as in other British colonies and dependencies outside of Ireland. However, locating Meanys with the same first names in Tipperary in the seventeenth century or earlier is still quite difficult to do since Roman Catholic records that can be put online are lacking for the turbulent times that included the wars inside Ireland led by the English general and Puritan leader, Oliver Cromwell, during the 1640s until his death.

Although I have family stories suggesting that ancestors of our Meanys, Maineys, and Mooneys may have lived in County Tipperary before the mid-1600s, I cannot conclude that the Catholic landholders had been permanently or only temporarily displaced from living in that county for some years after the fighting stopped. If they had been forced to move out of their homes but later came back, I have not yet been able to find records showing where they were living in the interim. However, property tax records for the mid-1600s do provide evidence that there were Meaneys and Meanys living in Tipperary County at that time and afterwards which can be seen by studying tax lists that showed the number of hearths that people were able to use inside their homes in order to keep the premises in good condition.[3]

The leader of the British army, Cromwell, had no love lost for the English king or for the Catholic establishment in Ireland. Cromwell had already demonstrated his military prowess, as well as his antipathy to the English king and to Catholics in general in his conduct of multiple wars in England and Scotland before he brought his army to Ireland in 1649. The result, after most of the dust cleared, was that Charles I, king of England, had been beheaded by people who held power because they were allied with Cromwell. Then, the Irish Catholic Confederacy government, which included leaders from the Norman side, as well as the native Irish side, were easily defeated, and most Catholics of whatever ethnicity — whether Norman-Irish or Old Irish — lost their civil rights, as well as some or all of their lands and other peoples' properties, in the process.

Then, after Cromwell died and Charles, the old king's son, was able to return to England from exile in Europe and became King Charles II of England, Ireland, and Scotland. All of this turbulence lasted from 1641 to approximately 1661, and there was still more to come. People in Ireland, like people in Scotland living on the

---

[3] This information has to be placed within a timeline summarizing an Anglo-Norman invasion of Ireland that had resulted in the settlement of French-and-Gaelic-speaking Catholics some five hundred years earlier and that, after their arrival in Ireland, the newcomers had begun collaborating with their co-religionists. It was this confederacy with the Normans that worried English Protestant governmental officials resident in Ireland during the 1600s.

western islands and onshore habitations in the Scottish highlands, listened for details from local Gaelic poets or bards who held important posts in society. People could also learn about important historical events affecting them through the work of another local official, the sennachie or historian/genealogist, who would read out records in oral form on important occasions. When they did not have access to census or church records, the Irish sennachies had to settle for creative census substitutes.[4]

Before the English developed their own courts and bureaucracies, Scottish clan chiefs and important people in Gaelic Ireland could rely on officials whose job it was to tell stories about victories, defeats, and other happenings in the past on ceremonial occasions. We have already seen the creative way that a man wrote his book by asking his neighbors in Malagawatch, Nova Scotia (NS), to tell him stories about who lived on each piece of land in the mid-1800s. I have also found a family genealogist, who was part of the Maney family group and acted as a kind of informal sennachie, collecting information about people in the Irish community of Providence, RI, as late as the 1980s, which makes her work remarkably similar to the Nova Scotia case. On a parallel track, as the timeline moved forward from the seventeenth to the twentieth century, written records containing information about Maneys in Ireland appeared more regularly.

Help Provided from "The Source" to Find the Property Tax Results

The key to unlocking this information was finding and consulting a reproduction of the original tax book that survived

---

[4] When reading what I have written below, the reader should be prepared for multiple spellings of Irish last names that all sound the same to our ears, such as Mainey, Meaney, and Mooney. Below I use the same spelling that the Irish had in their own birth and marriage records and also how they were referenced in English records, e.g., what the name of our ancestors looked like in British census records.

both the upheavals of the Cromwellian period and the Irish civil war in the 1920s. A helpful librarian at the Source Library and Arts Center in Thurles, Tipperary, which is located close to the town of Cashel, showed me these land records during a visit I made to Ireland in the fall of 2019. This book of hearth tax locations in County Tipperary recorded which of the county's Irish Catholic households had to pay a special land tax imposed by the British government on their homes starting in 1665. Like the minister's census done on Scotland's Isle of Coll in 1776, this set of records shows the names of male heads of household. The result is a list of locations in which Meanys were recorded along with the names of the towns and villages where Irish families of a similar income were living throughout the county. The British government levied this tax on native Irish people who could afford indoor hearths or fireplaces and chimneys. Both were telltales that the owners were not poor but had middle-class backgrounds.

These hearth records show the names of the heads of households throughout Tipperary County who had indoor hearths and the amount of tax each was required to pay. I was particularly interested in the locations of people with similar-sounding names or spelling variations for Meany, Meary, and Mooney. The families I found were spread over nine Tipperary administrative jurisdictions or baronies — Middlethird, Eliogarty & Ikyryn, Iffay & Offay, Slievardagh, Kyllnomanagh, Owney & Arrar, Upper Ormand, and Clanwilliam — in the first year that the tax was levied. From the record books, we know only the first and last names of the heads of these families. But that is enough to make a case that some of these people were likely members of the Meanys I was interested in because most of the locations where the hearth tax records showed Meanys living in the mid-1660s were within about fifty miles or less of locations in which John MacLean Maney's direct line of Tipperary ancestors married and baptized their children during the eighteenth and nineteenth centuries when church records of baptisms and marriages were more safely kept.

Examples of the towns mentioned in both hearth tax records from the seventeenth century and the church records of the eighteenth century include well-known places such as Cashel, Templetouhy. Ballingarry, Killenaule, Gortnahoo, Moyne, and Fethard, all of which had Meany and Meaney connections that had been recorded in the past and continued to be recorded for some of the same places in later times. Also, I noticed that the first names of Meany heads of household in these tax records often compared closely with the names of the fathers or husbands in later church records showing names of the women whom Meany men married and of their children who had been baptized. For example, the men and boys had baptism names such as Thomas, John, James (Jacob), and William in the 1665 data, and the mini-trees for this chapter show the same names as our Maney families gave to their own sons.

A follow-up search also showed many similar family names for the men and women who married into Meany families; their own families had last names such as Doran, Dwyer, Fogarty, Heffernan, Meagher, Power, Eustace, and Sexton. These are also names that Catholic records showed to be Meaney and Meany spouses in the eighteenth and nineteenth centuries. Thus, the names mentioned in the Tipperary hearth tax records book make a good case that some Meanys, Mooneys, and Mearys listed in the towns and villages of these baronies in 1665 may have inter-married locally with branches of the families listed above and continued doing so during the eighteenth and nineteenth centuries. In other words, it is likely that Meany parents were making marriages for their sons and daughters with children of other tax-paying families in the1600s and continued to do so in the centuries to follow. Land tax records in the nineteenth century, such as Tithe Applotment records and Griffith's Valuation (GV), also include some of the same last names and tend to confirm these findings.[5]

Where official records are missing, the best situation may be to have stories that confirm and supplement informal source materials, especially if they can be backed up by governmental, church, or other official records. As with the MacLeans and other Scottish families living on Coll and in Malagawatch or East Lake Ainslee in Nova Scotia, the information presented here supplements governmental records and links the event to a wide variety of written materials, such as oral histories, newspaper accounts, land records, family stories, memories of neighbors, and the like. While the information consulted in this chapter is mostly focused on people in John MacLean Maney's direct family line whose members were living mainly in one or the other Irish counties of Tipperary and Meath, there are similar records from nearby counties such as Kilkenny, Clare, Waterford, Cork, and Laois. And of course, written records tell more information about these Maneys after the children of John Maney (1849-1932) and his mother, Anastasia Doran, came to live in Connecticut, Rhode Island, and Massachusetts.

The written records consulted also rely on knowledge that my siblings and I have gained from proving DNA matches with descendants of our great-grandfather, John Maney (1849-1932) and similar DNA matches with people inside Ellen Reilly Maney's (1852-1933) maternal line of Dalys and her children's paternal line of Reillys, including DNA matches that Ellen Reilly shared with her sister, Catherine Reilly Bishop (1854-1930). The result

---

[5] Griffiths Valuation (GV) is regarded as an invaluable census substitute for the Famine period because it shows three pieces of evidence in one record: 1)the name of the owner of a piece of property on the eve of the Famine times; 2) the name of the occupier or tenant for most residential pieces of land in all of Ireland during the 1850s; and 3)which owners' rents were in arrears because of the widespread agricultural and economic distress that forced tenants to flee from their homes.

is three sets of stories that illustrate important events: about 1) Meany families who lived in County Tipperary; 2) Reilly relatives in County Meath, many of whom reacted to the famine by staying in Ireland or going temporarily to work in England; and 3) Dalys from County Meath, some of whom arrived as a big group in Ontario, Canada as the Irish Famine was just getting started.

The mini-trees shown below incorporate baptism and marriage records from the 1700s and suggest areas for further exploration. The list of Maney heads of households begins early in the eighteenth century with the record for a Jacob Meany (1720-?) whose grandparents may have lived through the hardships of the Cromwellian period of the 1660s. The same list continues through the life of my father, John MacLean Maney, who was born in Lawrence, MA, in 1914. The names of the wives of this line of Johns —women whose family names included Brennan, Eustace, Gleason, Heffernan, Doran, Dwyer, Power, Maher, Meagher, and Eustace —as well as locations where the baptisms of the parents and children in this line took place, also track with the hearth tax records. The territory outlined includes places near Tipperary's eastern borders with County Laois, known before Ireland's independence as Queen's County, as well as places located in or near Kilkenny and Waterford Counties. In Tipperary County it also included places such as Fethard, Clonmel, Cashel, Thurles, and others.

As in the other family chapters, the mini-trees below show parents and children in John MacLean Maney's (1914-1985) direct line in each generation. What is notable about this list of Meanys and Meaneys is that the first-born male child is named John in each case and in all but two cases reflect the line of descent to the big family of Maneys living in Lawrence, MA, in 1900 and working in the mills there from the mid-1870s. In one of the exceptional cases, the first male child mentioned is named Jacob, not John; in the other exceptional case, the first son was a John Meany (1832-?) When we take up this issue later in this chapter, I will argue that this first John died when he was a teenager and the same name,

John, was given by his parents to the next male child, my great grandfather, John Maney, (1849-1932), who was born after the first John had died.[6]

Meany and Meaney Mini-Trees Tell More of This Story

Jacob Meany, 1720-? who was born in Killenaule, Tipperary, married **Margaret Heffernan**, 1725-1797. Their child: **John Meany** was born in 1751 in Killenaule.

John Meany, who was born in Tipperary County in 1751-? married **Unknown.** Their child: **John Meany** was born in 1780 in Tipperary and died in abt.1820 in Cashel, County Tipperary.

John Meany, abt.1780- abt.1820, was born in Tipperary and married **Margaret Eustace,** 1789- Their children born in Cashel: **John,** 1809-1886**;** Alice, 1811-? Margaret 1812-? Judith, 1814-? Edmund, 1816-?; and Patrick, 1819-?

John Meany, who was born in Cashel in 1809, died in Thurles, Tipperary, in 1886. He married **Anastasia Doran** in Clonmel, Tipperary, in 1833. She was baptized in Gortnahoe, Tipperary, in 1809 and died in Providence, RI, USA in 1889. Their children: **John**, who was baptized in Clonmel, Tipperary in 1832, and probably died between 1840 and 1849; Ellen, who was baptized in 1833 and may have died in Philadelphia, PA in 1916; Katherine, who was baptized in 1836 and died in New Haven, CT, in 1925; Mary, who was baptized in 1838 and died in

---

[6] More information about this John Meany born in 1832 is part of the *Maney Family Archive.*

Providence, RI in 1919; Thomas, who was baptized in 1840 in Clonmeen Parish, Tipperary, and died in Tipperary after 1901; **John**, who was baptized in 1849 near Moyne, Tipperary, and died in Lawrence, MA in 1932; William, who was baptized in 1854-55 in Stockport, England, and died in 1935 in Providence, RI.

John Meany, who was baptized in Tipperary in 1849 and died in Lawrence, MA, in 1932, married **Bridget Ellen Reilly,** who was baptized in 1850 in Bohermeen, Meath, and died in Lawrence, MA, in 1933. They married in Providence, RI, in 1874.

Their children, all baptized in Lawrence, MA or the neighboring city of Methuen, MA: **John Joseph**, 1875-1942; William, 1877-1878; Marie, 1878-1948; Thomas, 1879-1957; Edward, 1882-1956; Helen, 1883-1922; Hugh, 1885-1885; Annie, 1886-1887; Joseph, 1887-1969; Leontine, 1888-1963; Anna, 1889-1952; Theresa, 1892-1893; and Matthew, 1896-1978.

John Joseph Maney was born in Lawrence, MA in 1875 and died there in 1942. He married **Sarah Harriet "Ruth" MacLean,** who was born in Prince Edward Island, CA, in 1876 and died in Lawrence, MA, in 1939. Their surviving child: **John MacLean Maney** was born in Lawrence, MA, in 1914.

John MacLean Maney was born in Lawrence, MA, in 1914 died in Amesbury, MA, in 1985. He married **Ethel Louise Bradstreet** in 1940. She was born in Danvers, MA, in 1917 and died in Milwaukee, WI, in 2005.

There are several interesting puzzles about these Maney families that are hinted at in the mini-trees. First, you can see from the trees that the people in the main family line had stopped living in or near Killenaule by the first decade of the nineteenth century when John Maney (1780-1820) moved to Cashel and began raising a family there with his wife, Margaret Eustace (1789-abt.1870).[7] At least one of the couple's children migrated from Ireland to Wales and another to North America before and during the famine times and others continued to do so until the end of the nineteenth century; in particular, their number included children of the sons Edmund and Patrick. Nor do we know how Ellen (1833-), Catherine (1836-1925), and Mary (1838-1919) — all daughters of John Maney (1809-1886) and his wife, Anastasia Doran (1809-1889) — found their way to Stockport, England, which is near Manchester and where members of this family lived during the worst of the Famine times, as shown in the 1851 and 1861 censuses for Stockport.

Maybe one or more Maney sisters had been working in a mill in Queens County, Ireland, or in County Clare and then found places in the mills of Stockport during the time when famine was wreaking havoc over all of Ireland. Or perhaps all of the children except for Thomas accompanied their mother, Anastasia Doran Maney, to Stockport, including her baby son, John[8] (1849-1932),

---

[7] It may be that some of the daughters of John Meany and Anastasia Doran Meany started working to support the Maney family during the Famine times in textile mills in Ireland and later found their way to mills in Stockport. England. R.F. Foster, in his *Modern Ireland 1600-1921* published in 1989, has written that the Irish had a centuries-old tradition of seasonal migration so that people could go for part of the year to places like Manchester and Glasgow from certain places in Ireland in order to earn money and return back home. Later, of course, in the Famine times, that tradition allowed the Irish to have a sense of themselves, Foster wrote, as "part of an international community, centered on a small island that still claimed a fiercely obsessive identification from its migrants" (p. 372). In the twentieth century per Foster, emigration was a continuing mechanism that helped Ireland survive by creating a mechanism to leave Ireland for the "young, the single, and those who lacked access to a farm or to textile skills" (p. 353).

[8] It is not certain when the daughters took possession of the apartment in Stockport or if they lived there before the birth of John, 1849-1932, my great-

my great-grandfather. In any event, there were five Maneys living in the apartment in Stockport at the time that the 1851 census was conducted. In 1854, Anastasia gave birth to another son, William Joseph Maney (1854/55-1935), whose baptism took place in Stockport per Roman Catholic records there. The Maneys living in Rhode Island and Massachusetts, who are in the direct line from Anastasia and her husband, learned about the Stockport census record from a cousin who had researched her relative's Maneys from Cashel and passed the information along to my father, John MacLean Maney. Maneys living in Lawrence later sent this information back to their Providence counterpart including William Maney's big family there.

Spotlight on Three John Maneys and One Thomas Maney

Some other questions deserve answers as well. For example, where was Anastasia's husband at the time that the other members of his family lived for several years in Stockport, and what was his occupation if he was living in Ireland during that time? However, I can now say confidently that when he was baptized in Moyne, Tipperary, Ireland, in 1849, my great-grandfather John (1849-1932) was the second child to have been named John in this family. This might have happened because his parents had baptized their first son as John after he was born in 1832. However, later he had probably died, perhaps at the age of about 15 years according to one record. The same parents also gave birth to three daughters between 1833 and 1838, whom they named Ellen, Catherine, and Mary, before a second son, whom they named Thomas (1840-?) arrived. When they learned that the first son had died, they probably gave the name John to their next son in keeping with the similar custom used in Scotland's Gaelic lands. An Irish police

---

grandfather and one of the immigrants. Nor is it clear at this point in time when Anastasia and my great-grandfather (John 1849-1932) arrived there.

record posted in the Ancestry.com online card catalogue suggests that the British maritime police arrested a John Meany, born in 1832, and sentenced him as a teen-ager to service in the British maritime navy.[9] Perhaps the family assumed that their son had died or never would become a free man.

Another question that needs an answer is why Anastasia's husband, John (1809-1886), did not move with the family to Stockport in order to escape the dangers of famine in Ireland or take up permanent residence in another part of England or Wales near Stockport. My answer to that question is mostly circumstantial but may well be true. The birth of another son in Stockport in 1854 indicates that the father probably visited his family when he could, but it seems that Anastasia's husband spent most of his time in Tipperary with their second son, Thomas, who was born in 1840 and would have reached adulthood by the end of the 1850s. The most likely explanation was that the father was involved in business activities that needed his attention in Ireland and that Thomas acted as his assistant.

Most likely, the business was working as some kind of agent for Catholic landowners or businessmen, as the name of John Meany (1809-1886) is attached to plots of land where he was sometimes listed as the owner and sometimes as the occupying renter of another person's property. After the return of his wife and his two youngest sons from England, my second great-grandfather (1809-1886) and his wife, Anastasia Doran (1809-1889), continued

---

[9] All of these documents are important parts of the *Maney Family Archive*. Here is the URL for the birth of John in 1832. See also John's police record and his British maritime service record: https://www.ancestry.com/imageviewer/collections/61039/images/02461_03_0150?pId=2968973
Here is the second record: https://www.ancestry.com/imageviewer/collections/61943/images/ire_prisr_rs00018280_4492665_00514?pId=1209984; and the maritime service record is below: https://www.ancestry.com/imageviewer/collections/60609/images/42482_6130000_0002-00069?pId=102073

living in the part of Tipperary between Cashel, Thurles, and towns near the border with Kilkenny and Queens (Laois) Counties. Thomas married and had a family whose first son the parents also named John. Of the three daughters in John and Anastasia's family, Catherine and Mary married Irishmen while they lived in England and later emigrated to the USA with their families. In the 1870s, both brothers, John and William, emigrated separately to the USA.

When he got his US citizenship, my great-grandfather, John Maney (1849-1932), gave his last address in Ireland as Johnstown, Kilkenny. He may have been working in the same business as an assistant to his father and brother Thomas, but was happy to be leaving Ireland. As he repeatedly told his grandson, John MacLean Maney, he "would never go back if they built a bridge." Before turning to some Maney immigrants who settled in New England, including John Maney (1849-1932) and Ellen Reilly (1850-1933), let's come forward in time with some Maneys who stayed in Tipperary. The 1901 and 1911 censuses for Tipperary show Meanys and Meaneys living in and around the same area we have considered as their home ground in this chapter, especially in Cashel and Thurles and near the border of Counties Tipperary and Kilkenny.

Descendants of Edmond Maney, (1816-?), who was my second-great-grand uncle had operated a tailor's shop in Cashel, and descendants of his brother, Patrick (1819-?), owned a liquor store in Cashel according to the 1901 census of Ireland. By the time of the 1911 census, the store had become a pub. When a visiting Maney from the USA showed up in Cashel in 2019, Patrick's friends and neighbors remembered him and his Meany family. In addition, the current owner of the pub remembered that Edmond's brother Patrick Meany (1819-?), the pub owner, had also sold milk from his farm in the back yard of the pub. When asked about this Patrick Meany, the owner of a nearby pharmacy insisted on showing the American visitors the cemetery where, he said, generations of the extended Meany family, as well as people in his own Dwyer family line, were buried. The census records also show some of the occupations of the sons of these Meany families. These Irish Meanys and Meaneys included in their number several small entrepreneurs and business owners in Cashel, as well as some farmers.

Anastasia Doran also had some stories about her Maney family which she told to relatives in the extended family in North America when she arrived in Providence, RI, after leaving Ireland for good. One concerned her youngest son, William, who had come home one day when he was a teen-ager and showed his mother a gold coin that he had gotten from a British navy recruiter. He went on to tell her that he wanted to join up. His mother, perhaps thinking about how the eldest John in her family had gotten separated from the family and never had been seen or heard from again, immediately took charge. She got William a ticket on a ship preparing to leave for the USA, and he arrived safely at his destination.

At first he lived in Lawrence, MA, near his brother, John, and they both worked in the city's textile mills. The last person to emigrate in this particular family was Anastasia Doran, the mother of both sons named John, plus Ellen, Catherine, Mary, Thomas, and William Maney. Once she reached the USA, it is assumed that Anastasia re-united with all of the adult children of her extended family. Her decision to settle in Providence was probably because her daughter, Mary, and son, William, already lived there. Another daughter, Catherine, lived in New Haven, CT which was not far away. It is also likely, but not yet proven, that Anastasia's daughter Ellen may have lived in Philadelphia with her family, a city about a day's journey away from Providence by train at that time.[10]

---

[10] Information in the *Maney Family Archive* shows DNA matches between Ancestry.com members who descend from John and William Maney and also include a contingent who are great-grandchildren of Catherine Maney Beesley, the daughter of Anastasia and John Maney (1849-1932), who lived in

Results from the first full censuses of Ireland done in 1901 and 1911 also allow us to identify where Meaneys and Meanys continued to live in Tipperary after decades of emigration by their children, parents, sisters, brothers, and cousins out of Ireland in the second half of the nineteenth century. A search of the census of 1901 for Tipperary County shows 94 individuals in that year with the last name of Meany or Meaney. The same census also shows 1,392 people with Meany or similar names for all of Ireland, male and female, young and old, for that year. This picture of family names can also be compared to the populations of Meanys and Meaneys in counties bordering Tipperary in 1901, including Clare (308), Cork (1720), Galway (5), Limerick (173), Kilkenny (172), Waterford (12), and Queens (12).[11]

Finding Maney Cousins in Lawrence and Methuen, Massachusetts

Finding the many families related to John Maney (1849-1932) and Ellen Reilly (1850-1932) and tracking their children was the easiest part of researching this chapter, as John and Ethel Maney and their children already knew about several second cousins: grandchildren of John and his brother William's surviving sons and daughters. Several times each year, my siblings and I would visit aunts, uncles, and cousins in Lawrence, Methuen, and nearby suburbs in northern Essex County, MA. Also interesting is what the members of John's big family did for work in Lawrence. Successive census and city directory records

---

Connecticut.

[11] There were also 39 Meanys and Maneys living in County Wexford, which is nearby Tipperary. Perhaps the James Maney who came to the USA in the 1700s was an indentured servant who fought for the American cause as many did, after finishing or escaping from their indentures. That would explain the DNA match and connection that my siblings have with the Irishman from Wexford who may have received a land grant based on his wartime service in the Revolutionary army.

held at the Lawrence History Center for the period from 1880 to 1930 show John, the immigrant, and his growing family in residence there. In these records, John Maney (1849-1932), was listed variously as an "operative" or machine operator in the textile mills. At about age 70 in 1920, he had a different job, as an elevator operator in one of the city's mills. His wife, the former Ellen Reilly, usually was described in census records as keeping house, but she was really the boarding house keeper of the place where her big family lived in 1900 with their younger children and as many as thirteen boarders, the number recorded in the U.S census for that year.

The female children of John Maney and Ellen Reilly who lived into adulthood included Marie (1878-1948), Helen or Ellen (1883-1922), Leontine 1888-1963), and Anna Katherine (1889-1952); all of them married and with at least one child in each of their families. Of the men, only two married: the oldest, John Joseph (1875-1942), and the youngest, Matthew (1896-1978). Seven other children either died in infancy or didn't marry. Both of Ellen and John's sons who did marry had only one child each instead of big families like the ones in which they had grown up. Here is information taken about John and Ellen's children compiled from the census in 1900:

John Joseph, born in 1875 – medical doctor
Marie, born in 1878 – milliner
Thomas, born in 1879 – clerk, insurance agent, and salesman
Edward, born in 1882 – cloth finishing operator, cotton mill worker
Helen, born in 1883 – dressmaker (worked out of her home)
Joseph, born in 1887 – mill laborer, carpenter
Leontine, born in 1888
Anna Katherine, born in 1889

Matthew, born in 1896 – carpenter, trade union leader, and assistant commissioner of the Massachusetts State Department of Corrections

The children of John MacLean Maney (1914-1985) and Ethel Bradstreet Maney have been sharing genealogical information with cousins born to people who emigrated from Ireland to Rhode Island, Massachusetts, and Connecticut. Seeing DNA match results with other cousins is helping us strengthen the connections already established by written records of kinship as we work toward the goal of identifying and confirming more Maney cousins as part of the *Maney Family Archive*. Learning about cousins from Ellen Reilly's family and their Daly relations is also proceeding, as shown in the next section.

Coming to America from County Meath: Ellen and Peter Reilly

Born Bridget Ann Reilly (1850-1933), John MacLean Maney's other grandmother preferred to be called Ellen.[12] Here is the story that she told her children about coming to America. She was traveling with her brother, Peter Reilly (1847-?) when they left Ireland. As their ship approached port in New York City, she got ready to disembark. Unfortunately, however, she lost contact with her brother and always said that she never saw

---

[12] Her voyage to New York City in the mid-1860s did not go as well as those of her future husband and his brother, but Ellen kept her wits about her and solved problems as they presented themselves. Numerous ship lists have been consulted to find out exactly which year Ellen and Peter came, and I have also looked at many bank records with the names of Bridget, Ellen, and Anne Reilly for the different years that my great-grandmother said that she arrived in New York City. For example, the year of her arrival is given in the 1900 census as 1866 and John's arrival is given as 1872. In the 1920 census she said she arrived in 1865. Part of the problem may have been that Reilly is a common last name, especially in Meath.

him again. No answer was ever provided to my father's questions about what may have happened to Peter. Records show that Ellen was baptized in 1850 in Bohermeen parish, a part of County Meath, which is near the town of Navan. The ship bringing her to New York harbor probably arrived in about 1865. John MacLean Maney (1914-1985) told his children that Ellen had instructions from her mother or some other family member about what to do after she arrived; if any trouble arose, she should show the address of the family that was expecting her to someone in authority and get help.

Ellen also told her grandson that she had followed the instructions she had been given to locate the nearest Catholic Church and ask for help after she had gone through immigration at Castle Garden, which was located near the southern tip of Manhattan. When she arrived at the church, the priest probably did for her what he did for other people who knocked on the door of his parish hall every day: he helped her contact the people who were expecting her. Probably some extended family member or friend from Meath was the contact person who helped Ellen get a job as a maid in New York City and later on in Providence, RI. New York City records show her marriage to John Maney there in 1874, and another set of marriage records in Providence showed that they were married again the same year in Providence.

It has been possible in recent years to piece together additional information from members of Ellen's family who continued to live in Bohermeen parish and nearby towns. These relatives confirmed information contained in census records for 1901 and 1911 that Ellen's next younger sister, Catherine Reilly (1854-1930), married a local man, John Bishop (1841-1929), and that the Bishops had raised a big family in nearby Kells in Meath County. With the assistance of a local expert who heads up the Roman Catholic parish historical society for Bohermeen, some interesting information has come to light about Catherine and John's youngest son, Peter Bishop (1898-1974). This Peter, along with his parents and siblings, are shown in the 1901 and 1911 censuses. Moreover, Peter also served as a military engineer in the Irish revolutionary armed forces during the war for independence, which ended successfully in 1922.[13] While staying in nearby Navan, I met cousins who were descendants of Peter Bishop. Since that meeting, two women from Catherine Bishop's family have been in contact with the Maneys in the U.S. because we have common DNA matches through a common ancestor, Maria Daly Reilly, who was the mother of Ellen Reilly Maney and Catherine Reilly Bishop.

Finding Other Irish Families: The Dalys from County Meath

The third group is also an interesting family. My siblings and I have proven DNA matches with many Dalys.[14] Most of these DNA matches were related to Ellen Reilly Maney on her mother's Daly side, and the story of how this Daly family came to Canada and the USA is an important one. The parents of Ellen's maternal grandfather, Matthew Daly (1795-1848), were Malachy Daly (1775-1852) and Judith Green (1775-1823). Both of them were from the part of Meath that is near Navan and Kells in the northeast part of the Republic of Ireland. When you look at the entry for the mini-tree below that was prepared about the Daly family, you can see that Matthew was the only child in this family when his father, Malachy, disappeared. Several records

---

[13] Even before achieving independence in 1922, Ireland had a modern census system that ran well in both 1901 and 1911. That meant that information was available about who lived where in Ireland during those two decades and also that it was possible to find another Irish nation living abroad in most parts of the world, including in England, Scotland, New Zealand, Canada, Australia, and the USA.

[14] It seems that there are more Maney DNA connections with Dalys and MacLeans than with any other families highlighted in this book.

suggest that Malachy Daly — or someone with the same name — was arrested by the police or some other arm of the British government, tried, and convicted in Cork for some crime, and then sentenced to serve a life sentence in Australia, where the British were increasingly relying on Irish convict labor sent by the Anglo-Irish police forces to serve their sentences. It is hard to be sure if the Malachy Daly who was the convict was the person in Ellen Reilly's tree, since the sentence was pronounced in Cork, which is the county west of Tipperary and more than one day's travel from the place where he had lived in Meath.[15] It seems that the family knew that he was "disappeared."

He may have been arrested elsewhere for participation in some political crime or disturbance and shipped out from the port for the city of Cork, which is the largest port in southern Ireland. Known as Queenstown then, and Cobh today, it was often the first port of call for ships leaving Liverpool bound for cities such as Boston and New York City, as well as where local authorities shipped out convicts to serve their life sentences in Australia. There is an island in the middle of Cobh harbor in County Cork that served as a prison under British rule. Whatever happened to Malachy would have remained an unsolved mystery, except that all of the children of John MacLean Maney and Ethel Bradstreet have DNA matches with cousins living in Australia who have

---

[15] On this website is one image for a Malachi Daly record in Australia. Meath County, Ireland, was one of the places where an attack on the British was put down in 1898. ancestry.com/imageviewer/collections/61039/images/04173_01_0066?pId=3145834
This is a census record, which suggests he was no longer in prison but couldn't leave Australia and go back to his home. ancestry.com/imageviewer/collections/1214/images/CSAUS1841A_081764-00597?pId=9139
This record also shows him alive, which may help explain how and why some of John MacLean Maney's children have a DNA connection with this particular Irishman living halfway around the world. ancestry.com/discoveryui-content/view/60131:1657?ssrc=pt&tid=24430911&pid=172011574318

Daly ancestors from that time. The most likely scenario is that Malachi was one of these convicts. You can see in the Reilly mini-tree that Ellen and her sister Catherine came from a big family; that their father was a Patrick Reilly from Dunshaughlin; and that their mother was a Maria Daly who was related to Malachi Daly through his son Matthew.

Reilly Family Mini-trees in County Meath

Patrick Reilly, **who** was born in Meath, married *Catherine Finnegan,* 1770-?

Their children: **Edward** was born in 1790; Mary was born in 1793.

Edward Reilly, who was baptized in Dunshaughlin, Meath about 1790-? married *Cath Judden* born in Meath in 1795-?

Their children born in Dunshauglin: **Patrick,** who was baptized in 1814-? John, who was baptized in 1816 and died in Oldcastle, Meath in 1893.

Patrick Reilly (1814-?) married *Maria Daly* (1816-?).

Their children baptized in Bohermeen, Meath: Margaret, 1826-? Edward, 1838-?; Eliza ,1841-? Mary, 1843-? Peter, 1847-? *Bridget Ann "Ellen,"* 1850-1933; Catherine, 1854-1930; Jane, 1855-?; Patrick 1856-?; and Matilda, 1859-?

Bridget Ann "Ellen" Reilly (1850-1933) married *John Patrick Maney* (1849-1832).

Their children born in Lawrence or Methuen, MA: *John Joseph,* 1875-1942; William, 1877-1878; Marie, 1878-1948; Thomas, 1879-1957; Edward, 1882-1956; Helen,1883-1922; Hugh, 1885-1885; Annie, 1886-1887; Joseph, 1887-1969; Leontine, 1888-1963;

Anna Katherine, 1889-1952; Theresa, 1892-1893; and Matthew, 1896-1978.

John Joseph Maney (1875-1942) married ***Sarah Harriet "Ruth" MacLean*** (1876-1939).
Their surviving child: ***John MacLean Maney,*** 1914-1985.

John MacLean Maney (1914-1985) married ***Ethel Louise Bradstreet*** (1917-2004) in 1940 in Danvers, MA.

The Daly mini-tree introduces us to Malachi's wife, Judith Green, who is also important for this story. Judith connects the Maneys and the Reillys to additional Dalys, as will be shown in this part of the Daly family mini-tree. Back in Meath after Malachi Daly's disappearance, Judith and other family members believed that Malachi had either died or had been transported to serve a life sentence in Australia. Either of those outcomes meant that he would probably never be able to return to his family. Accordingly, the family followed an interesting local custom which was sanctioned by the Roman Catholic authorities: Judith married one of Malachy's brothers, Loughlin Daly. Judith and Loughlin then had a family of at least six children, including Peter Daly (1802-abt1850). In his turn, this Peter became the patriarch of a family of many sons and daughters whose descendants are related to Ellen Reilly through her maternal Daly family line. The children of John Maney (1849-1932) were connected to Peter through his mother, Judith Green, who had been Malachy's wife; and we are also related directly to Peter Daly through Malachi's brother, Loughlin Daly.

Details about Peter Daly's life in Ireland are contained in records held in the city library in Navan, Meath. The local history librarian there collects information about Peter Daly which he enthusiastically shared with visitors from the USA. Peter was well-educated for the early 1800s, when young Roman Catholic children were still not allowed to attend local public schools in Ireland. As a young man, Peter spent some years teaching in an unofficial school for children in Bohermeen parish under the patronage and protection of the local priest, who let Peter live in the belfry of the church. The classes that he taught were held in a type of illegal school known in Ireland as a hedge school, since the lessons were frequently given outdoors because no system of public instruction was allowed by the British authorities for Roman Catholic families at the time.

Instead, teachers such as Peter wrote on a chalkboard or slate of some kind to an audience of children gathered around him. After some time teaching in Bohermeen and nearby, Peter married and the couple had a big family. Peter died in about 1850 after he and his wife shepherded their family out of Ireland. In the Canadian censuses of 1851 and 1861, Peter's widow and some of their children can be seen living in Ontario. As adults, some of these Daly children remained in Ontario while others filtered across the St. Lawrence River into the state of New York or settled in other parts of Canada and the U.S. west. John MacLean Maney and Ethel Bradstreet's children have more DNA matches with people named Daly than they do with those whose last names were Reilly. Peter Daly is a third-great-granduncle, and his family had the most sons who had religious occupations of all the families described in this chapter, including some sons working as priests and others as Protestant ministers. Peter and Margaret's first-born son, another Loughlin, became a parish priest in New Haven, CT, after arriving in the USA. In addition, at least two other sons became Protestant ministers and left big families of their own.

Daly Family Mini-tree
Loughlin Daly, born in Meath (1758-?), married **unknown.**
Their child: **Malachy Daly** was born in Meath, 1775-?

Malachy Daly, who was baptized in 1775, married **Judith Green,** 1775-1823, in Athboy, Meath in 1795. Their child: **Matthew Daly** was baptized in 1795-?
Matthew Daly, 1795-1848, married **Mary Daly,** 1793-1816.
Their child: **Mary Daly** was born in 1816-?

Mary Daly, who was baptized in Dunshaughlin, Meath, in 1816-? married **Patrick Reilly,** who was baptized in Dunshaughlin in 1814-?
Their children baptized in Bohermeen: Margaret, baptized in 1826-? Edward baptized in 1838-? Eliza baptized in 1841-? Mary baptized in 1843-? Peter baptized in 1847-? **Bridget Ellen** baptized in 1850 and died in Lawrence, MA, in 1933; Catherine baptized in 1854-? Jane baptized in 1855-? Patrick baptized in 1856-? And Matilda baptized in 1859-?

Bridget Ann "Ellen" Reilly, 1850-1933, married **John Meany,** 1849-1832 in New York City and also in Providence, RI in 1874.
Their children, who were born either in Lawrence or Methuen, MA: **John Joseph,** 1875-1942; William, 1877-1878; Marie, 1878-1848; Thomas, 1879-1957; Edward, 1882-1956; Helen, 1883-1922; Hugh, 1885-1885; Annie, 1886-1887; Joseph, 1887-1969; Leontine, 1888-1963; Anna Katherine, 1889-1952; Theresa, 1892-1893; and Matthew, 1896-1978.

John Joseph Maney, 1875-1942, married **Sarah Harriet "Ruth" MacLean,** 1875-1940, in Boston in 1909.
Their surviving child: **John MacLean Maney,** 1914-1985.

John MacLean Maney, *who* was born in 1914 in Lawrence, MA, died in Amesbury, MA in 1985. In 1940 he married **Ethel Louise Bradstreet,** who was born in Danvers, MA in 1917 and died in Milwaukee, WI in 2004.

Summing Up: The Impact of Continued British Rule on These Irish Families

This chapter ends with the author understanding more of the negative effects that British rule had on the lives of Irish people living in Meath, Tipperary, and other nearby counties throughout the period under study.[16] The English government had already started "planting" settlements of English and Scotch settlers as allies of their government in Ulster near County Meath in the last decade of the sixteenth century and in Tipperary, which is historically part of Munster. By that time, the British were looking for ways to "enclose" the native Irish people away from the Roman Catholic gentry, landowners, and their Norman co-religionists who were trying to establish an alternative government of Roman Catholic families under the name of an Irish Confederacy[17] and were rising up in the first in a series of rebellions that continued the resistance.

British rule and a lack of democratic norms and rules continued during three more centuries. Conflicts erupted

---

[16] After finishing this chapter, the reader is invited to suggest one or two people whose lives you are interested in spotlighting. Maybe it might be Peter Daly or Ellen Reilly Maney following one of the frameworks for spotlighting used in chapter 1 of this book.

[17] The Irish Confederacy had fought Cromwell's army and we are amassing information in the *Maney Family Archive* about the damage that this failed rebellion caused for Confederacy leaders. In this chapter we have also shared information about Roman Catholic people in Tipperary who may have gotten their houses back in the mid-1660s while others had to be content to live as tenants in the houses that they had formerly owned.

periodically during the eighteenth and nineteenth centuries, which the British government continued to put down by harsh policies against the native Irish backed up with military force. Just as important as full rebellion was the kind of police harassment and military takings that could severely alter their lives if people fell prey to them. In the eighteenth century, rebellions featured alliances between some Irish Catholic and Protestant leaders who hoped to see a revolution in Ireland similar to the successful War for Independence won by the colonial army in the British colonies after 1776 which delivered full citizenship rights to most European Americans, though not to Native peoples trying to remain as residents, African slaves living in the same communities, and, of course, women, given their status in all of white North America. Irish patriots also took courage from the events that established the French Republic after 1789.

When rebellion flared up again in and around Meath in 1798, it was quickly and brutally put down. As a result, many Meath men were killed, and it may have been the case that participation in this rebellion had been the reason for the arrest, conviction, and transportation to Australia of Malachi Daly, Ellen Reilly's great-grandfather, by the British. Then, in 1848, near the time and place where John Maney (1849-1932) was born, a new rebel group ended up in a gunfight that continued for several hours after they holed up in a house in Ballingarry, Tipperary. Ballingarry is close to Cashel and to Tipperary County's border with County Kilkenny and is also part of the region in which successive generations of Maneys had lived. Among the Irish leaders of this revolt was a man named Thomas F. Meagher, whose grandfather came from Killenaule, another place where Meanys later lived in Tipperary County.

Meagher was convicted by the British government in Ireland and transported to serve a life sentence in Australia but escaped and made his way to the USA, where he continued working for Irish independence in New York City and other U.S. cities with large populations of immigrants from Ireland. Meagher also served as a Brigadier General in the U.S. Army during the American Civil War, which was followed by a brief stint as the territorial governor of Montana. Uprisings continued in Ireland in the second half of the nineteenth century, but two other developments also stand out. The first, of course, was the departure of millions of Irish people who voted with their feet by emigrating from Ireland to England, North America, Australia, and many other countries in the face of famine conditions at home and greater economic opportunities offered elsewhere in the mid-1800s.

Also important for the ultimate victory of independence from Britain in the early twentieth century was the establishment and growth of a clandestine revolutionary army inside Ireland. John Maney (1849-1932), the immigrant, certainly wanted to be rid of Ireland and frequently affirmed that he would never go back there. However, that the people who stayed in Ireland finally forced the British government to affirm Ireland's calls for independence is due to the struggle for freedom waged by Irish people there. Thus, while visiting with Reilly second-cousins in County Meath, I heard an evening of stories that showed the pride of these distant relatives in the wartime service of Peter Bishop and his grandfather's service in the Irish Republican Army that followed.

Maney family English census, 1851 when family was living in Stockport, near Manchester, England

of ...ation	Rank, Profession, or Occupation	Where Born	Whether Blind, or Deaf-and-Dumb
72		*Ireland*	•
17	Factory Hand, Cotton Mill	*Ireland*	
16	Do Do	Do	
12		Do	
8		Do	
1	Labourer (Jobbing)	Do	
1	Factory Hand, Cotton Mill	Do	
20	Stay Maker	Do	
30	Factory Hand, Cotton Mill	Do	
15		Do	
16	Factory Hand Do	Do	
1	Labourer Jobbing	Do	
25		&c	
	General Practitioner, Licentiate of the Apothecaries Company	Cheshire Stockport	
52		Do Do	
27		Do Do	
24		Do Do	
17		Do Do	
15			

Annastatia Doran Maney, "Rhode Island, Deaths and Burials, 1802-1950"

Name:	Annastatia Doran Maney
Gender:	Female
Burial Date:	
Burial Place:	
Death Date:	15 Feb 1889
Death Place:	Providence, Providence, Rhode Island
Age:	68
Birth Date:	1821
Birthplace:	
Occupation:	
Race:	
Marital Status:	Married
Spouse's Name:	John Maney
Father's Name:	John Doran
Father's Birthplace:	
Mother's Name:	Mary
Mother's Birthplace:	
Indexing Project (Batch) Number:	I01177-5
System Origin:	Rhode Island-EASy
GS Film number:	2023152
Reference ID:	2

Citing this Record

"Rhode Island, Deaths and Burials, 1802-1950," index, *FamilySearch* (https://familysearch.org/pal:/MM9.1.1/F8ZH-8ZB : accessed 25 Oct 2013), Annastatia Doran Maney, 1821.

Map of Tipperary showing baronies and main towns.
Note: Kilnamanagh Upper incorporates the former baronies of Ileagh and Kilnalongurty.

A Stockport Heritage Postcard

Stockport during the Industrial Revolution (c 1845)

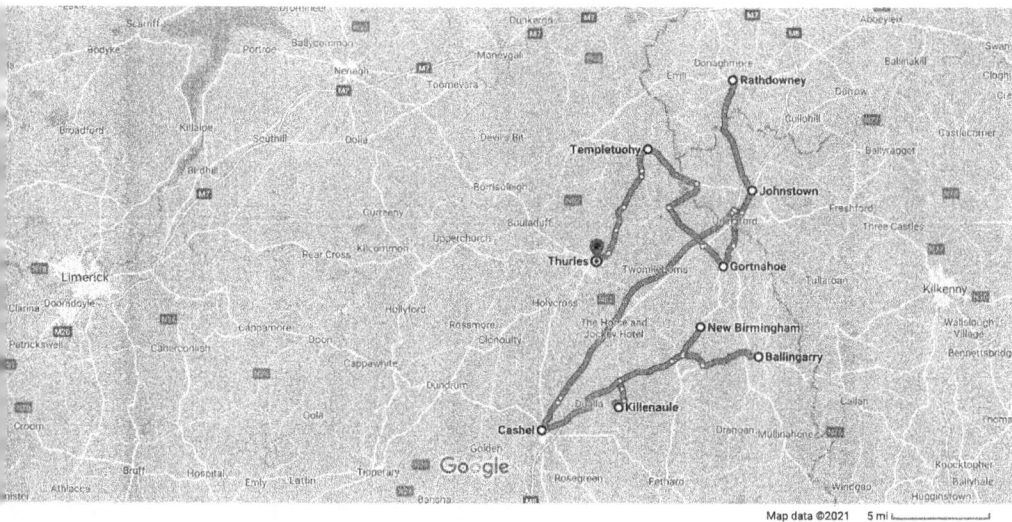

Google map showing short distances between the villages where the same Maney families lived over generations

M500	
Family name	Given name or names
MANEY	JOHN
Address	
Lawrence	
Certificate no. (or vol. and page)	Title and location of court MASS.
37-257	SUP.CRIM.CT.ESSEX CTY.SALEM
Country of birth or allegiance	When born (or age)
Tipperary, Great Britain	Aug. 7, 1850
Date and port of arrival in U. S.	Date of naturalization
	Oct. 23, 1882
Names and addresses of witnesses	

U. S. DEPARTMENT OF LABOR, Immigration and N̶̶lization Service. FORM NO. 1-IP. 14—2202
CF

Naturalization card for John Maney, 1850-1932

Genealogy organizations are publishing more research about women's issues at work

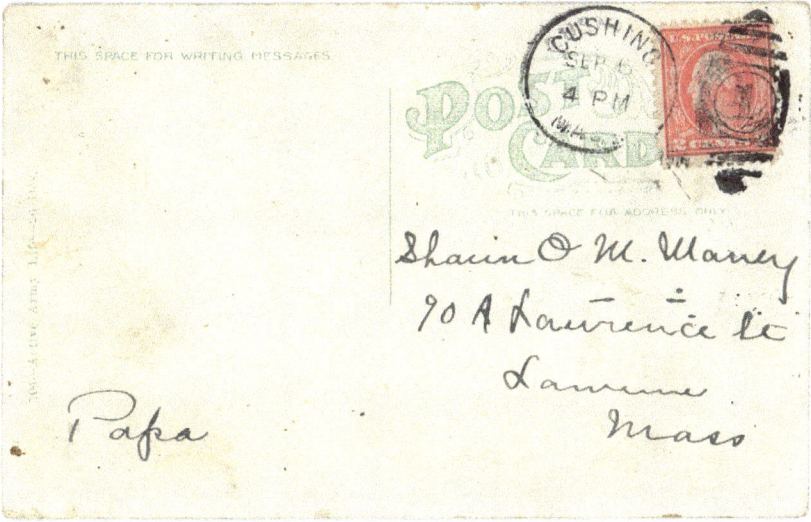

Postcard for John MacLean Maney from "papa" (back of card)

Cavalry training for War work

COPY. BY UNDERWOOD & UNDERWOOD, N.Y.

WW I postcard from Ruth to John MacLean Maney (front of card)

06

The Mothers of Us All

Introduction to Ethel Bradstreet's Maternal Line

I had two main goals for this chapter. First, I wanted to follow all of the women in Ethel Bradstreet's maternal line back in time until I had evidence about when the first of these women came to North America with her parents and/ or her own family. A second goal was to identify from public records, if I could, that woman's family members, including her parents as well as her female and male siblings and children. I used standard genealogical practice for searching records in England and New England on Ancestry.com and stopped after I found records showing a baptism certificate for one of them, Ethel Bradstreet's 9th great-grandmother, Bridget Chester (1587-1647), who was born in England and died in Newbury, a town in the northern part of the Massachusetts Bay Colony (MBC). Bridget Chester's dates clearly put her life inside the common starting period for all of this book's family chapters beginning with her birth in the last part of the sixteenth century or the first part of the seventeenth century. Information about Chester's daughter, Rebecca Swayne,[1] in turn, led me to the

---

[1] This Massachusetts document summarizes Rebecca Swain's history in England and in the Mass Bay Colony. ancestry.com/imageviewer/collections/61401/

English town of Salisbury in Wiltshire County, located near Stonehenge in the west of England.

The mini-tree information presented in this chapter also considers the historical context in which these women and their sons and daughters lived in each generation: information about women's child-rearing responsibilities and information about earnings, if any, from occupations practiced outside the home.[2] I focus first on the range of opportunities available for girls and women to do useful work for their families given the locations and time periods from the seventeenth century onward. Later in the chapter, I look for changes and continuities in women's status in New England from the seventeenth through the twentieth centuries and consider what some women and girls in my mother's maternal family tree had been doing to get paid and unpaid work inside their own families and in the communities where these families lived in Massachusetts Bay Colony.

In sum, I wanted to know as much as I could about the approximate place each woman occupied in her local community and if the situation of women and girls had changed over time. It also means that we will hear more in this chapter about work inside the home in northern Essex County during the 1600s and the possibilities for paid work for women and girls outside their homes, whether they came to what is now Essex County from places in England, Scotland, Ireland, other colonies in British America, and/or Newfoundland.

Mini-tree Information about Women, Their Spouses, and Their Children

Here is the mini-tree for my mother's maternal line. As in the other chapters, there is also a section included for discussion and

---

images/dvm_primsrc000094-01097?pId=1512310

[2] As was the case in the other chapters, such an approach could work also with materials I will continue to use from the *Maney Family Archive*.

analysis of what happened about women's work done for people both inside and outside of the nuclear family. It will also help readers re-visit what we have learned about other women whom the reader has already met. Unlike in the other chapters, however, this chapter puts only the daughters' names in italics in the mini-trees. Please note that the name of the daughter in the direct line to Ethel Bradstreet is listed in each of these tree entries and the other daughters are also shown.

Ethel Bradstreet's Maternal Mini-tree

Bridget Chester, who was born in Bristol, England, in 1587 and died in Newbury, MA in 1647, married Bennet Swayne in England in 1616. Bennet was born in Sarum, Wiltshire, in 1572 and died in Wiltshire County in 1630 Their children all born in England: *Bennett* Swayne and *Richard* Swayne and any other older children who may have been included in the travel to the MBC.
Rebecca born in 1616.

Rebecca Swayne, who was born in Salisbury, Wiltshire, EN, in 1616, died in 1695 in Ipswich, Essex, MBC, married John Hall who was born in England in 1611 or 1611 and died in 1647 in Salisbury, MBC.
Their children: **Susannah** born in 1642 in Salisbury, Rebecca Swayne had first married a man named Byley, then John Hall, then Rev. William Worcester, and, finally, MBC Lt. Gov., Samuel Symonds.

Susannah Hall, who was born in 1642 in Salisbury, Essex, MBC, died in Salisbury, Essex, MA, in 1730, after her marriage to *Timothy* Worcester in 1663. Timothy was born in Salisbury, MBC, in 1642 and died there in 1672.

Their children: **Sarah** born in 1667, **Susanna** born in 1671.[3]

Sarah Worcester was born in 1667 in Salisbury, MBC, and died in Hampton Falls, NH, in 1720. In 1690 Sarah married Benjamin Sanborn who was born in Hampton, NH, in 1688 and died there in 1740.
Their children: **Joana** born in 1692, **Sarah** born in 1694, **Abigail** born in 1700, **Jemima** born in 1702, **Susanna** born in 1704, *Benjamin* born in 1706, and **Judith** born in 1708.

Sarah Sanborn, who was born in 1694 in Hampton, NH, and died in Hampton Falls in 1756, married Reuben Sanborn in 1714 in Hampton Falls, NH. Reuben was born in Hampton, NH in 1692 and died in Hampton Falls in 1756
Their children: **Anna** born in 1715, **Mary** born in 1725, **Abigail** born in 1731, and **Phoebe** born in Hampton Falls, NH, in 1736.

Phoebe Sanborn, who was born in Hampton Falls, NH, in 1736 and died in Weare, Hillsborough, NH, in 1816, married Samuel Philbrick 1760-1792 in 1758 in Hampton Falls.
Their children: **Sarah** born in 1760, **Mary "Mollie"** born in 1765, *Jonathan* born in 1767, and **Mehitable** born in 1774.

Mary "Mollie" Philbrick, who was born in 1765 in Raymond, Rockingham, NH, and died in Barnstead,

---

[3] For Ancestry's information about Susannah Hall's parentage, marriages, and children, see https://www.ancestry.com/family-tree/person/tree/46577678/person/340000694244/facts

Belknap, NH, in 1855, married James Pickering, who was born in Portsmouth, NH, in 1758 and died in Belknap, NH, in 1837.

Their children: *Jacob* born in 1784, *Levi* born in 1788, *John* born in 1790, *Samuel* born in 1791, Mehitable born in 1797, *Jonathan* born in 1799, **Elizabeth "Betsy" Pickering** born in 1802, and *Moses* born in 1806.

Elizabeth "Betsy" Pickering, who was born in 1802 in Barnstead, Belknap, NH, and died in Boston, Suffolk, MA, in 1879, married Dudley G Colbath, who was born in Newington, NH in 1792 and died in Boston in 1881. Betsy and Dudley married in 1822.

Their children: **Louisa A Colbath**, born in Boston, MA in 1822, *Charles* born in 1823, **Mary** born in 1824, *Mark* born in 1826, *Eleazer* born in 1828, **Betsy** born in 1836, *Dudley J* born in 1839, and *Jonathan* born in 1842.

Louisa Colbath, who was born in Boston, Suffolk, MA in 1822 and died in 1891 in Wrentham, Norfolk, MA, married Thomas N. Guild, who was born in 1817 in Wrentham, MA and died in N. Attleboro, MA, in 1898. They married in Boston, MA, in 1841.

Their children: *William* born in 1842, **Elizabeth** born in 1844, *Wilson* born in 1850, **Maria** born in Wrentham, MA in 1852, *Henry* born in 1855, **Sarah** born in 1857, **Mary** born in 1859, **Emma** born in 1862, **Emma** born in 1866, *Thomas* born in 1868, and *Franklin* born in 1874.

Maria Guild, who was born in 1852 in Wrentham, Norfolk, MA, and died in Beverly, MA, in 1935, married Eben Francis Lovett in 1882 in Beverly. Eben was born in Beverly, MA, in 1848 and died in Beverly in 1923. Their children born in Beverly: **Bertha F** born in 1883 and **Ethel** born in 1885.

Bertha F. Lovett, who was born in Beverly, MA, in 1883, died in Danvers, MA, in 1971. In Beverly, in 1908 she married Alvah J Bradstreet, who was born in Danvers, MA in 1862 and died in Danvers, MA in 1960.
Their children born in Danvers, MA: *Dudley* born in 1909, *Alva* born in 1911, and **Ethel** born in 1917.
Ethel Louise Bradstreet, who was born in 1917 in Danvers, MA and died in Milwaukee, WI in 2005, married **John MacLean Maney**, who was born in Lawrence, MA in 1914 and died in Amesbury, MA, in 1985. They married in Danvers in 1940.

Analyzing Ethel Bradstreet's Maternal Line

Organizing a family along the maternal line – whether we call the result a tapestry, mosaic, or a weaving holding all of these women and their families together – gives hints about what constituted "women's work" for those women profiled in this chapter who came from Europe with their families during the seventeenth and eighteenth centuries. I was also interested in finding out how "women's work" changed when mothers and their daughters began getting paid for work done outside the home before and after the women married. By the mid-nineteenth century, census records show what work was available to them in Essex County besides what women did for people in their immediate households and how that changed when manufacturing expanded to an industrial scale in Essex County.

When we look at young women after 1850, we will see some of them working at trades related to weaving and working in cotton and woolen mills and also for shoe companies while boarding with fellow female workers in apartments in Lynn and Beverly, MA, as their counterparts in Europe were doing at the same time in Ireland, Scotland, and England, not to forget Lynn, Danvers, Lawrence, and elsewhere in Massachusetts, other parts of New England, and also in Canada. And we already know that some Scottish women from the Highlands and Islands continued to travel to the lowlands of Scotland to find work in the summer and at harvest time and later left their birth families in Nova Scotia and Prince Edward Island for better-paying jobs in Massachusetts.

In addition to records about births, baptisms, marriages and deaths, this chapter uses records and stories collected by New England historians who have identified information about the everyday tasks that women fulfilled inside and outside their homes, especially in the period from 1650 to the middle of the following century. Laurel Taylor Ulrich's book, *Good Wives*,[4] focuses not only on women's reproductive labor, but also on the household work of women some of whom we have already met in the Massachusetts-based chapters of this book. That list includes Anne Dudley Bradstreet and her sisters and daughters, as well as women who married into the Lovett, Guild, and Colbath families during the last quarter of the seventeenth century. As a result of Ulrich's research, we know a lot more about the responsibilities that women in the English families in the Massachusetts Bay Colony had from the last half of the seventeenth century, including why and how women's situations in the family might

---

[4] Ulrich's book has a long title which is useful to see here in its entirety: *Good Wives: Image and Reality in the Lives of Women in Northern New England, 1650-1750*. What is described as northern New England included towns such as Ipswich, Andover, Salisbury, Topsfield, and Rowley, all towns that still exist today. There are also occasional references to life in Salem, MBC. Most of these women lived in Hampton, Hampton Falls, and other nearby towns in the MBC's northern border with NH, however. Other families lived along or near the coast of Maine.

be different in frontier villages like Salisbury, MBC, and more settled larger towns such as Salem.

In *Good Wives*, Ulrich argues that wives in northern Essex County functioned as homemakers, artisans, and sometimes took on other important roles in Puritan households from the time of the first land grants and settlements. From about 1620 until 1750 Ulrich's research shows examples of a slowly expanding realm of work for women outside the nuclear family. Sometimes these women – and their children – worked at home for cash or bartered goods with neighbors and local shops; sometimes they even did paid work outside the home, especially when a woman's husband died at a young age. We have already seen that Ulrich suggested widows sometimes claimed considerable honorary status as a "deputy husband," i.e., when these women supervised the work of the oldest son until he was old enough to do the work that the head of a household would have done.[5]

The geography within which these women and their daughters and sons, grandchildren, great-grandchildren, and second great grandchildren, etc., moved is also interesting. This particular maternal line, for example, shows families spreading out to adjoining places in northern Essex County, such as Newbury, Ipswich, and Salisbury from the ones mentioned most often in previous chapters. Then, the families in Ethel Bradstreet's maternal line moved into coastal and central New Hampshire until Louisa Colbath (1820-1891), one of Ethel Bradstreet's great-grandmothers, lived in rural and urbanizing towns like Dedham and Wrentham, Massachusetts, not far from the western and southern boundaries of Essex County. Finally, in the last part of the nineteenth century, we will see Maria Guild Lovett (1852-

---

[5] Information available from several other important works comes from Mary Blewett. She focused on textile work and shoe manufacturing in places like Lynn, Lawrence, Fall River, Lowell, Manchester, NH, and other smaller places like Haverhill, Danvers, and Beverly.

1935) and her daughter, Bertha Lovett Bradstreet (1883-1971), living out their lives in Essex County in the bustling towns of Beverly and Danvers.

Origin Points for These Women and Their Families

The second mother in this maternal line, Bridget Chester's daughter Rebecca Swayne, was born in the west of England and came to the Massachusetts Bay Colony with her husband, John Hall (1611-1647), and her own mother, Bridget. Shortly after the family's arrival, Rebecca's daughter, Susannah Hall (1642-1730), was born in Salisbury MBC. After Rebecca's husband died, Susannah and her mother lived with the family of Rebecca's next husband, Rev. William Worcester (1601-1662), the minister in Salisbury, MA. Susannah later married Timothy Worcester (1642-1672), William's son by a previous marriage. Ulrich's research showed that women and girls who came to northern Essex County from the west of England seem to have had similar economic backgrounds to those who arrived in the 1630s, and some were also born into families of the minor gentry like the first generation arrivals.

The families settling in northern Essex County are important for several reasons. First, the lives they led helped keep the Puritan community experiment going during a period when in-migration to the MBC paused for a decade while the Civil War in England, Scotland, and Ireland raged during the 1640s and 1650s. Indeed, life was not settled until the mid-1660s for women and their families in Ireland since, as we have seen, historians have reported that many Roman Catholic Irish families had been forced out of their homes and some could only came back to their former properties as tenants of the new owners. Since the English Civil War discouraged people from emigrating in the numbers that had been common before, it also helped that newcomer families had sufficient funds to pay their own passage to British North America and held sufficient status in their communities that they could procure land grants from the towns in which they wanted to settle.

People coming from the west of England constituted a big share of the starting population of such northern Essex County towns as Newbury and Salisbury and their numbers spilled over into some of the first towns and villages in New Hampshire, such as Hampton, Hampton Falls, and Portsmouth. It was also important that members of the first generation of Puritan settlers from the east coast of England, who lived at first in coastal towns like Ipswich and Salisbury in the Mass. Bay Colony, were getting used to living near people who came later to northern New England from the west of England. As time went on, English ports serving the western coast of that country, like the coastal Massachusetts ports of Salem, Gloucester, Marblehead, and Beverly, were also becoming the home base for fishing fleets based in Massachusetts and New Hampshire in order to travel to Newfoundland and back each year. The goal of course was to bring cod from the Grand Banks to coastal communities in England's colonies in Massachusetts as well as other colonies in British North America.

Many people from the West of England came from Salisbury in Wiltshire County, England, and settled in or near Salisbury in Essex County in what became New England. It seems that they wanted to start up their own communities and not take on the tasks expected of fisher folk such as those whose numbers had helped expand Essex County's fishing industry centers in Salem, Marblehead, and the towns on Cape Ann, including Beverly, Gloucester, and Ipswich. Also the movement of families from place to place was typical of the choices that many families still make today when the decision is taken that family members would follow the husband to a new job location rather than choose among the same or nearby locations. So, some of the women moved came from the MBC and married men who had gotten land in New Hampshire. By then, northern Massachusetts was running out of land for husbands to provide a portion of their land to each son, a problem that Scots Canadians faced later in Nova Scotia. In this sample, the main indicator of how much "women's work" was done by high-status women in small settlements such as Salisbury seems to have been based on the economic and social status that their birth families held, along with the status of their husbands in the new colony.

While some of the families in Ethel Bradstreet's maternal tree had difficult times, many of her female ancestors married husbands who were freemen, landholders, or tenants. That meant that their fathers or husbands had gotten land and their sons had good prospects for getting land as well. If that happened, a wife did not have to depend on older female children working inside the household, as shown in the autobiography that a Lovett relative, Lucy Larcom, wrote about her own early education in the first half of the nineteenth century.[6] In telling these stories I am focusing on the work that ordinary women of a certain class did every day in Essex County in the first two hundred years after the coming of the Puritans to British North America, including what wives and mothers did for pay in their communities for work they may have done inside and outside of their homes in Essex County and how that changed after the industrial age arrived in the nineteenth century. In short, the new work and business opportunities that adult women and their daughters began to pursue were logical responses to their families' economic needs and interests.

_____

[6] In her autobiography, *A New England Childhood*, Lucy Larcom, who was born in Beverly in 1824 and was a distant relative of Ethel Bradstreet and her children, wrote about how local women used to earn money in their own homes when Lucy was a girl. For example, one woman operated a combination of school and day care center in Beverly, so neighbor women could get their own work done at home while the younger children were 'at school.' Lucy started her education at this school when she was about one year old. And she also began borrowing books to read at home from the teacher's lending library. Both Larcom and her mother would be good candidates for Spotlight profiles.

Ordinary Women: 'Good Wives' in Puritan New England

The subject matter of this section comes from the title of Ulrich's book, *Good Wives*, which studied the economic activity of families in northern Essex County until approximately 1750. Ulrich cautioned readers that the situation for women was different in high status families, such as those coming later to New England and then resided in the northern part of the MBC compared with what wives and mothers faced in middle class families or in the homes of laborers. Women in most Puritan farm families depended on help from their own older children or the mother's unmarried sisters. In wealthier households, the female householder may have also paid – or bartered – for help to do her household tasks within her family from female neighbors in their town.

And in some instances, women from households with more economic clout would have had more say about life in the home outside of the wife's traditional sphere, especially if they came from families of senior government or religious leaders. Rev. William Worcester, a leading minister in Salisbury, whom Rebecca Swayne married after her second husband died, is a good example. It is not surprising that this poem by Anne Bradstreet captured some of the responsibilities of 'good wives' for that time.[7]

> *When each of you shall in your nest*
> *Among your young ones take your rest,*
> *In chirping language oft them tell,*
> *You had a dam that lov'd you well.*
> *That did what could be done for young,*
> *And nurst you up till you were strong,*
> *And fore she once would let you fly,*

---

[7] See Ulrich, p. 163 and the biography of Anne Bradstreet authored by Charlotte Gordon, *Mistress Bradstreet: The Untold Life of America's First Poet*. Boston: Little Brown, 2005 in the bibliography prepared for this book.

She shew'd you joy and misery;
Taught what was good, and what was ill,
What would save life and what would kill.
Thus gone, amongst you I may live,
And dead, yet speak, and counsel give.

This ideal of motherhood is one strand in the tapestry that Puritan women in New England pursued while they waited for what they expected would be personal rewards in the next world. Another kind of transaction was practiced in towns like Ipswich, as we can see when a well-to-do woman hired as a maid one or more daughters of her financially-pressed neighbors, just as their husbands might choose apprentices from among the boys of the town who wanted to learn a trade. The main difference, of course, was that an apprentice or indentured worker could start up his own business after living in the family of his employer until he had learned his trade.

On the other hand, women working as maids did not have an employment ladder to use except marriage, after doing domestic work in someone else's home. There were some special exceptions in the middle of the seventeenth century for enterprising women with a talent for dressmaking or hat-making, who could take orders for work to be done in their own homes from women in the town or village where they lived. That was also the option which Ethel Bradstreet's maternal grandmother, Maria Guild, followed in the late nineteenth century as a dressmaker. Another milliner was one of John MacLean Maney's aunts, Leontine Maney, as shown in the Lawrence City Directory published in 1888 and discussed in chapter five.

Ulrich provides additional information about a family in Newbury, MBC, which shows how busy the wife was having babies and notes how this woman was treated as a widow in the terms of her husband's will after he died. His will confirmed his love for her, as well as for his children and grandchildren. However, reading the will today you may see that he went along with the common practice which favored sons over daughters in dividing up his estate, that is, male children were given land, female children were given possessions, and his widow received housing and income for the rest of her lifetime.[8] In the first hundred years, few financial records survive showing women and men working at home in New England. If the family got any cash money for making shoe parts or products, for example, the money would go to the head of household. In the case of his wife's work, money given to the apprentice would normally go to the husband as well.

Ulrich and other historians agree that a lot of bartering was going on for goods made by adults but it was less visible when done by women working in their own domain, i.e., inside the house where the herbs were processed, food prepared, woolens woven, etc.[9] Another vignette took place in Ipswich during an earlier marriage of Lt. Gov. Samuel Symonds (1590-1678) before he married Rebecca Swayne. Symonds and Martha Read, his wife before he married Rebecca, were the subject of a court case. An overheard conversation at a family gathering in the Symonds house showed that wives in this kind of high-status family sometimes were able to speak up to contradict their husbands in front of other family members and household members like the apprentices and the maids.

On this occasion, Martha Read appealed to her husband, Samuel Symonds, to confirm that the two Irish apprentices[10] had

---

[8] Ulrich, *Good Wives*, 146-159.

[9] More of a paper trail attached itself to products made by a husband who was a blacksmith, barrel maker or practiced some other trade. Ulrich noted that some men and women kept records about these barter transactions in rural places like Topsfield and also in towns like Salem and Beverly. After all, keeping records current was vital to showing who was ahead or behind in these never-ending barter transactions.

[10] It is unusual to hear stories about Irish indentured servants living in New England in the mid-1600s. This is a reminder that such people existed in

fulfilled the time specified in the indenture and therefore should get their freedom and the customary grant of a specified sum of money as severance pay. Symonds' wife was requesting that the indentured servants be allowed to speak at household gatherings. In this example, Symonds' wife may have had some additional social status from her parents, as she seems to have had the ability to raise a counter to her husband's views on a topic which would usually have been in his domain, since it was related to how the farm, not the household, should function. Information useful for family historians about how marriages and families really work may, it seems, sometimes be unveiled in court cases, wills, and/or from family diaries kept by local history societies.[11]

It is also possible to see how a wife acted on behalf of her husband if he was a fisherman or mariner in a town like Beverly or Salem. In those cases his wife needed to be able to act in his place while her husband was away from home on sea voyages or was somehow incapacitated. If so, the wife was sometimes given a pass by the enforcers of norms in their Puritan world. In Beverly and Salem by 1750, women might be expected to keep the books and do other work if or when their husbands were away on long sea voyages. The conversation in the Symonds household referenced above occurred in 1661, however, and resulted in a court case brought by the indentured servants, which was tried in Ipswich before a jury of Lt. Gov. Symonds' peers and friends,

---

northern MBC, which makes this story even more interesting. Likewise, we have suspected that James Maney may have been an indentured servant in Virginia at about the same time and we know that families with means like the Bradstreets brought servants and men under indenture with them when they came to the end of their voyage from England to British America.

[11] Symonds' wife, Martha Read, stood up for the Irish indentured servants to say their peace in that day's meeting. However, Symonds won the court case against the indentured apprentices with the help of Simon Bradstreet and other powerful political patrons from Ipswich who sat as members on the jury of Symonds' peers.

including Simon Bradstreet. The servants lost the case coming out of the conversation in the Symonds household meeting that day. However, the indentured servants did not have to leave Ipswich after they finally were released from their indentures. Instead, they formed their own families, bought land, worked that land, and continued to live in Ipswich.

Ordinary Women: More Paid Work Available for Women, 1750-1850

Changes finally started coming in men's and women's workforce roles in the 1800s. First of all, it was more possible for men to make their way in the world as the nineteenth century got underway in an independent country. The factors which spurred young men such as Jeremiah Jones Colbath to break free of the requirement to work his neighbors' land to pursue education and successfully promote their own causes need to be compared with the obstacles that their sisters faced before they could develop and act on similar ambitions with as much likelihood of success. Let's compare Jeremiah Jones Colbath's situation with that of a woman who was born at about the same time in Beverly and faced difficult conditions supporting herself after the death of her betrothed. When this woman, who was born into a family related to the Lovetts, received word that the man whom she had expected to marry had died of consumption after a long sea voyage from New England to San Francisco, she turned inward and spent the rest of her life living with her sister's family and helping out as a caregiver. Here is an excerpt from a gloomy poem written by Lucy Larcom (1824-1893), about someone she knew, a certain Sarah Trask, who was in a similar situation and Lucy kept Sarah in mind[12] as she wrote this poem.

---

[12] The full version of Lucy Larcom's poem can be found online at https://www.bartleby.com/102/163.html accessed on 25 November 2020

Hannah Binding Shoes
Poor lone Hannah,
Sitting at the window, binding shoes.
Faded, wrinkled,
Sitting, stitching, in a mournful muse.
Bright-eyed beauty once was she,
When the bloom was on the tree.
Spring and winter.
Hannah's at the window, binding shoes.
Twenty winters:
Beach and tear the ragged shore she views
Twenty seasons:
Never one has brought her any news.
Still her dim eyes silently,
Chase the white sails o'er the sea.
Hopeless, faithful,
Hannah's at the window, binding shoes.

Shining a Spotlight on Lois Barrett And Her Daughter, Lucy Larcom

The person who wrote this poem was definitely someone who would seek a path to a different life that could be pursued by other girls and women during the first half of the nineteenth century. Lucy Larcom was a distant ancestor in Ethel Bradstreet's maternal line. Shoe-binding was something that girls and women did in the homes of Lucy's friends on a regular basis. However, Lucy and her sister became part of an unusual and unplanned work experiment which her mother, Lois Barrett Larcom (1786-1868), created for them. As a result of these experiences, Lucy, her mother, and her sisters embarked on a change in their lives that they might never have thought possible. The change started in 1832 when Lucy's mother faced a dilemma after her husband, Benjamin Larcom (1776-1846), died unexpectedly at a young age. He had been a Beverly sea captain and trader going back and forth on voyages from Beverly and Salem to East Asian ports.

For many years he sailed his own ship along the Atlantic coast to the Bahamas, then to Brazil, and after crossing the equator, headed toward Cape Town and then stopped in several East Indies ports before coming back from each trip with a treasure trove of silks, satins, and spices. By about 1820 Benjamin had given up making these trips himself and instead remained at home in Beverly where he operated as a trader and bought and sold the same types of goods that other sea captains from Beverly or Salem brought back on their ships. Unfortunately, Benjamin died unexpectedly and at a young age, without leaving a will.

The steps that his wife took in his place show that women and girls had more options in the early 1800s in a town like Beverly than would have been possible – or even thinkable – for their grandmothers to have done in earlier generations. Lois decided to move her family to the nearby Essex County town of Lowell and start up a new kind of woman-led business that would bring two kinds of income into the family which she hoped would yield a reliable income for herself and her children. Lucy tells readers in her autobiography that her mother started by corresponding with a Lowell mill owner who wanted to employ young women and girls for jobs in that city's burgeoning textile mills.

Lois' willingness to take on the role of a 'deputy husband' making decisions on behalf of her family can be seen as an inflection point in the lives of other women too in this part of New England. Both of Lois' daughters went to work in Lowell's mills and brought in small amounts of pay from this work. Lois also earned money from the mill owner by taking care of other young women who boarded in her apartment in Lowell. Lucy went on to create a career for herself as a writer, an occupation which would probably not have been possible before the middle of the nineteenth century when a large audience of women readers had been created in the U.S.

Lois Barrett Larcom liked that the mill owner wanted to attract young women as workers and also was promising he would provide a school in which they could study basic subjects after their work at his mill finished each day. Nor was Lois the only widow applying to run a boarding house for a mill owner. Once the family had settled into their new home in Lowell, Lucy made friends with a girl whose mother had had the same idea.[13] Lucy later became a teacher, poet, and is perhaps best known for her book, *A New England Childhood*, which was set in Beverly. Lucy also supported her literary work by teaching in a series of women's seminaries in Illinois where one of her married sisters lived with her own family. We know that Jeremiah Jones Colbath, a cousin of Louisa Colbath in Ethel's maternal line, was able to re-invent himself as Henry Wilson, someone who later died in office as vice president of the United States during the term he held with Ulysses S. Grant. However, this is the first example I have found of a woman, Lucy's mother, re-inventing herself in middle age, as a woman with a large family of daughters, and as a widow.

Ordinary Women: Moving Away from Home & Inventing Their Own Lives, 1850-1940

In this section, we broaden the lens to include lives led by girls and young women from families featured in other chapters of this book before we return to those in Ethel Bradstreet's direct maternal line in the 1800s. By the mid-nineteenth century, young women were traveling long distances on their own or with friends and/ or relatives in order to take up jobs to help themselves and their families. Much of the movement of girls and women in their late teens or early twenties came from places in rural Massachusetts towns in nearby counties to larger towns and cities where industrialization was already underway. The first mention in this book of young women living away from home for periods of time in order to help support their families came from young Scottish

---

[13] This other woman's daughter, Harriet Hanson, became a journalist and women's suffrage advocate after working, like Lucy did, in one of the Lowell mills as a teenager.

women, like those in John MacLean Maney's tree, who worked harvest jobs in Scotland, which also attracted their brothers and cousins from the highlands and islands in the 1700s.[14]

One of Ruth MacLean's (1876-1939) Nova Scotia aunts, Christiana MacLean (1843-1905), is an example of Scots-Canadian girls or young women coming to cities and towns in Essex County from Nova Scotia as domestic workers. A few years later, Christy married a farmer's son from Ipswich. After that, she may never have gone back to Nova Scotia except for short visits. Soon her sister, Mary MacLean, married a Maine fisherman, James Greenleaf, whom she likely met in Cape Breton, Nova Scotia, when he was working on a fishing vessel. Soon after their marriage she and her husband were living in Maine and later in Ipswich, Massachusetts. In the early 1860s, Mary's sister, Flora, who was to be the mother of my grandmother, Ruth MacLean Maney, also lived near Mary and her family in Maine for a year before Flora and her husband, Charles, returned to NS with their first daughter and settled on land that they had bought on Prince Edward Island.

We also know that Ellen Reilly (1850-1933) from County Meath had been a domestic worker for families in New York City and Providence, Rhode Island, before marrying John Maney (1849-1932) in 1874 and that after she married she kept a boarding house for female and male millworkers in the city of Lawrence in northern Essex County. Finally, we should note that all three of John Maney's (1849-1933) sisters had done mill work in Ireland and in Stockport, England, before they married and left Ireland for a new life. Besides these examples of expanding

---

[14] We know about this practice because some members of the Scottish clergy had written disapprovingly about it in the reports they had to send for the government's Statistical Accounts, information that contributed to the bigger picture about their parishes' strained economic condition at the end of the 1790s.

economic opportunities for women in the growing industrial economy of Essex County towns and cities, there seems to have been greater stress placed on how children could assist their families financially in the middle of the nineteenth century in Essex County than before.

By the mid-1800s, families in Essex County, especially families in which the husband had died and the mother was the breadwinner, as Lois Barrett Larcom had been, needed additional income and were becoming increasingly dependent on the wages that their daughters, as well as sons, contributed to the family budget while living at home. And much of this work was shoe-making and textile industry work. Some of the occupational information presented about the Bradstreet and Lovett families in the middle of the nineteenth century is captured in data collected from the 1850 and 1860 censuses which hinted at changes in the occupations listed for girls and young women. Examples included women listed as teachers and shoe binders in the mid-nineteenth century censuses in Essex County. At the same time, the main women in Ethel Bradstreet's family tree, plus their sisters and female cousins, also can be seen pursuing traditional female occupations such as dressmaking and millinery. Soon, teaching and nursing would be added to that list.

More Women's Occupations: A Focus on Women as Nurses

Nursing was among several new occupations offering opportunities for women in the USA and England, especially after the end of the American Civil War. Four examples are given here. John MacLean Maney's mother, Ruth MacLean (1876-1939), was the first in her family to complete advanced training and receive professional certification in the field of nursing which was done in those days by individual hospitals. When Ruth left Nova Scotia for Massachusetts in the late-1890s, she started working in a hospital in the Boston area while living with the family of one of her sisters,

237

another Flora, who lived with her family in Newton, Massachusetts. A few years later, Ruth moved to Lawrence, MA, and was accepted into the nurses' training program at Lawrence General Hospital which was where she met her husband, John Joseph Maney, MD (1875-1942), the oldest of Ellen Reilly and John Maney's (1849-1932) children.[15] The second person in this list of women who became professional nurses, Sarah Corning (1872-1969), was born near Yarmouth, Nova Scotia, in 1872, about one hundred years after her seafaring family had left Beverly before the American war for independence started.

Like Ruth, Sarah left her home in Nova Scotia for the Boston area and graduated from a nurses' training program offered at a hospital in Springfield, MA, just a few years after Ruth began working as a nurse at the hospital in Lawrence. After satisfying all the requirements for receiving her nursing certificate, Sarah Corning became a Red Cross nurse and served in Europe during World War I. See for example information about the Sara Corning Centre for Genocide Education, the successor to the Corning Centre, the organization that continued the relief and peace-making work that Sarah Corning had done in war-torn regions in Greece, Turkey, Armenia, and the Balkans at the end of World War I.

According to all accounts, Sarah Corning was both resourceful and fearless in assisting and supporting refugees, especially children, and getting them placed in orphanages that Corning helped start up while violence continued to rage after the war had officially ended. She went from organizing resources for these orphanages to getting official government approval from the U.S., Britain, and other wartime allies to move children out of harm's way in the

---

[15] After graduation Ruth continued working at Lawrence General Hospital and then started a private practice specializing in occupational health and safety injuries for both women and men. Most of her clients in this practice were likely to have had injuries which occurred from mill work. It was an especially-needed specialty in Lawrence because mill workers with those medical problems were plentiful in a textile city which was dependent on highly specialized machinery.

face of campaigns of ethnic cleansing which were happening in parts of Armenia and Greece. Sarah continued her postwar work in collaboration with relief organizations, moving from hotspot to hotspot during the period leading up to World War II. For the rest of her life, she divided her time between doing international work from her base in Massachusetts and her home town of Cheggogin, near Yarmouth, Nova Scotia.

At least two more nurses are connected to Maney families in this big family tapestry. Less is known about the older of the two, Ellen Maney (1888-1914). Ellen, who grew up in Providence, was a daughter of William Maney (abt 1854-1935) and Sarah Jane Guilfoyle (1855-1948). Records in the *Maney Family Archive* indicate that Ellen was married and that she and her husband were the parents of at least one child. Both parents worked at a state hospital and perhaps died in the flu epidemic in 1918. If so, Ellen was what Americans would have termed an essential worker in 2020-2022 and her medical work deserves to be included in this group. Maney relatives in the Rhode Island branch of the Maney family believe that other sisters and/or cousins of this woman may have also worked as nurses. The other nurse whom we know about with certainty was a first cousin of John MacLean Maney, Helen Marie Manock (1920-?), who was born in 1920 and grew up in Lawrence, MA. During World War II, she entered a nurse's training program sponsored by the U.S. Army which worked at multiple locations in the U.S.

She took the courses she needed at Columbia University in New York City. The military services expected to employ as many nurses with modern training as they could get, as World War II dragged on. Helen Marie did not serve in the war after all, as her qualifying certificate program didn't end until 1945 when the fighting was already winding down. However, she took advantage of an offer to study at Columbia for one additional year during which she completed a master's degree in nursing. After that, she returned to Massachusetts and worked professionally as a nurse at Danvers State Hospital and later as an instructor in the School of Nursing which was established at Boston College. She also developed a professional specialty in psychology and was in demand as a speaker on psychology and religious topics for audiences from Catholic women's organizations in addition to her appointment as a professor of nursing at Boston College.

What Else Does this Maternal Line Show?

Women like Lucy Larcom and her mother, besides Sarah Corning, Ruth MacLean Maney, Helen Marie Manock, and the other women cited above, created and filled interesting and unique occupational niches during their lifetimes, but the list is not yet complete. All of these women were able to work outside their homes due to their ability to: pursue additional specialized education and training; receive support from family members, including spouses; and, in the case of Ruth MacLean Maney, because she was able, at the beginning of her career, to live with a sister who, herself, contributed to the well-being of her own family through her profession of dressmaking. There are DNA tests for sale by many providers that will search someone's maternal line for people interested to know where that line goes and if it gives similar or different information. In the case of the four sets of families that we have followed here, the maternal line from the mother to her mother and so on was done in the same way that the other family trees shown here were originally constructed, i.e., by searching for birth, baptism, marriage, births of children, census records, wills and probate, and other documents referred to in the earlier chapters. The results suggest that similar topics show up in all four families, especially when the topic is expansion of occupations for women and girls during the period from 1850-1940.

Once the occupational framework for a new type of job like nursing was developed, we also see young women taking part in establishing new professional conditions in specialties such as industrial nursing, psychology, and others. Analysis of the DNA results for all of Ethel Bradstreet and John MacLean Maney's children confirm the main findings of each mini-tree created for this chapter. But it needs to be said again that the maternal and paternal line trees used in this book look different from one another in important ways. Going back in time from now, Ethel Bradstreet's maternal tree focused most recently on Beverly, then jumped to Maria Guild's birthplace in Wrentham and Boston, MA, then back to NH, and the coast of northern New England. Meanwhile, John MacLean Maney's maternal line starts with his mother's birth in Prince Edward Island and his grandmother' birth in Nova Scotia. Before that, their births and lives were lived on the Isle of Coll before 1776.

A Spotlight on the Lives of Maria Guild and Eben F Lovett

It is now appropriate to take another look at the life and times of Ethel Bradstreet Maney's maternal grandmother, Maria Guild, who moved to an urban environment from a town in Massachusetts which was still rural when she and her siblings were born in the middle of the nineteenth century. In the 1880 census she is listed as a dressmaker and her name appeared regularly in local city business directories where her occupation of dressmaker is always described in the same way. In the census records, we can see three Guild siblings, William, Maria, and Mary Anna, moving to Beverly in search of work. Both William and Maria lived the rest of their lives in Beverly while Mary Anna married and moved with her husband to Providence, Rhode Island, which was his home town. The apartment which Maria Guild shared with her female friends is described as household #843 in the 1880 census.

Living in the same building at #842 was a second household headed up by Ellen Lovett, who is recorded as living with two of her brothers and a servant. One of the brothers was the Beverly town clerk and the other gave his occupation as working in an electrical factory. It is likely that Ellen and/or one of her brothers received the house as a bequest after the death of someone in the big Lovett family tree. Most likely, Ellen came from the "John" side of the family tree, the other main branch of the seventeenth century immigrants, John Lovett and Mary Grant. All four of the female boarders shared space which was somewhat like what the writer, Virginia Woolf, would have termed a place where a woman could be recognized as having her own creative, living, and working space, i.e., "a room of one's own." Two of Ellen Lovett's female boarders used the apartment that they shared for their businesses, dressmaking and tailoring, and the other reported working for a shoe shop, which could have meant doing stitching and sewing at home.

Unlike in earlier times, Ellen was a female resident of Beverly who had had real estate left to her by her father or mother on the Lovett side of their family tree. In later life, Maria Guild and her husband, Eben Lovett, continued renting apartments – or maybe they got free rent in exchange for providing some goods or services, as Lucy Larcom explained in her autobiography was common in Beverly in previous generations. One of the main goals of the Puritan experiment had been to establish "competencies," which Ulrich and other historians described as the foundation for the success of Puritan lives and livelihoods; however, by the 1880s, except for Ellen Lovett, the other women had to find work that they could do to support themselves without the economic stability that land grants, land purchases, homes, and careers in public or community service had provided for men in both Lovett lines.[16]

However, by the mid-nineteenth century, it seems that the goal of owning a family house was becoming out of reach for ordinary people in places like Beverly after three hundred years had passed and the era of governmental land grants had ended in that part

---

[16] In his book, *Farmers and Fishermen*, Vickers emphasized the John line of the big Lovett family when he listed such Beverly merchant maritime families as the Obears, Cabots, Lovetts, and Thorndykes. See p 193. More often than not, the norm for Ethel Bradstreet's Lovett line is more like what Vickers describes for the other line of the Lovett family in Beverly, i.e., people working at a range of different jobs over their lifetimes.

of the country. Sarah Corning[17] was a distant relative in Ethel Bradstreet's tree when Sarah's parents lived in Beverly and Salem before moving to Nova Scotia. Neither the 1850 census nor the 1860 census records for Eben Lovett's father, Ebenezer Lovett, Jr. (1822-1882), shows that Ebenezer, Jr., owned any real estate either. In the 1860 census, his occupation was listed as shoemaker and the amount of money he earned he estimated at $300/year. In communities west of Boston, like Wrentham or Dedham where Maria Guild had grown up, her father, Thomas Guild, did not volunteer any value for land, although perhaps he had already transferred his land ownership to one of his sons.

In later censuses, we see entries for Maria and Eben when both were over age sixty showing that they were still working to support themselves economically by jointly running a grocery store. We may also assume that they continued plying multiple home-based trades at the same time. For example, Maria was making high-end dresses and Eben advertised himself as a "poulterer" by which he may have meant filling special orders for fresh poultry, hares, and game for customers at the corner grocery store which the couple jointly operated for their daughter's husband, Alvah Bradstreet. The marriage that Eben and Maria had was a different one than what their Puritan ancestors had planned. Indeed, looking at this marriage from the twenty-first century it appears to be one which depended on a kind of social compact among the male and female partners; both worked hard at paying jobs and or professions during their entire adult lives. In some respects they lived their lives as gig workers long before that term was even dreamed about.

---

[17] The connection showed Sarah's descendant was my 7th cousin 1x removed and there are DNA matches with other people in Sarah's family as well. This information comes from the *Maney Family Archive* which parallels what is presented in this book and keeps track of the family trees created for the book project.

Spotlight on Women Developing Jobs and Careers in Industrial New England

Searching Ethel Bradstreet's maternal family was done by identifying her female ancestors back to Rebecca Swayne and Bridget Chester who came to British North America from Wiltshire, England. Evidence from probate and other records indicate that their families, like the Bradstreets, had upper-middle class status in their seventeenth century communities in England and in the Mass. Bay Colony. They and their daughters usually had their father's last name until their marriages: Rebecca Swayne, Susannah Hall, Sarah Worcester, Sarah Sanborn, Phoebe Sanborn, Mollie Philbrick, Betsy Pickering, Louisa Colbath, Maria Guild, Bertha Lovett, and Ethel Bradstreet. In addition to names, other vital records, and the locations where they lived, there has been a focus on the roles that these "working women" played as wives and mothers, and where appropriate, as breadwinners. Often they worked inside their households, sometimes for cash, and sometimes they bartered goods that they made at home and sold or bartered with people outside of their families who needed these goods.

At the end of the day, there are no records showing that any of Ethel Bradstreet's maternal ancestors practiced occupations inside the family that they were able to use to increase the family's income, except for the last two in the line. Those two, Bertha Lovett Bradstreet and Ethel Bradstreet Maney, on the other hand, worked paying jobs as teachers.[18] Among the other women named in this chapter who did bring in enough money to get "rooms of their own," the main way was through creating careers as boardinghouse keepers, dressmakers, nurses, and writers. Besides what women were doing inside the family, there were other examples. For example, Ethel Bradstreet's Lovett ancestor, Lois Barrett Larcom, took her

---

[18] We should also include income earned by Ellen Lovett, Lois Barrett, and Lucy Larcom from their respective work as breadwinners even if they are not in Ethel's direct maternal line.

family of young girls to work in the mills of Lowell, and Ellen Lovett, who had the Puritan competency of inheriting property, which Ellen used to take female boarders into the house that she inherited in downtown Beverly.

Indeed, all of Ethel's "mothers" starting with Rebecca Swain and ending with Louisa Colbath seem to have made comfortable upper-middle class marriages without having to secure paid work of their own outside of the home. The notable exceptions are the most recent ones, Ethel's grandmother, Maria Guild, her mother, Bertha Lovett Bradstreet, and herself. The emphasis on occupations in this chapter also has brought back some of the same women and men whom you have already read about in the four main family chapters. The writers that we know about include two published poets, Anne Bradstreet[19] and Lucy Larcom. The next group to salute are the boardinghouse keepers who supported their families by generating additional family income from taking in tenants: this group included Ellen Lovett, Lois Barrett Larcom, Anastasia Doran Maney, Ellen Reilly Maney, and probably more whom we still do not know about.[20]

Spotlight on DNA Matches in Ethel Bradstreet's Maternal Line

When I decided to do a maternal family tree for this book, I did not anticipate that I would be able to successfully connect so many individual families with each other through DNA matching. The first step was to complete all of the work usually done to fill

---

[19] Anne Bradstreet also deserves mention for her efforts to keep communication going between the different world of Puritan England and the Puritans of the MBC, as Richard Round sees it in his *By Nature and By Custom Cursed*. Hanover, NH, University Press of New England, 1999, which celebrates Anne Bradstreet's role in keeping cultural discussions going in very difficult times for all concerned. See especially pp 174-204 and https://www.ancestry.com/discoveryui-content/view/1490241:61157?ssrc=pt&tid=46577678&pid=7028290904

[20] I expect that there will be additional examples of female boardinghouse keepers among Maney women I haven't found yet.

out information needed for a family tree by finding and reading the kinds of records which are familiar to amateur and professional family historians. After that task was complete, I looked at my own DNA matches to confirm each part of the tree. As it turns out, I have DNA matches for all of these "mothers" beginning with Bridget Chester, my 10th great-grandmother and her daughter Rebecca Swain, my 9th great-grandmother. Rebecca was born in 1616 near Stonehenge in Wiltshire County, England. She married four men over her lifetime, including John Hall, the father of Susannah Hall, who is shown in the maternal tree in this chapter.

Another of Rebecca's husbands was Samuel Symonds, who was at one time the deputy governor of Massachusetts. Now I also have DNA matches for Susannah Hall, one of my 8th great-grandmothers; Sarah Worcester, a 7th great-grandmother; Sarah Sanborn, a 6th great-grandmother; Phoebe Sanborn, a 5th great-grandmother; Mollie Philbrick, a 4th great-grandmother; Betsy Pickering, a 3rd great-grandmother; Louisa Colbath, a 2nd great-grandmother; Maria Guild, my maternal great-grandmother; followed by Bertha Lovett, my grandmother; and Ethel Bradstreet, my mother.

Many of these women grew up in big families and often raised their own big families, so it turned out not to be very difficult to uncover people from their families who are alive today and have taken the DNA test used by Ancestry.com or another of the big DNA testing companies. If they did take the test, it would show up as an Ancestry DNA match with the mothers who are our common ancestors. That clearly happened as the various "mothers" ranged from a low connection of 6 cMs to a high connection of 26 cMs. Besides "thanks" and "cheers," which need to be raised to Rebecca Swayne and her mother, Bridget Chester, both of them deserve to be included in the last sentence of this book since they were clearly the mothers of us all.

Maternal line map

Eng → Ipswich,² Newbury,³ Salisbury,⁴ Hampton,⁵ Portsmouth, ⁶ Hillsborough,⁷ Barnstead, ⁸Boston, ⁹Wrentham, ¹⁰Beverly, ¹¹Danv

1. Ipswich, MA
2. Newbury, MA
3. Salisbury, MA
4. Hampton Falls, NH
5. Portsmouth, NH
6. Hillsborough, NH
7. Barnstead, NH
8. Boston, MA
9. Wrentham, MA
10. Beverly, MA
11. Danvers, MA

Lake Winnipesaukee

*Wolfeboro

7. *Barnstead

5. *Portsmouth

*Manchester NH
6 *Hillsborough (4) *Hampton Falls

(3) *Salisbury

*Newburyport

*Lawrence

*Andover   2 *Newbury

*Topsfield 1 *Ipswich

*Manchester

11 *Danvers

10 *Beverly

9 *Salem

*Lynn   8 *Boston

*Rockport

*Gloucester

*Wrentham

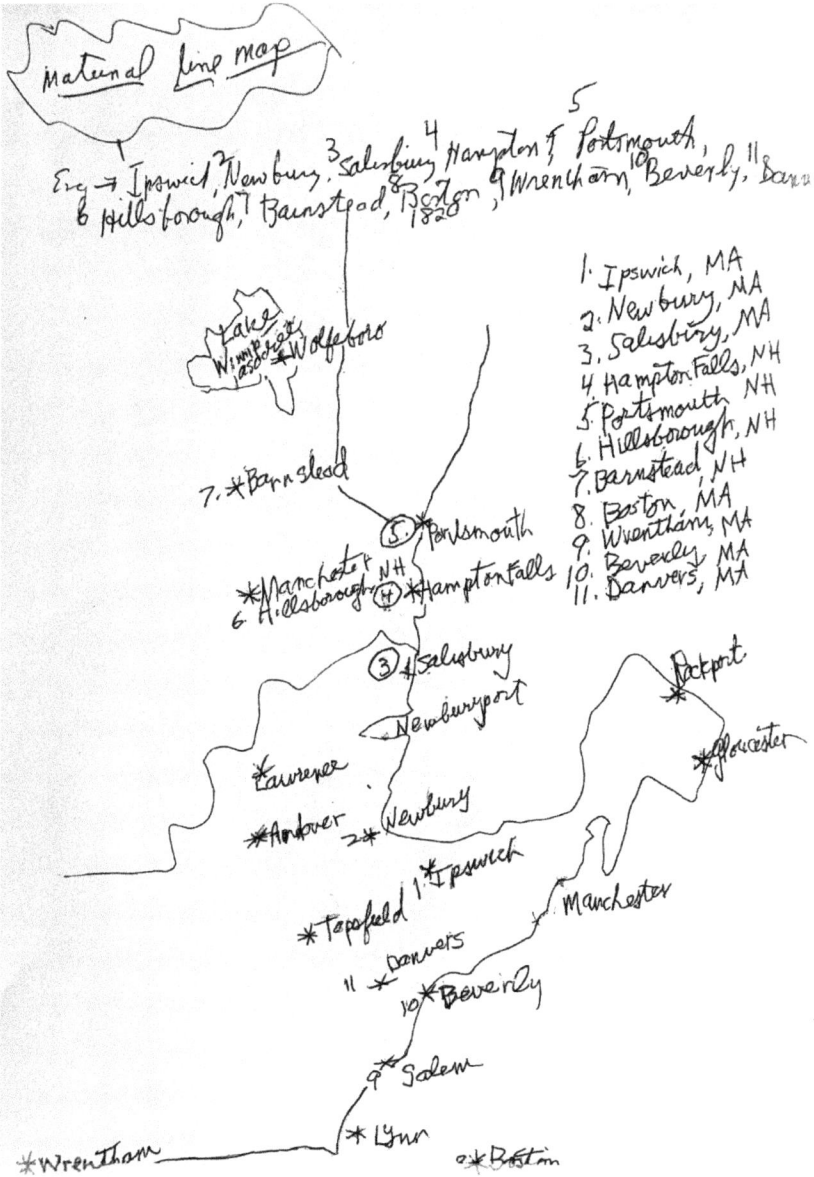

Maternal Line Map during the 1600s, drawn by the author

Maria Guild and her dressmaking tools

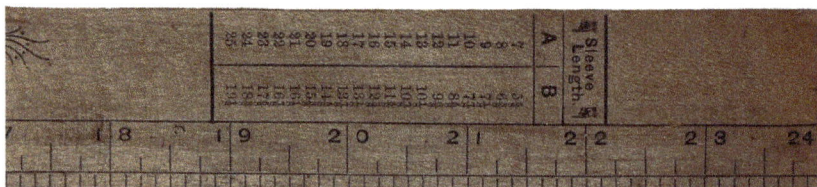

M. E. QUINN'S
NEW AND ONLY
Mechanical Tailor System of Square Measurement
For Cutting Ladies' and Children's Garments.
FALL RIVER, MASS.

Ethel Bradstreet and her family at her wedding in 1940

Ethel Bradstreet and some guests at her wedding in 1940

John Maney and Ethel Bradstreet on the wedding day of one of their daughters

Mary Pukui who was born in Hawaii was proud of her Bradstreet heritage.

Warren G. Harding's Presidential Yacht, 1920s

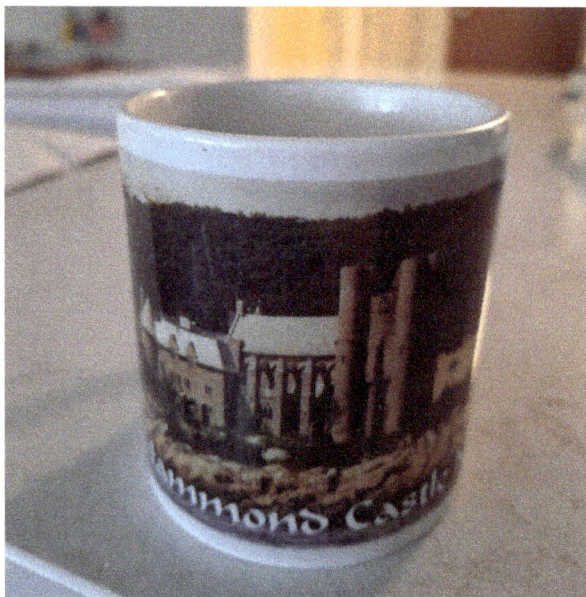

Mug from Shop at Hammond Castle

Interior View of Hammond Castle

John Jack Maney and His Sisters

Bibliography

Anderson, Robert Charles. *The Great Migration Begins, 1620-1633*. Vol. 1-3. Boston: New England Historical Genealogical Society, 1999.

_____. *The Great Migration Directory: Immigrants to New England, 1620-1640: A Concise Compendium*. Boston: New England Historical Genealogical Society, 2015.

Anderson, Virginia DeJohn. *New England's Generation*. Cambridge, England: Cambridge University Press, 1991.

Bailyn, Bernard. *The New England Merchants of the Seventeenth Century*. Cambridge: Harvard University Press, 1955.

_____. *The Peopling of British North America: An Introduction*, NY. Knopf, 1985.

Blewett, Mary H. *Constant Turmoil: The Politics of Industrial Life in Nineteenth Century New England*. Amherst and Boston: University of Massachusetts Press, 2000.

_____. *The Last Generation: Work and Life in the Textile Mills of Lowell, MA, 1910-1960*. Amherst: University of Massachusetts, 1990.

_____. *Men, Women, and Work: Class, Gender, and Protest in the New England Shoe Industry, 1780-1910*. University of Illinois Press. Urbana and Chicago, 1988.

_____. *We Will Rise In Our Might: Working-women's Voices From Nineteenth Century New England.* Ithaca: Cornell University Press, 1991.

Bliss, Robert M. *Revolution and Empire: English Politics and the American Colonies in the Seventeenth Century.* Manchester, UK: Manchester University Press, 1993.

Boyce, D.G. *Ireland, 1828-1921: From Ascendancy to Democracy.* Oxford, UK: Oxford University Press, 1980.

Boydston, Jeanne. *Home and Work: Wages and the Ideology of Labor in the Early Industrial Revolution.* NY: Oxford University Press. NY, 1991.

Bradstreet, Alvah J. *The Life and Times of Alvah J Bradstreet.* Edited by John M. Maney and Ethel Bradstreet Maney. Danvers, MA, 1949.

Breen, Louise A. *Transgressing the Bounds: Subversive Enterprises Among the Puritan Elite in Massachusetts, 1630-1692.* Oxford: Oxford University Press, 2001.

Breen, T. H. *The Character of a Good Leader: Puritan Political Ideas in New England, 1630-1730.* New Haven, CT. November, 2008.

_____. *Puritans and Adventurers: Change and Persistence in Early America.* New York: Oxford University Press published as an ACLS Humanities E-Book, 1982.

Bumstead, J.M. *The People's Clearance: Highland Emigration to BNA 1770-1815.* Edinburgh: Edinburgh University Press, 1982.

Cameron, Ardis. *Radicals of the Worst Sort: Laboring Women in Lawrence, MA, 1860-1912.* Urbana: University of Illinois Press, 1993.

Campbell, R.H. "The First Phase of Clearances," 91-108. In T.M. Devine and Rosalind Mitchison, eds., *People and Society in Scotland*, 1988.

Canny, Nicholas. *Making Ireland British 1580-1650.* Oxford: Oxford Academic Press, 2001.

Carroll, Charles J. *The Timber Industry of Puritan New England.* Providence, RI, 1973.

Clark, Andrew Hill. *Acadia: The Geography of Early Nova Scotia to 1760.* 1968.

Cott, Nancy F. *The Bonds of Womanhood: Women's Sphere in New England 1780-1835*, Yale University Press. New Haven, CT, 1977.

Cregeen, E.R. *Tiree Bards and Their Bardacht.* Ed. by Margaret Bennett. "The Poets in a Hebridean Community," Coll, 1978.

_____ and D.W. MacKenzie. *Recollections of an Argyllshire Drover*, Ed. by Margaret Bennett. Edinburgh: John Donald, 2004.

Cressy, David. *Coming Over: Migration and Communication Between England and New England in the Seventeenth Century.* Cambridge, UK, 1987.

Cullen, Louis M. and Thomas C. Smout, eds. *Comparative Aspects of Scottish and Irish Social History 1600-1900.* Edinburgh: John Donald, 1977.

Daly, Mary and David Dickson, eds. *The Origin of Popular Literacy in Ireland, 1600-1900.* Dublin: University College, 1900.

Dawley, Alan. *Class and Community: The Industrial Revolution in Lynn, Massachusetts, 1780-1860.* Cambridge, MA: Harvard University Press, 1976.

Devine, T. M. *The Great Highland Potato Famine: Hunger, Migration and the Scottish Highlands in the Nineteenth Century.* Edinburgh. John Donald, 1996.

_____ and Rosalind Mitchison, eds. *People and Society in Scotland.* Edinburgh: John Donald, Vol.1. 1988.

Dickson, David. *New Foundations: Ireland, 1660-1800.* Cork: Irish Academic Press, 1987.

Dodgshon, Robert A. *From Chiefs to Landlords.* Edinburgh: Edinburgh University Press, 1998.

Donnelly, James S., Jr. *The Great Irish Potato Famine.* Dublin and Portland, OR: Irish Academic Press, 2010.

Dublin, Charles. *Women at Work: The Transformation of Work and Community in Lowell, MA, 1826-1860.* New York: Columbia University Press, 1981.

Faler, Paul. 1981. *Mechanics and Manufacturers in the Early Industrial Revolution. Lynn, Massachusetts, 1780-1860.* Albany: State University of New York Press, 1981.

Foster, R.F. *Modern Ireland 1600-1972.* London: Alan Lane Penguin Press, 1989.

Godfrey, William. *Pursuit of Profit and Preferment in Colonial North America: John Bradstreet's Quest.* Waterloo, Ontario: Wilfrid Laurier University Press, 2006.

Gordon, Charlotte. *Mistress Bradstreet: The Untold Life of America's First Poet.* Boston: Little Brown, 1980.

Haldane, A.R.B. *The Drove Roads of Scotland.* Edinburgh: Nelson, 1952.

Hall, Frank. *The Lovett Genealogy* https:///www.familysearch. for/library/books/records/item/294187-a-lovett-genealogy-eogramt-ancestor-john-lovett-of-beverly-massachusetts-landed-from-england-prior-to-1639-and-allied-families-of-rea--jordon-thorndyke-larkin-woodbery-dodge-proctor-hale-hall

Harper, Marjory and Michael E. Vance, eds. *Myth, Migration, and the Making of Memory: Scotia and Nova Scotia, c.1700-1990.* Edinburgh, 2006.

Hazard, Blanche Evans. *The Organization of the Boot and Shoe Industry in Massachusetts Before 1875.* Harvard University Home Economics Studies, 1921.

Hill, Christopher. *The World Turned Upside Down: Radical Ideas During the English Revolution.* NY: Penguin, 1991.

Hochschild, Adam. "The Cruelties of Empire," *New York Review of Books.* 55-57, 2023.

Innes, Stephen. *Creating the Commonwealth: The Economic Culture of Protestant New England.* New York: Norton, 1995.

_____. *The Cod Fisheries: Work and Labor in Early America.* Chapel Hill, NC: University of North Carolina Press, 1988.

_____ and Philip Round. *By Nature and Custom Cursed. Transatlantic Civil Discourse and Cultural Production, 1620-1660*. University Press of New England, 1989.

Johnson, Samuel. *A Journey to the Western Isles of Scotland*. UK. Penguin Classics, 1984.

Kelley, Sean M. *American Slavers: Merchants, Mariners, and the Transatlantic Commerce in Captives, 1644-1865*. New Haven: Yale University Press, 1989.

Knowlton, Christopher. *Cattle Kingdom: The Haddon History of the Cowboy West*. Boston: Houghton Mifflin Harcourt, 2017.

Larcom, Lucy. *A New England Childhood*. Boston: Northeastern University Press, 1985.

Lepore, Jill. *The Name of War: King Phillip's War*. NY: Vintage, 1999.

Litton, Helen. 2018. *Irish Rebellions*. Dublin: The O'Brien Press, 2018.

The Lovitt Genealogy. Undated. *The Lovitt Family of Yarmouth*. Yarmouth, Nova Scotia, Canada. Last entry is about Hon. John Lovitt 1832-1908.

MacDougall, J.L. *History of Inverness County, Nova Scotia* at: https://electricscotland.co/canada/inverness/index.htm 1922.

Marshall, Tim. 2021. *The Power of Geography*. N.Y. Scribner, 2021.

Martin, John Frederick. *Profits in the Wilderness: Entrepreneurship and the Founding of New England Towns in the Seventeenth Century*. Chapel Hill, NC: University of North Carolina Press, 1991.

McCusker, John J. and Russell R. Menand. *The Economy of British America, 1607-1789*. Chapel Hill, N.C. and London: University of North Carolina, 1985.

McGreachy, Robert A.A. *Argyll 1730-1850: Commerce, Community, and Culture*. Edinburgh: John Donald, 2010.

Norton, Mary Beth. *Founding Mothers and Fathers: Gendered power and the Forming of American Society*. N.Y. Knopf, 1996.

Oakes, James. 2023. "Ships Going Out." Review of Kelley. *American Slavers*. Review in *New York Review of Books*. 21 September 2023. Pp. 58-60.

O'Callaghan, Sean. *To Hell or Barbados: The Ethnic Cleansing of Ireland*. Dingle: Brandon, 2001.

Ohlmeyer, Jane H. *Making Ireland English: The Irish Aristocracy in the Seventeenth Century*. London, Yale University Press, 2012.

O'Reilly, William. "Movements of People in the Atlantic World, 1450-1850," 305-323. Ch. 18. In *The Oxford Handbook of the Atlantic World*, Edited by Nicholas Canny and Philip Morgan. Oxford: Oxford University Press, 2011.

Oxford English Dictionary in the 1971 edition, vol. II, P-Z on p. 2726 for definition of sennachie.

Perley, Sydney. *The History of Salem vol 3, 1671-1716*. Salem, MA: Higginson Book Co., 1924.

Power, Thomas P. *Land Politics and Society in 18th Century Tipperary*. Oxford: Clarendon Press, 1993.

_____ and Kevin Whelan, eds. *Endurance and Emergence: Catholics in Ireland in the Eighteenth Century*. Dublin: Irish Academic Press, 1990.

Reid, John G. *Acadia, Maine, and New Scotland: Marginal Colonies in the Seventeenth Century*. Toronto: University of Toronto Press, 1981.

Ross, David. *Scotland: History of a Nation*. New Lanark: Lomand Books, 2003.

Rothschild, Emma. *The Inner Life of Empires: An 18th Century History*. Princeton: Princeton University Press, 2011.

Round, Phillip H. *Transatlantic Civil Discourses and New England Cultural Production 1620-1660*. Hanover: University Press of New England, 1999.

Russell, Howard S. 1976. *A Long Deep Furrow: Three Centuries of Farming in New England*. Hanover NH: University Press of New England, 1976.

Simington, R.C. *The Transplantation to Connacht 1654-58*. Dublin: IUP, 1970.

Smyth, William J. *Map-making, Landscapes, and Memory*. Notre Dame: University of Notre Dame Press, 2006.

Stone, Edwin M. *History of Beverly From Its Settlement in 1630 to 1642*. Boston: James Munroe and Company, 1843.

Ulrich, Laurel Thatcher. *Good Wives, Image and Reality in the Lives of Women in Northern New England 1650-1750*. N.Y. Vintage, 1991.

Unknown. Unofficial ship list for trip of the Dunlop of Greenock departing from Tobormory, Scotland, on June 25, 1820. Ship's destinations were Nova Scotia and PE. The list of passengers is incomplete and unofficial. The ship departed Tobermory, Mull, on 25 June 1820 and discharged some passengers in NS before leaving for PE.

Vickers, Daniel. *Farmers and Fishermen: Two Centuries of Work in Essex County, Massachusetts, 1630-1850*. Chapel Hill and London: University of North Carolina Press, 1994.

Vital Records of Beverly Massachusetts to the end of the year 1849. 1907. Topsfield Historical Society, Topsfield, MA, Vol. II. *Births*. And Vol. VII. *Marriages and Deaths*, 1907.

Whelan, Kevin. *The Tree of Liberty: Radicalism, Catholicism, and the Construction of Irish Identity? 1760-1930*. South Bend, IN: University of Notre Dame Press. December, 1998.

_____. *Fellowship of Freedom: The United Irishmen and 1798*. Cork, Ireland: University of Cork, 1998.

Young, Christine A. *From "Good Order" to Glorious Revolution: Salem, Massachusetts, 1628-1689*. Ann Arbor, Michigan, 1980.

About the Author

I had a wonderful career teaching local government and women in politics and administration from my perch in the Political Science Department at Iowa State University. I cherish the opportunities that I had as an ISU faculty member to write serious research papers and books during my career, based on work that I did during stays in Washington, DC, New York City, and in state and local government archives in various parts of the USA. I also would like to thank the Iowa State Extension Program for giving me outreach opportunities that I delivered in small cities and towns inside Iowa, as well as making it possible to do work trips in the Cote d'Ivoire, the Czech Republic, Hungary, Kenya, Lithuania, Slovakia, Russia, Kenya, and the country of Georgia.

I also appreciated getting genealogical information provided by family and friends such as Robert Lovett, a cousin on my maternal side who was a senior business researcher at Harvard University's Baker Library, as well as stories from Alvah Bradstreet, my maternal grandfather. The people who helped me connect with others from the countries mentioned above are too many to mention separately here. As the reader may have already understood, I also have enjoyed learning about the Atlantic Ocean all of my life. So, it should not be a surprise to know that I am currently living in Milwaukee, WI, high above the city harbor and the sea lines through Lake Michigan and the other Great Lakes that go to Europe and the world beyond.

—Ardith Maney, Milwaukee, April 2024

www.ingramcontent.com/pod-product-compliance
Lightning Source LLC
Chambersburg PA
CBHW051256020426
42333CB00026B/3235